Betrayal U

THE FEMINIST WIRE BOOKS

Connecting Feminisms, Race, and Social Justice

ALSO IN THE FEMINIST WIRE BOOKS

Frontera Madre(hood): Brown Mothers Challenging Oppression and Transborder Violence at the U.S.-Mexico Border, edited by Cynthia Bejarano and Maria Cristina Morales

Black Women and da 'Rona: Community, Consciousness, and Ethics of Care, edited by Julia S. Jordan-Zachery and Shamara Wyllie Alhassan

Lavender Fields: Black Women Experiencing Fear, Agency, and Hope in the Time of COVID-19, edited by Julia S. Jordan-Zachery

A Love Letter to This Bridge Called My Back, edited by gloria j. wilson, Joni B. Acuff, and Amelia M. Kraehe

Black Girl Magic Beyond the Hashtag: Twenty-First-Century Acts of Self-Definition, edited by Julia S. Jordan-Zachery and Duchess Harris

The Chicana M(other)work Anthology, edited by Cecilia Caballero, Yvette Martínez-Vu, Judith Pérez-Torres, Michelle Téllez, and Christine Vega

Them Goon Rules: Fugitive Essays on Radical Black Feminism, by Marquis Bey

BETRAYAL U

The Politics of Belonging in Higher Education

EDITED BY REBECCA G. MARTÍNEZ AND
MONICA J. CASPER

THE UNIVERSITY OF
ARIZONA PRESS
TUCSON

The University of Arizona Press
www.uapress.arizona.edu

We respectfully acknowledge the University of Arizona is on the land and territories of Indigenous peoples. Today, Arizona is home to twenty-two federally recognized tribes, with Tucson being home to the O'odham and the Yaqui. Committed to diversity and inclusion, the University strives to build sustainable relationships with sovereign Native Nations and Indigenous communities through education offerings, partnerships, and community service.

ISBN-13: 978-0-8165-5472-0 (paperback)
ISBN-13: 978-0-8165-5471-3 (ebook)

Cover design by Leigh McDonald
Cover art by Octavio Quintanilla

Publication of this book is made possible in part by the proceeds of a permanent endowment created with the assistance of a Challenge Grant from the National Endowment for the Humanities, a federal agency.

Library of Congress Cataloging-in-Publication Data
Names: Martínez, Rebecca G. (Rebecca Gilda), 1967– editor. | Casper, Monica J., 1966– editor.
Title: Betrayal U : the politics of belonging in higher education / edited by Rebecca G. Martínez and Monica J. Casper.
Other titles: Feminist wire books.
Description: Tucson : University of Arizona Press, 2025. | Series: Feminist wire books | Includes bibliographical references and index.
Identifiers: LCCN 2024032676 (print) | LCCN 2024032677 (ebook) | ISBN 9780816554720 (paperback) | ISBN 9780816554713 (ebook)
Subjects: LCSH: Discrimination in higher education—United States. | Belonging (Social psychology) | Betrayal. | LCGFT: Personal narratives.
Classification: LCC LC212.42 .B48 2025 (print) | LCC LC212.42 (ebook) | DDC 378.7308—dc23/eng/20241227
LC record available at https://lccn.loc.gov/2024032676
LC ebook record available at https://lccn.loc.gov/2024032677

Printed in the United States of America
♾ This paper meets the requirements of ANSI/NISO Z39.48-1992 (Permanence of Paper).

In loving memory of Dr. Adele E. Clarke—
an extraordinary mentor, scholar, and woman

CONTENTS

Part II. Gender-Based Violence, Sexual Assault, and Title IX

Part III. Belonging

Afterword

Betrayal U

Introduction

Monica J. Casper and Rebecca G. Martínez

A colleague, the only Black woman department chair in a land grant public research institution, seeks promotion to full professor. The all-white leadership staff in the dean's office tells her she is "not ready" because her new book is not yet under contract and her edited book will not count. This is the message despite a research workload of only 20 percent (a typical research load at Research 1 institutions is 40 percent), her exemplary and excessive service record, and her award-winning teaching. A doctoral student one of us mentored begins a tenure-track position, only to be harassed by a male colleague to the point of a near breakdown. She leaves academia after a bruising "investigation" that results only in more harassment; she does not return, instead making a career as a consultant and nonprofit director. Another colleague, at an agricultural university in Texas, is in a protracted battle with her institution for decades of under-compensation, overwork, and gender-based harassment. Her public information requests are stonewalled. And one institution in Arizona, known for being "innovative," has a long history of not granting tenure to women of color, especially those who engage in significant community service and outreach.

This is a book about institutional betrayal in higher education—an issue about which we know far too much as scholars, leaders, colleagues, and ethnographers. Each of the stories above is an example of institutional betrayal, which we define more fully below. We came to this project from different vantage points that intersected in the harmful spaces where institutions, and many leaders within those institutions, fail embodied people—specifically, where institutions fail to make room for Brown and Black bodies, female-gendered bodies, nonbinary and transgender bodies, disabled bodies, bodies with mouths and hands that speak and write hard truths, bodies that neither look nor act like the bodies of the people who created the institutions in the first place. In myriad ways, many people are made to feel unwelcome, uncomfortable, and unworthy within spaces that, at least on the surface, profess to want them (Ahmed 2012; Gutiérrez y Muhs et al. 2012; Niemann, Gutiérrez y Muhs, and González 2020).

And when institutions fail people, they are adept at making it seem as if it is the fault of the people who are harmed or are forced to leave, rather than the fault of institutions (and outside political influences) themselves. They point often to "impostor syndrome" or "fit" or "goal alignment" or "metrics," and very rarely to their own shortcomings as institutions or as leaders within those institutions. Indeed, it is much easier to name and reject the misfit as a "troublemaker" than it is to refit, retrofit, or make fit the institutional spaces through which diverse people move (Ahmed 2021). This is especially true as higher education has become increasingly influenced by outside forces, including donors and politically appointed boards of trustees (Hirsch and Kessler 2023), alongside corresponding reductions in state and local funding for education (Allegretto, García, and Weiss 2022). With its democratic ethos, promise of social mobility, and vaunted "ivory towers," higher education has long been considered special. It turns out that higher education is also *not* so special, with institutional harms that mirror (or even surpass) those of other industries.

Especially notable, in our view, is the failure of institutions to welcome and retain the people that they claim to want in their obligatory and ubiquitous diversity, equity, and inclusion (DEI) statements and strategic hiring plans: women, people of color, LGBTQIA+ people, people with varying abilities, multilingual people, people who might upend the status quo and actually do the work required for social and cultural change. Is there a campus in the United States, or anywhere, that has not attempted to create a DEI plan or to hire more people of color and then crow about it, or to appoint a DEI officer only to witness high turnover and burnout in the role due to lack of support (Abrica and Oliver Andrew 2024)? Leaders in higher education know they need "diversity," but few have the courage to make room for—or to listen to—that diversity once hired. Sara Ahmed notes that diversity "can be emptied of its more antagonistic content—i.e., the entire point of it—but that emptying can also be used strategically" (Binyam 2022). Political context has a great deal to do with this—senior leaders have been publicly humiliated and professionally harmed by taking stances supportive of DEI efforts (Gay 2024). And media spin can both obscure and sensationalize the underlying reasons why leaders are removed from their positions.

We call this broad type of harm *institutional betrayal*, as conceptualized by psychologist Jennifer Freyd (2008, 2018), whose lived experiences and professional contributions have deeply influenced this edited collection, including our original call for contributions. The term *institutional betrayal* refers to the harms done by institutions to people who are dependent on those institutions, primarily employees and students (Freyd and Birrell 2013). It also includes the failure to prevent or respond adequately to harms done *by* individuals (or groups) *to* other individuals (or groups) within institutions. Often, this refers to sexual harassment or gender-based violence that occurs within institutional contexts. But it can also refer to other kinds of harm, such as racism. Importantly, betrayal can occur through both *practices* and *processes*, which are *structural* in their manifestations (Smith and Freyd 2014). While people harm people in all sorts of ways, they often do so in contexts—including families, communities, and workplaces—that may shape, reward, and/or punish certain behaviors, while ignoring or even amplifying others.

Freyd, a psychologist, is a professor emerit at the University of Oregon, and her research foci include betrayal trauma theory, institutional betrayal and courage, workplace sexual assault and harassment, DARVO (deny, attack, and reverse victim and offender), disclosures of abuse, minority discrimination, and much more. She is the founder and president of the Center for Institutional Courage (Courage), a nonprofit "dedicated to transformative research and education about institutional betrayal and how to counter it through institutional courage." She has published widely, and her theories and methods have been taken up by scholars across multiple disciplines (Christl et al. 2024). In 2024, Freyd was presented with the Gold Medal Award for Impact in Psychology by the American Psychological Foundation. Importantly, Freyd sued the University of Oregon on the basis of sex discrimination under the Equal Pay Act—and won. As the senior psychologist in her department, she earned much less than the men (Bartlett 2021). Her lawsuit alleged that retention raises disproportionately benefit men, who are more likely to go on the market, leading to a significant loss of earnings for women over time. In settling the lawsuit, Freyd received a monetary award and a contribution to Courage from the University of Oregon (Powell 2021).

Significantly, Courage maintains an extensive, ever-growing database of the theoretical and methodological travels of institutional betrayal and courage. As of March 2024, the database included more than two hundred academic articles and papers on a variety of topics, including sexual assault and harassment, bullying, gender and racial harassment, financial fraud and exploitation, torture, intimate partner violence, and moral injury and distress. Institutional categories include education, corporations, the military, health care, law enforcement, government, churches, the judiciary, and more. (As gender scholars, we are not surprised that so many of the studies included in the database focus on sexual assault and harassment in educational contexts.) Courage has also funded more than twenty research projects focused on betrayal and courage. Beyond these academic treatments of the concept, it also appears (often uncited) in media, including around public cases of harassment and assault (Eckstein 2024).

Courage's website defines institutional courage as "an institution's courage to seek the truth and engage in moral action, despite unpleasantness, risk, and short-term cost. It is a pledge to protect and care for those who depend on the institution. It is a compass oriented to the common good of individuals, institutions, and the world. It is a force that transforms institutions into more accountable, equitable, effective places for everyone." What strikes us, as scholars who have been attending to these issues for many years, is how *infrequently* institutions display true courage. This is not to say that people *within* institutions fail to display courage—as the contributions to this edited collection show, there is abundant courage in the face of betrayal and adversity. Yet institutions themselves, by which we mean people leading these institutions, often take the path of least resistance. Confronted with expectations of boards of trustees, donors, and elected officials, as well as the security (and lucrativeness) of their own employment, many leaders may choose a CYA (cover your ass) approach to conflict, while others may throw folks lower on the food chain under the proverbial bus to save their own skins. Neither approach displays courage and, in fact, are certain to cause harm.

The most tragic outcome of institutional betrayal is, sadly, the fatal kind, and we would be remiss not to discuss this here. On January 8, 2024, Dr. Antoinette Candia-Bailey, who was vice president of student affairs at Lincoln University of Missouri, a historically Black university and her alma mater, took her life (Lawrence 2024; Nittle 2024). In an email she wrote that day to the university president, a white man, she cited his ongoing workplace bullying as greatly contributing to her declining mental health. The all-too-often toxic work environments for Black women in higher ed (Hollis 2021) was a familiar subject; Candia-Bailey's dissertation examines the very obstacles and problems she herself faced. Even though she sought help from the university's board of curators to intervene and also sought accommodations for "severe anxiety and depression" (Hollis 2024), her institution failed her. Just five days before she ended her life, Candia-Bailey had been fired and told to vacate her office immediately. After taking a paid leave of absence, the university president was reinstated after the board of curators, in a closed-door meeting, found no wrongdoing on his part. The bullying was not acknowledged, and this appalling example of institutional betrayal sends a strong message to Black women that they will not be protected.

The Political Context of Betrayal

The stories, art, poems, and research compiled in *Betrayal U* take place in the context of ongoing attacks on DEI efforts in institutions of higher education, including assaults on critical race theory and the rolling back of affirmative action measures. Broadly speaking, these attacks on efforts to combat racism, sexism, ableism, heteronormativity, transphobia, and classism have a long history. The most recent iteration—amid backlash against the Barack Obama presidency, the election of Donald Trump, and Trump's 2024 reelection—has included a flurry of fast-moving right-wing efforts to dismantle DEI efforts on (and off) college campuses. These attacks are organized and far reaching, with multipronged efforts at individual, local, state, and national levels. They are also personally and often viciously directed at scholar-activists who speak openly and publicly about gender, race, and identity on social media, in the classroom, and in congressional hearings. Any popular social media scholar can experience hate-fueled assaults (Cottom 2015), but people of color, especially women, often bear the brunt of onslaught by conservative activists who claim that educating about race and racism teaches hate (Waxman 2022).

One such example of these conservative efforts is the highly public right-wing assault on critical race theory (CRT) (Jaleel 2021; Alexander 2023). During President Barack Obama's bid for the presidency and first term in office, Andrew Breitbart, who ran a far-right conservative website, was particularly dogged in his public outcries against CRT, a concept he clearly did not fully understand but was certainly eager to decry and debunk. By linking Harvard Law School professor Derrick Bell (1989, 1992, 2008), who developed the theory, to President Obama, who had been Bell's student, conservative television, radio, and social media outlets claimed that CRT espouses racist hate against white people. This rhetoric caught on in right-wing circles, implicating President Obama and other progressive leaders as "racist" against white people (Samuels and Lewis 2022). Even with Obama's victories in 2008 and 2012, the disingenuous grievances around CRT have remained ever present.

A decade later, the 1619 Project, marking the four-hundred-year anniversary of the beginning of slavery in what is now the United States of America, would become a target of the ongoing campaign against CRT. Nikole Hannah-Jones, a Pulitzer Prize–winning journalist for the *New York Times Magazine*, was denied tenure in her position—specifically, the Knight Chair in Race and Investigative Journalism—at the University of North Carolina at Chapel Hill (UNC) after the university's board of trustees took the highly unusual step of failing to approve the journalism school's affirmative recommendation. Instead, they offered Hannah-Jones a five-year renewable contract. This was odd because the two previous Knight Chairs in Journalism at UNC were awarded tenure along with their positions (Robertson 2021). The university's trustees sided with right-wing social media pundits that attacked her professionally and personally. Again, the false and tired anti-CRT tropes were used in the barrage of hateful rhetoric.

In June 2021, after sustained pressure and public criticism from other academics, journalists, and supporters, the board of trustees reversed its decision and voted to offer Hannah-Jones tenure. The blistering critique of the trustees by the collective Knight Chairs, who hold positions at universities throughout the country, perhaps carried the most weight: "The lesson the Board of Trustees has delivered is that far too often women and persons of color are told to accept a discount ticket to a seat of power" (Kiesow 2021). Shortly thereafter, Hannah-Jones declined the tenure offer and instead accepted a tenured position at Howard University, a historically Black university. Although her professional career continued, Hannah-Jones weathered an onslaught of racist and sexist social media attacks. She is only one example among myriad scholars whose careers, family life, and personal safety have been compromised by right-wing groups (Kamola 2019). Because of her popularity, and the efforts of her supporters, Hannah-Jones's outcome was a welcome exception. Her highly visible case highlights issues of academic freedom, institutional and systemic racism and sexism, and other forms of marginalization in higher ed that are often obscured when they happen to lesser-known scholars. Other faculty, especially faculty of color, who write about race, gender identity, and/or reproductive justice, have not fared as well (Krupnick 2023).

Right-wing attacks on scholar activists—and on anything having to do with CRT, DEI, and gender studies—have been emboldened by a conservative-majority U.S. Supreme Court installed by former president Donald Trump. A massive blow was dealt to affirmative action on June 29, 2023, when the Supreme Court ruled that race as a status could not be a factor in college admissions. The decision severely limited and, one might argue, effectively ended race-based affirmative action in college admissions. The UNC and Harvard College cases filed in federal court by a conservative group, Students for Fair Admissions, were a successful attempt to overturn *Grutter v. Bollinger*. In that 2003 case, the court upheld the University of Michigan Law

School's contention that the consideration of race for applicants was one important factor in maintaining a diverse student body. However, this recent 6–3 ruling concluded that admissions practices at UNC and Harvard violate the Constitution's clause against racial discrimination by government entities (Howe 2023).

With a conservative-majority Supreme Court firmly in place, legislative attacks against the most marginalized people in the United States have gained momentum, with no promise of abating in the immediate future. The affirmative action decision has led the way for additional legislative attacks on DEI. Numerous bills have been introduced to limit or do away with DEI-related programming, including entire offices and divisions, thus severely affecting not only student learning and belonging but also staff and faculty employment. For those individuals who may already feel marginalized in predominantly white institutions, their sense of place is further compromised. Both the *Chronicle of Higher Education* and BestColleges.com (Bryant and Appleby 2024) have created up-to-date trackers to monitor the increasing number of anti-DEI bills that have been introduced. The *Chronicle* (2024) "is tracking legislation that would prohibit colleges from having diversity, equity, and inclusion offices or staff; ban mandatory diversity training; forbid institutions to use diversity statements in hiring and promotion; or bar colleges from considering race, sex, ethnicity, or national origin in admissions or employment."

Meanwhile, the conservative Goldwater and Manhattan Institutes have provided legislative models for dismantling DEI programming. Those models have been successful in helping lawmakers in 28 states construct and ultimately introduce over 85 bills; 14 have received final legislative approval, 14 have become law, and 49 have been tabled, failed to pass, or vetoed as of May 2024 (*Chronicle* 2024). The 3 most restrictive pieces of legislation that were signed into law are in Iowa, Texas, and Utah, targeting DEI offices, mandatory DEI training, diversity statements, and identity-based preferences. This means that DEI offices in these states must be dismantled, identity-based affirmative action admissions must be halted, and potential employees will not be required to submit diversity statements or to participate in mandatory DEI training. These laws use the phrase "differential treatment" to misrepresent and obfuscate the use of equity in DEI, as opposed to equality. The former takes into consideration historical and contemporary differential treatments based on race, ethnicity, sex, gender identity, national origin, religion, and sexual orientation, among other factors, that have resulted in social, political, and economic disparities and the creation and sustainment of marginalized populations. Equality means that populations are treated the same way, disregarding ongoing oppressions and blocking institutional mechanisms of support that would better support and uplift these groups.

Beyond these anti-DEI efforts, attacks on reproductive justice and bodily autonomy are also ever present. The ruling in *Dobbs v. Jackson Women's Health Organization* effectively overturned *Roe v. Wade*, throwing into confusion abortion (and contraception) laws across the country. Providers in many states are left with more questions than answers about how to manage difficult pregnancies, including those that necessitate terminations to save the lives of pregnant people. Further, access to reproductive health care, increasingly limited or nonexistent in many states, has become a metric by which students and their parents are making decisions about college. Some states, including California, have become sanctuaries for people seeking abortions and trans-affirming health care. Other states, including many across the U.S. South, are likely to see an outflux of progressives who have the economic means to migrate. Universities in states that are anti-DEI, anti-abortion, and anti-trans are in the unenviable position of having to navigate these treacherous waters, requiring the kind of courage in leadership that is quite rare. While some university leaders may issue statements, others are reluctant to wade into controversies that may result in their dismissal (Rivera 2024).

In short, whether the issue of the day is affirmative action, DEI, reproductive justice, religious fundamentalism, transgender rights, or the factuality of scientific data, the current political climate has created an oppressive context in which the lives of people who are not wealthy, white, able bodied, male, cisgender, or gender conforming are in peril, often extremely so. It is important to recognize that these conservative efforts are not merely discursive moves, symbolic acts, or fodder for headlines. Lives will be harmed and even lost from lack of access to care and the violence that often attends to racism, misogyny, and other forms of bigotry. Project 2025's tome, *Mandate for Leadership: The Conservative Promise*, advocates eliminating the U.S. Department of Education, alongside other regressive measures, promising that right-wing challenges to democracy, inclusion, and flourishing for everyone will remain salient for many years to come (Heritage Foundation 2023).

And so into these waters we wade.

Our (Partial) Stories of Institutional Betrayal

As women with doctorates, we each have our own stories of institutional betrayal—the lived experiences that brought us here, to each other as friends and colleagues, and to the making of this collection of heartfelt, painful, and galvanizing stories of rejection, harm, institutional malfeasance, and courage. Though no story is the same, because people are not widgets despite how institutions may treat them, the stories we offer here, both our own and those of our contributors, share common themes of betrayal, including dashed professional expectations, myriad forms of violence and harm, psychological abuse, racism, misogyny, classism, homophobia, ableism, elitism, hazing, and business as usual no matter the consequences. Universities are, in a word, dangerous—but not for everyone and not equally, as Candia-Bailey's story reveals. Higher education is as stratified as any other industry in the United States, despite its alleged ethos of inclusion, and inequalities have only deepened in the long pandemic. In 2021, for example, the *Chronicle of Higher Education* reported that only 2.1 percent of tenured associate and full professors in 2019 were Black women. The numbers were even lower at public flagship universities such as University of California, Berkeley, where Black women represent a mere 1.3 percent of tenured faculty (June and O'Leary 2021).

In sharing our own stories as a prelude and companion to the others in this collection, we aim not to be exceptional—indeed, we are anything but. Our experiences mirror those of so many other scholars at the margins, especially women. Some of what we share below is simply par for the course of academic life, the daily ins and outs of being employed in/by complex institutions. But some of what we share extends beyond the Sturm und Drang of academic life, into the realm of preventable harm and institutional malfeasance, even while we hold certain privileges. The American Association of University Women (n.d.) reports that only 36 percent of full professors are women, while women make up the majority of non-tenure-track lecturers and instructors. Malika Jeffries-El (2022) notes that "nonwhite groups are underrepresented in the academy, accounting for a collective total of only 25.1 percent of all faculty positions, despite representing nearly 40 percent of the U.S. population." She suggests the term *systematically marginalized groups* rather than *underrepresented minorities*, "because the underrepresentation of certain people in certain places is not coincidental, it is intentional" (Jeffries-El 2022).

Rebecca's Story

As the daughter of parents who never attended high school, as the daughter of an immigrant woman from Mexico, and as a woman of color who grew up poor, I was not supposed to be an academic. The ivory tower was never meant for people like me, like many of us whose stories are told in this anthology. We have fought for our inclusion and representation and, through our stories here, continue to illuminate exclusionary practices in higher education, so that we can spur change. When we do make it into the rarefied spaces of academia in a tenure-track position, the tenure process can be particularly alienating and harsh for women of color, who must deal with sexist and racist microaggressions from students, faculty colleagues, administrators, and staff, as well as the sexism, racism, classism, heteronormativity, and ableism that are built into the very structures of our "hallowed halls." Add to this mix of marginalization the fact that we also lack role models and mentors who understand what we experience and who can help guide us through it.

My own story focuses on my traumatic experience of the tenure process in a women's and gender studies (WGS) department at a public land-grant university in a politically conservative midwestern state. This experience still feels fresh at times, painfully so, though it happened several years ago. I was ultimately granted tenure, but I left that institution shortly after because I wanted to be back home in California. Significantly, being a woman of color in a WGS department in a red state was becoming untenable and unhealthy for me. Indeed, in 2015, my institution was featured in the national news for student protesters leading the way in calling out institutionalized racism on our campus. It was clear that the university president, chancellor, and board of curators would not have the backs of activist-scholars who drew the attention of state politicians for calling out oppressions. It was time to go, but first I needed to secure tenure, no small feat in an environment such as this.

Seeking tenure in a context of fear that my research, teaching, and service would be seen as "too political" made the process especially isolating and tumultuous. For scholars of color, the tenure process is often fraught: not only are there the usual pressures to publish a lot and quickly (especially at Research 1 institutions, such as mine), but the people evaluating our performance often hold the same biases that make up the fabric of our society. As Patricia A. Matthew (2016, 13) notes, "Since 'higher education institutions are greatly influenced by, and cannot be analyzed apart from, the larger social, historical, and cultural context,' and we have documented evidence that faculty and administrations hold problematic attitudes . . . how can they fairly evaluate their colleagues of color?" Moreover, the secrecy of the tenure process can be particularly disempowering for women of color, who are already marginalized in academia. Rather than uncritically accepting the process as isolating and secretive, WGS—given the avowed social justice emphasis of the discipline—would be assumed to push back against a model of tenure that is motivated to maintain hierarchical structures. Alas, as I learned through my own experience, this is a faulty assumption. For me, the opposite happened: my department embraced a patriarchal model of tenure that was non-agentive and reproduced practices of secrecy and isolation.

Our own departmental document on tenure and promotion, as well as organizational guidelines from the National Women's Studies Association (NWSA), were set aside in favor of murky "unwritten" rules. Matthew (2016, 10) explains: "The academy thrives on unwritten rules. Personnel processes in the academy are particularly opaque . . . from the processes departments use to decide what areas they want tenure-track positions in, to the composition of search committees, to mentoring of junior faculty through the tenure process." Our department was small and nearly every colleague, except another (white) woman who was also going through tenure, was involved in my process. This meant that there were few avenues through which I could seek support and encouragement.

During a particularly stressful time when my chair was changing goalposts for my tenure process, she questioned an anthology I had put on my curriculum vitae as "in progress." She asked if I was "really" working on it because she had not heard me talking about it. I explained that I had been formulating it for a while but was not comfortable adding it to previous iterations of my vitae because I had only just cemented my co-editors and laid out chapters with them at a recent conference. Humiliated by this interrogation, I reached out to one of my friend-colleagues, who was on my committee. I was shocked that my progressive white woman department chair, who knows about the biases women of color face in academia, was basically accusing me of padding my vitae. Meanwhile, my friend-colleague was worried that my talking to her could compromise my tenure process because our chair told my committee they were not to discuss *anything* tenure related with me. Thus, even though in my desperation to understand what my chair was doing, I began reaching out to other department chairs across campus with whom I felt safe, who told me her approach was "extreme." I learned that at least one department even provided senior mentors for faculty seeking tenure to advise them on putting together their dossier and discussing any concerns. By that point, I was completely isolated. I cried often. Even writing about this now, years later, causes a pit to form in my stomach and tears to roll down my face.

What I experienced during my tenure process was not necessarily explicit in its oppression but rather was part of the nexus of oppression that results from silence and collusion within a system and institution that were never meant to include me. The following are some of the things that were done for my "own good," so that I would be motivated (through fear) in the last year of my tenure process. I was told that my sole-authored book published by a top-ten academic press, that later won a major professional award, would not be enough for the "scientists" on the campus-wide committee, even though this book met the departmental and NWSA tenure guidelines. I was told almost nothing about the process itself, only offered guidance about "filling out tabs." I was informed that my edited volume would not count at a Research 1 university, even though WGS scholars regularly produce edited volumes. (The current collection is a case in point.) No one ever asked for my input into the process, thus making it secretive and non-collaborative. There was great insistence that I follow unwritten rules that were disconnected from our own WGS and NWSA disciplinary guidelines. This "advice" was presented as mentorship, but it only eroded my trust. WGS can and should do better. Mentorship should follow a feminist, antiracist model rather than one that reinscribes patriarchal principles. What makes WGS social justice oriented if we mimic hierarchical power and alienate women of color in our own internal practices?

Ultimately, I was tenured. And though I have been in therapy, I hope that one day I will truly be over the trauma of getting there. Yes, I "survived" the process, but the system is truly broken in that it is taken for granted that we talk about it this way, as *survival*. It feels especially vulnerable to be writing about my experiences in this context of curated stories of loss and betrayal, but I hope that through storytelling I can contribute to the conscious reimagining of a tenure process in WGS departments that is collaborative, based on our disciplinary vision and values, and centered in antiracist and feminist mentorship. As Audre Lorde (1984, 42) stated, "that visibility which makes us most vulnerable is that which also is the source of our greatest strength." In building on her legacy of empowerment through vulnerability, it is important to bring to light the invisible hand of patriarchy in WGS, a discipline established during the second-wave feminist movement to address persistent gender inequities.

A different sort of trauma continued after I earned tenure, when my partner and I decided to leave the midwestern institution to accept a position he was offered in California. Currently, I am financially privileged to be an independent scholar, but this was not the plan. I assumed I would be a "spousal accommodation" hire at my partner's school in the University of California system. (I am acutely aware that spousal hires accrue their own kind of privilege.) Yet a newly hired dean refused to contribute one-third of my not-large salary after the provost and dean of my partner's school had already agreed to put two-thirds toward my hire. The department wanted me, but ultimately the dean of my would-be college chose not to hire me. Later that year, I learned he had offered the department a two-year instructional hire, and it was hard not to take this rejection personally. Though the institution is designated as "Hispanic serving," its university-wide statistics on tenure-track and tenured faculty of color are abysmal.

Monica's Story

A first-generation scholar from a midwestern working-class family, I benefited from a world-class education at the University of Chicago, thanks to abundant scholarships, student loans, and a small (but large for them) financial contribution from my parents. I also worked throughout college, twenty hours per week during the school year, during every vacation, and full time in the summers. Only recently did I repay one of my student loans, at age fifty-six. My class status fundamentally shaped my undergraduate experiences and contributed to my interest in understanding—and working to ameliorate—inequality. At the same time, college profoundly changed my life, including my career trajectory and social mobility. I shifted from wanting to attend law school, a field legible to my family and to me, to becoming a professional sociologist. Until I entered college, I had no idea that one could make a living, or a difference, as a professor.

And yet institutions and the people within them have a way of pushing back and reminding people they do not belong. I will never forget the look of distaste on the face of a financial aid officer at my elite college when I sought an additional student loan so that I could purchase an Apple Macintosh computer—as if I was either not managing my money well or did not need a new technology that many other (more privileged) students already had. Classism in action! Nor will I forget, later during graduate school, sharing an airport shuttle with a few other folks after the annual conference of the American Sociological Association, when I was on the job market. A white male full professor asked, leeringly, if I wanted to share my vitae with him, so that he could "put in a good word" with the hiring powers. When I rejected his offer, he told me, "Well, nobody hires blonds anyway." Sexism in action!

A few years later, following tenure at the University of California, Santa Cruz, I took a leave of absence to pursue motherhood and nonprofit work. After I left, a colleague and friend (or so I thought) disparaged my departure in a faculty meeting as "blond ambition," according to another colleague who was there. (Notice the recurring gendered hair-color theme.) I ultimately did not return to Santa Cruz. Later, when I tendered my resignation from an administrative job at one Arizona university to accept a department chair position at another, my dean at the former university—who described herself dishonestly as a "feminist"—violated federal policy by having my health insurance canceled and also stopped my summer pay, even though *I was still employed*. I did not know my insurance had been canceled until my youngest daughter needed surgery, and we had none. When I sought legal counsel, I was told that my former institution "played dirty" and that, because I would continue to be employed by the Arizona Board of Regents, I should simply move on. Defeated, I did.

As a trauma survivor who has, for decades, lived with panic disorder and chronic anxiety, I have also had to manage an invisible disability in an industry built on the primacy of rational thought. I have done so incredibly well, or so it seems, given how frequently people tell me they are surprised that I have anxiety. I am, as they say, *high functioning*. But this does not mean that I have not canceled work trips when my anticipatory flight terror became too much, or missed important meetings, or turned down opportunities that would have interfered with my ability to take care of myself. It also does not mean I have not endured numerous meetings wondering where else I could be, sometimes unable to still my heart or catch my breath. I have frequently been physically ill from anxiety, and I have also needed to take an occasional "mental health day." A graduate school colleague once described me to a mutual friend as "flaky." Maybe. Or maybe I was simply listening to my body and/or later taking care of my daughters as a single mother. Early in my career, I chose to write publicly about my anxiety, in large part because academics with mental health challenges need role models, and hope.

There are numerous other examples of ways I was made to feel as if I did not belong, or had done something wrong by simply existing in a space not meant for me. (I will not even mention here what it means to be a mother in the academy—that topic requires its own volume.) Indeed, as a woman, these instances of small and larger injuries alike have escalated as I have ascended the academic food chain. If women should not be graduate students or professors, they certainly should not be deans. The College and University Professional Association for Human Resources notes that "women and minorities are woefully underrepresented among the highest-paid higher ed deans" (Kline 2019). Of course, associate deans or other support roles are acceptable—at a former institution, a colleague referred dismissively to the college's four women associate deans (including me) as "deanlets." Fortunately, our male dean firmly and publicly corrected them in a too-rare show of allyship.

I also understand that I enjoy many privileges that others do not. I am white. I am able bodied most days, though menopause, age, and a newly diagnosed chronic illness pose unbidden limitations. I am heterosexual and partnered (to a white man, so I also enjoy privileges by proximity). I am a tenured full professor. I am solidly upper-middle class, despite my working-class roots. And I have held many leadership roles through which I have gained and wielded institutional power, roles that have afforded some degree of protection to me while also serving as a means for enacting systemic change. Yet, it must also be said, on occasion I have been in the position of upholding questionable practices—Sara Ahmed (2022) calls this "institutional polishing"—a cost of leadership that has sometimes been untenable. At the Arizona institution I mentioned earlier, I ultimately resigned from my position because I was tired of being asked to throw other women under the bus and, on at least two occasions, to bend the law. (For the record, I refused to do so.) Stepping away from my role prompted retaliation from my dean and the woman administrator she hired to replace me.

I have also had many opportunities as a leader to witness institutional betrayal in action and to push back on these betrayals, sometimes to my own professional detriment. As a department chair, associate dean for faculty affairs and inclusion, and dean, I have lost count of how many people have been injured—morally, psychologically, economically, and physically—in the workplace. To be clear, one is too many, but when every third or fourth meeting involves discussion of some form of institutional betrayal and a box of tissues, we have a problem. I have counseled people to leave academia, for their own sanity and survival. I have encouraged women associate professors to seek promotion to full, despite subtle negative messages they received from department chairs and colleagues. I have listened in dismay and anger as untenured women of color have described microaggressions and worse from their white colleagues, men and women alike. I hold close many people's secrets about their divorces, marriages, affairs, and other forms of interpersonal disruption; their pregnancies, wanted and unwanted; the unceasing ineptitude of department chairs, deans, provosts, and presidents, an ineptitude that in some cases borders on criminal; and the ways damaged people hurt other people in systems not designed for care.

Overview of the Volume

It is these experiences, coupled with our belief that things can and should be better, that we offer this volume on institutional betrayal and courage in higher education. If any industry should put people first, it is ours, given our fundamental educational and socializing mission. We are here to serve others, full stop, and we firmly believe in this mission. Yet so many academics are fleeing for industries that are, surprisingly, proving to be kinder, more lucrative, more flexible, and more forgiving. Why? Because many universities have forgotten how to serve others, including the people within them—their employees—who keep things running. If students have become "customers," what does that make university employees? While not ready to turn our backs on higher education, given its promise of social mobility and its capacity to change people's lives, we are more than ready to pull back the veil, as many others have done before us, on its hostile and harmful practices.

We have organized this collection into five sections: (I) "Betrayal"; (II) "Gender-Based Violence, Sexual Assault, and Title IX"; (III) "Belonging"; (IV) "Disability, Health, and (Non)Normative Bodies"; and (V) "Resistance and Resilience." Many of the chapters fit into more than one category, and we hope that readers will gain insight from the connective tissue binding the sections. We have included original research, essays, stories, art, and poetry, recognizing that a multigenre approach offers our best hope for revealing varied local, institutional conditions alongside the macro conditions that cause people harm. Taken together, the authors gathered here present a powerful indictment of institutional betrayal in higher education and a call for systemic change. Individually, they offer texture and context, letting us into the often painful lived experiences of navigating the twenty-first-century university.

A powerful poem by scholar Amy Andrea Martinez, "Terca Pero No Pendeja," follows this introduction and sets the tone for the entire book. Her beautiful defiance in the face of oppression challenges the very terms of professionalism, who sets these terms, and who belongs. "We are here," she asserts, despite ongoing microagressions and "the boundaries and borders of confinement." Martinez's politics and poetics embody refusal and dignity as she creatively works to decolonize the academy, overthrow tradition, and honor the legacy of parents who "crossed deserts, climbed barbed wire fences, and swallowed many instances of white racism." Martinez is thriving, unapologetically and audaciously. Courage, in verse.

Part I, "Betrayal," includes seven contributions that speak directly to structural experiences of institutional betrayal. Poet Wang Ping's "Pity the Nation" fiercely calls out academia's spirit-destroying corporatism alongside political corruption, reminding us that "freedom is never free" and inviting us to "stand together for truth." Next, gender studies scholar Taylor Marie Doherty describes the harassment she experienced in a doctoral program as a queer, anticapitalist, working-class feminist. Refusing to be "a circus animal for any institution," Doherty encourages us to consider not only forms of institutional harms but also how we might strategically betray the institutions that betray us. Social work scholar Susan Hillock brings us to pedagogy and the ways that sharing personal and social identities to "welcome students in" may be unsafe for those who teach. Gendered and homophobic backlash in her case led to social and economic harms, leading Hillock to wonder how much more data about harm we need before systems change.

Next, Matthew Wills offers a lighter, though no less critical, touch with his poem "Vice-Chancellor Bliss-Simpson." Through the personification of a self-absorbed university administrator, Wills reminds us that harm comes not only from structures but also from the humans working inside and animating them. Innovation and strategic planning, though trendy, do not necessarily help those in need. Speaking of those in need, activist and poet Jasmine Banks tackles the politics of student debt, specifically the role of the Koch brothers and their many academic fronts in fostering inequality. In following the money, Banks reveals the oversized role of special interests in university business, with students the clear losers.

Celeste Atkins shares her experiences of being blacklisted at a community college in Arizona, including microaggressions from white women and male leaders. She offers an important example of how institutions may embrace "civility" without understanding or caring about its racist dimensions, and the ways that complaint processes favor the status quo. Particularly notable is her depiction of how marginalized faculty may be negatively impacted by reorganizations. And last in this section, Meg A. Warren and Samit D. Bordoloi offer an empirical study of male allyship in STEM fields, suggesting that it may be quite helpful for men to step up when women are experiencing institutional betrayal. They also show, however, that male allies may themselves experience pushback when they step up, revealing that institutions will not change through allyship alone. Structural reform is also needed.

Part II, "Gender-Based Violence, Sexual Assault, and Title IX," documents specific and chronic harms related to gender, sexuality, and power. It is not surprising that betrayal occurs in and through the very spaces set up to mediate such harms, especially when institutions themselves are sedimented with harmful practices. Sociologist Alanna Gillis narrates the sexual harassment she experienced as a graduate student, noting that while her male professor was found guilty, the complaint process itself reproduced harm. Forced to remain as his teaching assistant or lose her stipend, she was subjected to ongoing harassment. There was simply no room in the process for her protection.

Cierra Raine Sorin, who had been a doctoral student in the University of California system, offers a sadly similar tale of processes gone awry, showcasing the many harms stemming from her research and activism on sexual and domestic violence. An advocate for policy shifts, she notes that graduate students often fall through the cracks in policies and processes designed primarily for undergraduates. Addressing campus sexual violence head on, Connor Spencer, Chantelle

Spicer, and Emily Rosser—Students for Consent Culture Canada—describe their efforts to form a survivor-centered advocacy group, the avenues for their work opened by the Me Too movement, and the doors slammed shut when faculty were called out for bad behavior. Their Open Secrets Project revealed an academic culture that tolerates abusive faculty behavior and fails to protect students, underscoring the hypocrisy of institutions that claim to take oppression and violence seriously.

Part III, "Belonging," explores diverse aspects and spaces of inclusion and community, including those structures and practices that make belonging possible and those that exclude. Poet Wang Ping begins the section with "The Story of Ping," an autoethnographic poem/essay that poignantly connects her childhood in China to her quest for freedom in American higher education—a freedom that remains sadly elusive. But in living like a poet, Ping finds a purpose in the suffering and an element of freedom in swimming the river like a carp. Her words are both an indictment and a balm.

English professor Aparajita De also longed for freedom in the academy, yet was told that experiencing oppression and betrayal as a South Asian woman were the price of this American dream. Her commitment to students marked her as a cultural other, and colleagues disparaged her pedagogy, language, and scholarship. Even in a minority-serving institution, her perceived foreignness was cause for microaggressions related to race, ethnicity, and religion, leading her to suggest tangible changes in hiring practices and support for international students and faculty. Literary scholar Rashna Batliwala Singh confronted a different form of othering in the academy, specifically as an "international" faculty member writing and speaking on matters of U.S. politics. Inquiring how foreign faculty are actualized, she notes that "diversity initiatives seldom address xenophobia," and native-born faculty of all races and ethnicities may engage in harmful behaviors. Foreign-born faculty, she argues, "must become part of the national conversation without punitive consequences," while native-born faculty must become more conscious of their own biases.

Taking up questions of belonging in gender and women's studies, Kristina Gupta explores what happens when departments do not have explicitly antiracist and feminist policies and practices. In Gupta's case, questioning anti-Muslim racism led to retaliation and ongoing professional harm. Her chapter draws important attention to notions of willful ignorance and the framing of those who raise questions as troublemakers. We move next to a consideration of "teaching while Brown," by Mercedes Valadez and Alma Itzé Flores. Drawing from their own experiences, they point to numerous challenges faced by Latina faculty. Their firsthand accounts describe efforts to navigate environments shaped by inequity, including assumptions made by students and others about who belongs in the academy. Suggesting that "the disruption of racial-gendered microaggressions" should be a priority for institutions, they offer some possible ways forward.

From a different vantage as university research staff, Brandy L. Simula and Jessica Bishop-Royse take on the question of who can be a scholar. Though they each hold a doctorate in sociology, their career choices have been challenged in numerous ways by faculty. While their whiteness offers a degree of protection, their staff status does not, nor does their gender. Microaggressions abound, including untitling and uncredentialing, as well as lack of access to institutional resources. Simula and Bishop-Royse helpfully offer recommendations for affirming the value of staff scholars and their research. And last, African American studies scholar Jasmine L. Harris presents an empirical study of belonging for Black students at predominantly white institutions. Surveying 1,400 students, she found that Black students reported feeling less safe and connected on campus than white students. In order to create connections and foster belonging, Black students remap campus in ways that prioritize their own safety and experiences. She concludes that as universities seek to make campuses more inclusive, they need to better understand how Black students perceive belonging in their own terms.

Section IV, "Disability, Health, and (Non)Normative Bodies," draws our attention to the ways that embodiment intersects with inclusion and betrayal. Rachael McCollum and Krista L. Benson discuss institutional responses to their submission of a disability studies research project. Rejection of the project revealed both tacit and explicit ableism, which the authors describe as both institutional failure and disability injustice. Calling for the need to embed disability justice throughout higher education, the chapter thoughtfully highlights the personal and professional costs of ableism.

Sara A. Mata documents the experiences of women faculty with breast cancer. Through words, including quotes from Audre Lorde, and images, Mata shows how the women in her account were both visible and invisible in their cancer experiences. Institutions failed to make space for their illnesses, for example through inadequate sick leave policies, while breast cancer itself underscored the limitations of embodied gender. This chapter showcases the need for institutions to be more inclusive of a range of embodied experiences, including illness. Similarly, C. Goldberg shares what happened when university administrators instructed her to follow protocols to assess workplace accommodations during the COVID-19 pandemic. Rather than discuss the supports they might offer to enable her to keep teaching online, they ignored their appointed "employee well-being" specialist's assessments and recommendations, abruptly terminating her teaching assistant contract mid-semester. They did so without further consultation with her, telling her that she was being accommodated. Goldberg documents the harm and irony of having her own legally protected rights as an employee with disabilities violated by the same institution that subsequently invited her to TA a course on human rights in the workplace.

The final chapter in this section is from Doreen Hsu, who explores mental health among graduate students. Calling into question specifically a deficit model that implies such challenges are individual rather than contextual or structural, Hsu outlines the ways in which peer support becomes a de facto response. Unfortunately, in the absence of institutional responsibility, assuming that students will support other students may instead lead to competition and harm. The resulting stress and insecurity has implications for graduate student well-being, retention, and program completion.

Part V, "Resistance and Resilience," showcases some of the many ways that people push back against harmful institutions and behaviors. Black feminist and critical race scholar Jennifer M. Gómez describes her embodied presence on a search committee as a Black woman and the corresponding lack of recognition of her personhood. Critiquing the power of white mediocrity, she resists performative diversity by not resigning from the committee and not remaining silent about racism in the process. Courage is also found in self-affirmation of her soul and refusal to be just a body.

Sociologists Jennifer Lai and Angélica Ruvalcaba tell each other's stories as a way to document their lived experiences as BIPOC graduate students in a predominantly white institution. In sharing their experiences with each other, and in narrating them for this volume, they find that institutional compassion can create spaces for rest and recuperation for marginalized students. They encourage institutions to listen to and trust BIPOC and other marginalized students as experts that can help create safer, better learning environments.

Next, dancer and dance teacher Kathy Diehl's poem, "Out of the Shadows," explores starting over as a middle-aged woman after budget cuts and layoffs. Listening to her body's wisdom, she resists invisibility, dancing her way "out of the lies" and reclaiming what she knows. Her words offer hope for reinvention and freedom after harmful economic shifts in higher education. Shantel Martinez's poem, "*La*

Llorona of the Academy," reclaims—in her words—"the monster of *la llorona* into a figure of power, freedom, and beauty." Depicting herself as the "wailing woman" of academia, Martinez narrates the legacies of trauma, racism, sexism, and betrayal, forging a new, creative path of belonging and being. As with Diehl, she will not be silenced.

Sociologist James M. Thomas (JT) closes this section with a tale about how his 2018 tweet about migrant children spawned a right-wing harassment campaign. The ensuing hateful and threatening emails and phone calls necessitated placing a security detail in his academic department. That he was largely unbothered by this campaign bothered many. At the same time, he and his colleagues released a study of racial microaggressions that led to accusations of bias and questions about his research integrity, including from senior leadership at his university. In the face of institutional silence, JT chose to speak, to become a problem. This, too, is resistance.

Last, we invited Reshmi Dutt-Ballerstadt, notable public scholar and director of critical ethnic studies at Linfield University, to write an afterword to this collection. Her contribution focuses on the politics of complaint and what happens behind closed doors in university settings. Eschewing secrecy, she tweeted about an investigation of bias, which led to both internal repercussions and external attention. Drawing on the example of her own institution, she shows how institutions weaponize their human resources and other processes to silence and punish those who demonstrate institutional courage. The costs of exhibiting courage, though, are high, exacting economic, bodily, and other tolls on those who resist. Dutt-Ballerstadt writes that "being brave comes with a price." Her afterword underscores that, while resistance is important to institutional change, individuals cannot act alone; remaking institutions must be a collective endeavor that targets structural deficits in higher education.

•

You might ask, How should I read this volume? We suggest you read it any way that is most helpful and instructive to you and to those you care about. Some readers may travel from front to back, while others may read thematically by section or by individual authors. Our hope is that this book will be a valuable resource for those who seek to transform institutions, for those who have been harmed by institutions, and for those who care for and about those who are harmed by institutions. We especially hope that university leaders will take note, finding the courage to act differently or to make way for those who will. In fact, we encourage university presidents and provosts to assign this book to deans and department chairs, in much the same way that at one institution, Monica recommended that department heads read the groundbreaking volume *Presumed Incompetent* (Gutiérrez y Muhs et al. 2012). Our own intention with this collection is that universities endeavor to emphasize an equitable *culture of care* over a *culture of compliance*, though we understand that existing structures, policies, and procedures make this difficult. The voices herein offer numerous courageous examples of ways to name and overcome institutional harms and forge a more inclusive culture of belonging and humanity.

Acknowledgments

First and foremost, we thank our contributors, not only for their bravery but also for their patience, encouragement, and good humor. This project began many years ago and was derailed by the COVID-19 pandemic, our own institutional and geographic moves, the trials and tribulations of mothering (between us, we have five young adult children between the ages of twenty-one and twenty-six), loss of life of people dear to us, and a host of other roadblocks. And yet here we are, in no small part due to the people whose words and images are contained herein. We are grateful, too, for three helpful and affirmative reviews of this manuscript—we always learn from reviewers, and this project was no different. Kristen Buckles is an editor-in-chief extraordinaire and a valued friend and ally. We have enjoyed working with her and the University of Arizona Press team, even while they were forced to contend with our delays. Octavio Quintanilla, artist and poet, provided the beautiful cover image; we are so appreciative of his creativity. And last, of course, we thank each other—especially for the mutual love, concern, and understanding as we have navigated personal and professional challenges. Our texts to each other from near and far have often been lifesaving, or at least life affirming, and often great fun.

Works Cited

Abrica, Elvira Julia, and Ruth Oliver Andrew. 2024. "The Racial Politics of Diversity, Equity, and Inclusion (DEI) Work." *Journal of Diversity in Higher Education*. Advance online publication. https://doi.org/10.1037/dhe0000566.

Ahmed, Sara. 2012. *On Being Included: Racism and Diversity in Institutional Life*. Durham, NC: Duke University Press.

Ahmed, Sara. 2021. *Complaint!* Durham, NC: Duke University Press.

Alexander, Taifha Natalee. 2023. "Efforts to Ban Critical Race Theory Have Been Put Forth in All but One State—and Many Threaten Schools with a Loss of Funds." *The Conversation*, April 7, 2023. https://theconversation.com/efforts-to-ban-critical-race-theory-have-been-put-forth-in-all-but-one-state-and-many-threaten-schools-with-a-loss-of-funds-200816.

Allegretto, Sylvia, Emma García, and Elaine Weiss. 2022. "Public Education Funding in the U.S. Needs an Overhaul." Economic Policy Institute, July 12, 2022. https://www.epi.org/publication/public-education-funding-in-the-us-needs-an-overhaul/.

American Association of University Women. n.d. "Fast Facts: Women Working in Academia." Accessed September 20, 2024. https://www.aauw.org/resources/article/fast-facts-academia/.

Bartlett, Tom. 2021. "Why Are Colleges So Cowardly? Jennifer Freyd Has a Few Ideas." *Chronicle of Higher Education* 67, no. 24 (July 23): 40.

Bell, Derrick. 1989. *And We Are Not Saved: The Elusive Quest for Racial Justice*. New York: Basic Books.

———. 1992. *Faces at the Bottom of the Well: The Permanence of Racism*. New York: Basic Books.

———. 2008. *Race, Racism, and American Law*. 6th ed. Boston: Aspen Publishing.

Binyam, Maya. 2022. "You Pose a Problem: A Conversation with Sara Ahmed." *Paris Review*, January 14, 2022. https://www.theparisreview.org/blog/2022/01/14/you-pose-a-problem-a-conversation-with-sara-ahmed/.

Bryant, Jessica, and Chloe Appleby. 2024. "These States' Anti-DEI Legislation May Impact Higher Education." BestColleges, updated May 22, 2024. https://www.bestcolleges.com/news/anti-dei-legislation-tracker/.

Christl, Maria-Ernestina, Kim-Chi Tran Pham, Adi Rosenthal, and Anne P. DePrince. 2024. "When Institutions Harm Those Who Depend on Them." *Trauma, Violence & Abuse* 25, no. 4 (October): 2797–2813. https://doi.org/10.1177/15248380241226627.

Chronicle of Higher Education. 2024. "DEI Legislation Tracker." Accessed May 28, 2024. https://www.chronicle.com/article/here-are-the-states-where-lawmakers-are-seeking-to-ban-colleges-dei-efforts?sra=true.

Cottom, Tressie McMillan. 2015. "'Who Do You Think You Are?' When Marginality Meets Academic Microcelebrity." *ADA: A Journal of Gender, New Media, and Technology*, no. 7 (April): n.p. https://scholarsbank.uoregon.edu/xmlui/handle/1794/26359.

Eckstein, Griffin. 2024. "'Sexual Violence Is Such a Thief': Ashley Judd Speaks Out Against Overturn of Weinstein Conviction." *Salon*, April 26, 2024. https://www.salon.com/2024/04/26/sexual-violence-is-such-a-thief-ashley-judd-speaks-out-against-overturn-of-weinstein-conviction.

Freyd, Jennifer J. 2008. "Betrayal Trauma." In *The Encyclopedia of Psychological Trauma*, edited by Gilbert Reyes, Jon D. Elhai, and Julian D. Ford, 76. New York: Wiley.

Freyd, Jennifer J. 2018. "When Sexual Assault Victims Speak Out, Their Institutions Often Betray Them." *The Conversation*, January 11, 2018. https://theconversation.com/when-sexual-assault-victims-speak-out-their-institutions-often-betray-them-87050.

Freyd, Jennifer J., and Pamela Birrell. 2013. *Blind to Betrayal: Why We Fool Ourselves We Aren't Being Fooled*. Nashville: Turner Publishing.

Gay, Claudine. 2024. "Claudine Gay: What Just Happened at Harvard Is Bigger Than Me." *New York Times*, January 3, 2024. https://www.nytimes.com/2024/01/03/opinion/claudine-gay-harvard-president.html.

Gutiérrez y Muhs, Gabriella, Yolanda Flores Niemann, Carmen G. González, and Angela P. Harris, eds. 2012. *Presumed Incompetent: The Intersections of Race and Class for Women in Academia*. Boulder: University Press of Colorado.

Heritage Foundation. 2023. *Mandate for Leadership: The Conservative Promise.* Washington, D.C.: Heritage Foundation.

Hirsch, Lauren, and Sarah Kessler. 2023. "How Much Influence Should Universities Give Their Donors?" *New York Times*, October 21, 2023. https://www.nytimes.com/2023/10/21/business/dealbook/college-donors-israel-hamas.html.

Hollis, Leah P. 2024. "Dying To Be Heard?" *Inside Higher Ed*, January 22, 2024. https://www.insidehighered.com/opinion/views/2024/01/22/tragedy-workplace-bullying-opinion.

Hollis, Leah P. 2021. *Human Resource Perspectives on Workplace Bullying in Higher Education: Understanding Vulnerable Employees' Experiences.* New York: Routledge.

Howe, Amy. 2023. "Supreme Court Strikes Down Affirmative Action Programs in College Admissions." SCOTUSblog, June 29, 2023. https://www.scotusblog.com/2023/06/supreme-court-strikes-down-affirmative-action-programs-in-college-admissions/.

Jaleel, Rana. 2021. "Critical Race Theory and the Assault on Antiracist Thinking: What Counts as Racism?" *Academe* 107, no. 4 (Fall): n.p. https://www.aaup.org/article/critical-race-theory-and-assault-antiracist-thinking.

Jalonick, Mary Clare, Eric Tucker, Farnoush Amiri, Jill Colvin, Michael Balsamo, and Nomaan Merchant. 2022. "Trump 'Lit That Fire' of Capitol Insurrection, Jan 6 Committee Report Says." PBS, December 23, 2021. https://www.pbs.org/newshour/politics/trump-lit-that-fire-of-capitol-insurrection-jan-6-committee-report-says.

Jeffries-El, Malika. 2022. "How Do We Mitigate the Impact of Systemic Bias on Faculty from Underrepresented Groups?" American Association for the Advancement of Science, December 14, 2022. https://aaas-iuse.org/mitigate-the-impact-of-systemic-bias/.

June, Audrey Williams, and Brian O'Leary. 2021. "How Many Black Women Have Tenure on Your Campus? Search Here." *Chronicle of Higher Education* 67, no. 19 (May 27): n.p. https://www.chronicle.com/article/how-many-black-women-have-tenure-on-your-campus-search-here.

Kamola, Isaac. 2019. "Dear Administrators: To Protect Your Faculty from Right-Wing Attacks, Follow the Money." *AAUP Journal of Academic Freedom* 10:1–22. https://www.aaup.org/sites/default/files/kamola.pdf.

Kiesow, Damon. 2021 "Statement from the Knight Chairs in Journalism to UNC's Board of Trustees." Medium, May 21, 2021. https://dkiesow.medium.com/statement-from-the-knight-chairs-in-journalism-to-uncs-board-of-trustees-11023e51560e.

Kline, Missy. 2019. "Women and Minorities Lack Representation Among Highest-Paid Higher Ed Deans." College and University Professional Association for Human Resources, April 24. https://www.cupahr.org/blog/women-and-minorities-lack-representation-among-highest-paid-higher-ed-deans.

Krupnick, Matt. 2023. "Attacks on Tenure Leave College Professors Eyeing the Exits." Center for Public Integrity, December 19, 2023. https://publicintegrity.org/education/academic-freedom/attacks-tenure-college-professors-exits/.

Lawrence, Andrew. 2024. "'She Endured Cruelty': What Led to a Leader's Death at a Historically Black University?" *The Guardian*, February 28, 2024. https://www.theguardian.com/us-news/2024/feb/28/antoinette-candia-bailey-lincoln-university-death.

Lorde, Audre. 1984 "The Master's Tools Will Never Dismantle the Master's House." 1984. In *Sister Outsider: Essays and Speeches*, 110–14. Berkeley: Crossing Press.

Niemann, Yolanda Flores, Gabriella Gutiérrez y Muhs, and Carmen G. González. 2020. *Presumed Incompetent II: Race, Class, Power, and Resistance of Women in Academia*. Logan: Utah State University Press.

Nittle, Nidra. 2024. "'We Don't Want to Go Through the Same Heartbreak': An Administrator's Death Sparks a Call to Action at an HBCU." *The 19th*, February 23. https://19thnews.org/2024/02/lincoln-university-antoinette-candia-bailey-justice/.

Powell, Meerah. 2021. "Retired Professor and University of Oregon Settle Longstanding Lawsuit." Oregon Public Broadcasting, July 17, 2021. https://www.opb.org/article/2021/07/17/university-oregon-professor-settle-equal-pay-lawsuit/.

Rivera, Suzanne M. 2024. "The Presidential Voice." *Inside Higher Ed*, February 13, 2024. https://www.insidehighered.com/opinion/views/2024/02/13/its-time-reset-presidential-statements-opinion.

Robertson, Katie. 2021. "Nikole Hannah-Jones Denied Tenure at University of North Carolina." *New York Times*, May 19, 2021. https://www.nytimes.com/2021/05/19/business/media/nikole-hannah-jones-unc.html.

Samuels, Alex, and Neil Lewis Jr. 2022. "How White Victimhood Fuels Republican Politics." *FiveThirtyEight*, March 21, 2022. https://fivethirtyeight.com/features/how-white-victimhood-fuels-republican-politics/.

Smith, Carly P., and Jennifer Freyd. 2014. "Institutional Betrayal." *American Psychologist* 69 (6): 575–87. https://doi.org/10.1037/a0037564.

Waxman, Olivia B. 2022. "Anti-'Critical Race Theory' Laws Are Working: Teachers Are Thinking Twice About How They Talk About Race." *Time*, June 30, 2022. https://time.com/6192708/critical-race-theory-teachers-racism/.

1

Terca Pero No Pendeja

Amy Andrea Martinez

Me dicen que no me vista así
No crop tops
Dark-colored lipstick
Heavy makeup
Colored hair
Snapbacks
Grillz
Gold gauges

It's not professional
They would say

But the middle of my brown *pancita*
Abuelita chocolate matte lipstick
Carefully drawn eyebrows
Black-winged cat eyes
Leopard-print hair
Expanded earlobes
Let me make a bold statement

Estoy presente
We are here
I could give you Kehlani's sexy tomboy—urban—baggy clothes aesthetic

and I could give you my long Oaxacan *huipiles*
crystal necklaces
a spiritual *curandera* look
Or I could give you the carefully trimmed hot-pink blazer
American Apparel black disco pants
Moschino 500 leopard-print eyeglasses
and Steve Madden high-heeled white boots
with a light
nude
lip gloss
My aesthetic was not only a reclamation of space
It was a manifestation of my peoples' embodied and dignified spirit
A rebelde sin causa they would always say
Pero don't get it twisted
I was still a *doctora* in the making
Actively, intentionally, carving out my own way
Designing my own brownprint Toward
a dignified re-presentation of what and who a *Xicana* PhD is and looks
like
Willfully pushing against the boundaries and borders of confinement
And even when I got pushed out of UC Berkeley's Ethnic Studies department,
(A weak case of attempted spirit murder)
I still got up ten* and was accepted into another top-tier public
university
Retribution
You did not break me
A proud politics of refusal
Carefully outlined on the curvatures of my facial features
an old colonial logic of white professionalism
and aptitude
That constantly serves to remind me
You don't belong here

* A reference to rap star Cardi B's song "Get Up 10" from her 2018 *Invasion of Privacy* album.

Trying to psychologically
institutionally impose an *impostor syndrome*
But I always woke up feeling worthy
WE BELONG HERE
I allow my aesthetics to do the reclaiming
My parents crossed deserts, climbed barbed wire fences, and swallowed many
instances of white racism How dare I
—not honor their legacy of resilience?
Why
would I ever allow or willfully consent to
—pledge allegiance to—
an ivory tower, an institution
Built on
STOLEN

Indigenous land
By the hands
of Black
Brown
Indigenous people?
Incessant lies and broken promises
Institutional betrayals
Our dignity is not up for negotiation
As a petite chocolate-skinned *Xicana indígena*
I stand as an embodied audacious and strategic willful defiance
A testament
against white assimilation
Still walking through the white halls of a criminal justice department with
Crop tops
Dark-colored lipstick
Colorful makeup
Colored hair

Snapbacks
Grillz
Gold gauges

And ankle-high Timberlands
Still winning awards
Expanding networks
Publishing
Cultivating a modality of balanced self-preservation
in the face of colonial and delusional notions of success, (white) professionalism,
tradition, and meritocracy
Decolonizing the way we think about, practice, and embody
being an academic—in this white academy
You. May. Not. Understand. Me.
But just remember
I am only here to revert the colonial gaze back unto spirit murderers in these academic
colonial trenches
Unapologetically. *Subversively.* Willfully. *Audaciously.*
—Porque soy terca, pero no pendeja.
BITCH I'M THRIVING.

Part I

Betrayal

2

Pity the Nation

after Ferlinghetti

Wang Ping

Pity the nation whose freedom melts faster than Arctic ice*
Whose justice defends sex predators & puts children in jail
Pity the nation that sells academia into corporate fiefdoms
Whose presidents scream "Not enough" with their million-dollar
package
Who hike up tuitions to shackle students with debts
Who turn professors into adjuncts and intellectual slaves
Pity the nation branding youths with Divide & Conquer logo
Who get rewards for ordering professors to "take down the syllabi!"
Calling them "racists & appropriators" as public shaming
Pity the nation whose education becomes "just business"
Its giant machine squeezing hefty tuitions from Chinese
Who sell kidneys to send children to America for a degree
Oh pity the nation whose president churns lies like popcorn
Whose students get awards for banishing Native grandpas from the
campus
For yelling "You should feel lucky I find your words good enough to
plagiarize"

---

* This poem was originally published in the autumn 2019 issue of *World Literature Today* (https://www.worldliteraturetoday.org/2019/autumn/pity-nation-wang-ping). It is reprinted with the permission of the author.

To her professors who try to teach academic integrity
Pity the nation as her Lady weeps for children caged along the southern border
Her torch stolen to slow-burn truth tellers
Pity the nation that rewards cheaters and mediocrity
That condemns poetry for "manipulating emotions"
That bullies truth into silence
That gags science, deletes data, exiles facts into deserts
That wires classrooms with eyes and ears to break spirits
Oh pity the nation that builds its high tower
Upon the bones of the Natives, slaves, coolies, immigrant poets . . .
Oh pity!
Oh let's pity the nation with actions!
Let's stand together for truth
Freedom is never free
It wants our flesh and spirit
But it's worth it
Our reason to live

3

Reflections on Belonging and Betrayal from "One of Those Gender Studies People"

Taylor Marie Doherty

"Oh, you must be one of those gender studies people."

The disdain in his voice was palpable. His words dripped with misogyny. I was at an academic conference presenting my research on feminist economics and the gendered impacts of post-conflict economic reconstruction in Latin America. I had bumped into my discussant before the panel and was making academic small talk. He asked if I was presenting and I told him he was actually the discussant on my panel. He asked about my paper that I had sent him over a week before the deadline. Not only did he not read my paper—which I later found out was the only paper sent on time—he did not even know what it was about. When I told him about my research, he laughed and exclaimed, "Oh, you must be one of those gender studies people." When I told him we were in the same field—political science—he laughed again, as though gender is not always political. I walked away, hurt and dismissed. But I didn't dwell on it. I also felt hopeful and excited to begin my PhD program a few months later. After all, I was going to become a political theorist in a progressive, heterodox department!

This would be a new chapter. I still remember the parting words of my master's adviser. They came from a place of care, but they stung and were profoundly gendered. He told me I would be chewed up and spit out by academia because I care too much. He told me to stop caring about the world so much because there would be nothing I could do to change it. "You can only do your best and hope for the best for the world, Taylor," he said, "but you cannot change it." Of course, men are not told that they care too much because they are not expected to perform emotional labor.

Emotional labor, a concept theorized by sociologist Arlie Hochschild ([1983] 2012), refers to the management of one's own emotions in order to elicit emotional responses in others (Bellas 1999, 97). This reflection expands on this understanding of emotional labor to include often invisible and unpaid interpersonal care labor that occurs in universities. Women in the academy—faculty, graduate students, and staff alike—are called into roles of service and care at much higher rates than their male colleagues (Pyke 2011; Guarino and Borden 2017). Women of color are frequently expected to perform departmental service and emotional labor at significantly higher rates than their white counterparts (Bellas 1999; Beetham 2013; Hua 2018; Nash 2019). In naming and interrogating the gendered, racialized, and classed nature of emotional labor—and all academic labor—we can move toward valuing it as work. Redistributing the politics of caregiving can help disrupt the gendered norms and stereotypes at the heart of emotional labor.

In addition to the care we provide for our students, we are often called on to care for our male colleagues. In the first year of my PhD program, I was asked by multiple faculty members to help my male peers who struggled with their work. Some of them stole my coursework and presented it as their own. Others received numerous extra attempts at assignments. They were not and still are not held to the same standard, because emotional labor functions in specifically gendered ways.

During that first year, I experienced sexism from a professor at my institution and rampant queerphobia and sexual harassment from a man in my cohort. When I brought the latter matter to my university through formal processes, I was deemed responsible for my own harassment. I had been friends with him at one point, so according to them, everything he said was OK. The rumors he created were dismissed. His stalking of female professors was completely ignored. The comments on my sexuality were disregarded as inconsequential. I had enabled it by once being his friend. They cited instances of me getting coffee while studying with him as an indication that we had a relationship that warranted his comments. My multiple pleas for him to stop sexualizing me, to stop degrading my female professors, and to stop openly fantasizing about my queer professors meant nothing to the administration. I lost a summer of productivity meeting with investigators who actively used queerphobic language and blamed me for my harassment. The deans I had to meet with turned the investigation back on me. My department chair wrote things off as out of his hands. The final decision exonerated my harasser. I had egged him on because I was nice to him. There is so much more to tell, but my sad guess is that those of you reading this can imagine the rest of the story; it is a story we all know far too well. It became clear that my "progressive" department and flagship university were not without their flaws because, at the end of the day, the university is a site of incredible epistemic (and physical) violence that is gendered, racialized, classed, etc.

The university and academia function as a site of biopolitics: the power to make live or to let die (Foucault 1978). The university and academia become an enactment of institutional and epistemic violences and biopolitics thrust onto "others" who are violently staged as voices and bodies that are never meant to show up, yet are constantly called on, interpellated if you will, to perform intellectually reproductive labors of legibility. The neoliberal academy is dripping with death and erasure (Ohito 2020; Hong 2015). This means asking: On whose death or erasure does my (intellectual) life rest? Who am I silencing? Who gets to be a theorist? Who is relegated to the space of the artist, the activist, or the amateur? Who is taken seriously? What possibilities and conceptual horizons would appear (or reappear) if we were to take seriously as intellectuals those whom the university has discarded? How is the devaluation of certain subjugated knowledges (Collins 2009)—queer and Black feminist thought, for example—linked to social and material death?

In my department, people are too busy fighting each other over petty methodological debates to ask these questions and to fight the cis-heteropatriarchal white supremacy of the academy. We do not need to find common ground; we need to create a new intellectual constellation, a new intellectual commons—one that compensates us for the labor of our intellect and does not just extract the labor of our care. This new commons requires that we deromanticize and actively resist the ways that the capitalist, colonial, neoliberal university commodifies education and the bodies that produce it (Giroux 2013: Meyerhoff 2019). This also means fighting tooth and nail for better working conditions for contingent faculty and graduate students. This current configuration has betrayed so many of us and will continue to do so.

The institution of academia has betrayed me both intellectually and somatically by devaluing my work, safety, and general well-being. But—institutional betrayal goes two ways. I implore that we ask not only how the institution betrays us but how we MUST betray the institution of the university. In other words, can we imagine a configuration in which marginalized people are not both expected to fix the university and also face retribution when we do so? We do not reflect enough on who calls us to show up, who is called to show up, and with what consequences or costs. When we show up, who cares for us? When we show up, who harms us?

There are those who believe I do not belong in this institution. I am a queer, anticapitalist feminist from a working-class background who doesn't know the hidden or even the transparent rules of academia. I am not professionally correct most of the time. I have been punished and labeled as a problem by my department for standing up for our graduate student union rights. One of our department chairs called me disrespectful for speaking out and told me I would never find an academic job or get tenure, but really, he was criticizing me for not performing an appropriately affective mode of docile femininity. I do not want to be a circus animal for any institution—and certainly not for any man; I refuse to perform. I am here to create a disruption by bringing my politics and my lived experiences to the classroom and not treating teaching as a value-neutral endeavor. As scholars, we are obligated socially and morally to help build a better world. I do not know yet what the consequences will be for my disruptions, and that is terrifying. My greatest fear is that I will lose my sense of self in this institution, but I hope and believe that it is this very fear that will prevent me from doing so. I have made numerous promises to myself: I will never lose myself in this institution. I will never be of this institution, but I will occupy space in it. If the cost of a job or tenure one day is my silence, I will gladly become untenurable. I will speak up and make sure others get this chance too. I will never fully belong, and this is OK. I do not want to belong. I would rather burn it all down and build something beautiful in the ashes. I will continue to show up because they do not want me to.

My work in its purest, rawest form aims to be a love letter to queer women, fellow nonbinary femmes, first-generation academics, and the working-class writ large. Embracing my role as "one of those gender studies people" is how I am fighting back. I worry about finding an intellectual and institutional home. I want to tell stories, share narratives, and create things that are much bigger than the four walls of a broken institution. I want to be conceptually adventurous. I want research that doesn't just go outside the box—I want research that destroys the box and exists in the hinterlands. I want to play with words and creativity. I want to tell stories and paint pictures. I want to dare to think and dream against the grain of our prevailing configurations. I want to betray the institution that has betrayed me. And, you know what, being "one of those gender studies people" is the first step.

Acknowledgments

I am grateful to the reviewers for their gracious and helpful feedback. I would also like to thank Catie Fowler for generative conversations, comments, and, above all, for standing up with me in feminist solidarity. R. L., N. D., S. A., and A. D. helped me survive University of Massachusetts Amherst. Thank you for fighting for me, sticking your necks out, and believing me when no one else would. I am incredibly grateful to A. D., H. S., and A. W. for their mentorship and support in finding a new academic home. Lastly, I would not be here without my wife, Anna, and our fur babies, Leviathan and Hypatia.

Works Cited

Beetham, Gwendolyn. 2013. "The Academic Feminist: Women of Color, Racism, and Resilience in Academia." *Feministing*, May 13, 2013. https://feministing.com/2013/05/13/the-academic-feminist-women-of-color-racism-and-resilience-in-academia/.

Bellas, Marcia L. 1999. "Emotional Labor in Academia: The Case of Professors." *ANNALS of the American Academy of Political and Social Science* 561 (1): 96–110. https://doi.org/10.1177/000271629956100107.

Foucault, Michel. 1978. *The History of Sexuality*. Vol. 1, *An Introduction*. Translated by Robert Hurley. New York: Pantheon Books.

Foucault, Michel, Mauro Bertani, Alessandro Fontana, François Ewald, and David Macey. 2003. *Society Must Be Defended: Lectures at the Collège de France, 1975–76*. New York: Picador.

Giroux, Henry. 2013. "The Corporate War Against Higher Education." *Workplace: A Journal for Academic Labor*, no. 9 (February): 103–17. https://doi.org/10.14288/WORKPLACE.V0I9.184051.

Guarino, Cassandra M., and Victor M. H. Borden. 2017. "Faculty Service Loads and Gender: Are Women Taking Care of the Academic Family?" *Research in Higher Education* 58 (6): 672–94. https://doi.org/10.1007/s11162-017-9454-2.

Hill Collins, Patricia. 2009. *Black Feminist Thought: Knowledge, Consciousness, and the Politics of Empowerment*. 2nd ed. New York: Routledge.

Hochschild, Arlie Russel. (1983). 2012. *The Managed Heart: Commercialization of Human Feeling*. Updated with a new preface. Berkeley: University of California Press.

Hong, Grace Kyungwon. 2015. "Neoliberal Disavowal and the Politics of the Impossible." In *Death Beyond Disavowal: The Impossible Politics of Difference*, 1–34. Difference Incorporated. Minneapolis: University of Minnesota Press.

Hua, Linh U. 2018. "Slow Feeling and Quiet Being: Women of Color Teaching in Urgent Times." *New Directions for Teaching and Learning* 2018, no. 153: 77–86. https://doi.org/10.1002/tl.20283.

Lawless, Brandi. 2018. "Documenting a Labor of Love: Emotional Labor as Academic Labor." *Review of Communication* 18, no. 2: 85–97. https://doi.org/10.1080/15358593.2018.1438644.

Meyerhoff, Eli. 2019. *Beyond Education: Radical Studying for Another World*. Minneapolis: University of Minnesota Press.

Nash, Jennifer C. 2019. *Black Feminism Reimagined: After Intersectionality*. Next Wave New Directions in Women's Studies. Durham, NC: Duke University Press.

Ohito, Esther O. 2021. "Some of Us Die: A Black Feminist Researcher's Survival Method for Creatively Refusing Death and Decay in the Neoliberal Academy." *International Journal of Qualitative Studies in Education* 34, no. 6: 515–33. https://doi.org/10.1080/09518398.2020.1771463.

Pyke, Karen. 2011. "Service and Gender Inequity among Faculty." *PS: Political Science & Politics* 44, no. 1: 85–87. https://doi.org/10.1017/S1049096510001927.

4

A Ton of Feathers

Betrayals in Academia

Susan Hillock

Although the literature is replete with discussions about students' safety and trigger warnings, it rarely addresses instructors' safety, especially the safety of those who are untenured, sessional, or dare to live and teach from diverse perspectives, social locations, and identities (Hillock 2021; Gutiérrez y Muhs et al. 2012; Niemann, Gutiérrez y Muhs, and González 2020; Matthew 2016). Some have referred to this as teaching "from the margins" (Kirby and McKenna 1989). Brown and Strega (2005, 3) explain:

> Teaching and learning from the margins is, on the one hand, self-explanatory in a generation of teachers and learners familiar with the influences of civil rights, "waves" of women's movements, critical race theories, queer theory, theories of disability and equity rights and so on. On the other hand, an awareness of these contemporary social movements is only a beginning in understanding how these theories are reflected and engaged within our classroom spaces, either intentionally or unexpectedly.

In this essay, I share personal vignettes about what happens when those of us who are "othered" dare to transgress (hooks 1994), by choosing to teach openly and transparently from our personal standpoints, locations, and identities (or when we have no choice, as our differences are visible). What do I mean by transgressing? As a structural feminist, I live by the mantra that the personal is political (Levine 1989). Thus, as a role model, I try to be as open as possible about my social locations and identities as a middle-class, white-settler, bisexual, chronic-pain-suffering, cisgender female. So, as a social work professor, I often make disclosures about my coming-out stories, sexuality/identity changes over my lifetime, and gendered experiences of violence, body shame, and empowerment.

I believe that sharing who I am sets the stage for social work students to feel more comfortable in my classrooms and helps them reflect upon their own (and others') sexualities, identities, and experiences of privilege and oppression. Accordingly, instructor self-disclosure is consistent with feminist teaching (Hillock 2021), and as a teaching tool it "decrease[s] power and status differential . . . creates an environment of mutuality and nurtures a partnership in learning that allows students to join the instructor in risk-taking disclosure and challenges their personal beliefs" (Cain 1996, 56–57).

However, sharing who we are is not always safe, as institutions of higher education are not immune from inequality, discriminatory practices, and oppressive forces (Hillock and Mulé 2016; Superson and Cudd 2002). In addition, many students and faculty, who often come from privileged backgrounds, do not necessarily desire transformational learning experiences (El-Alayli, Hansen-Brown, and Ceynar 2018; Hillock 2011; Jeffery 2007; Lund 2010; Overall 1998). In agreement, Redmond (2010) and Schick (2005) argue that resistance to alternative paradigms, paradigms that attempt to interrogate and disrupt traditional knowledges, stems from the entitlements of whiteness, racism, sexism, and classism and how they are entrenched and maintained in academic institutions.

In direct contradiction to the social justice rhetoric that abounds in university policy statements, educators who actively and consciously try to identify their bias, name their social locations and identities, and center knowledge from the margins, are more likely to experience backlash (Chilly Collective 1995). Backlash manifests in many ways, including hostile reactions from students, classroom disruptions, harassment, complaints, and negative course evaluations. These responses to individuals, methods, and knowledges outside the mainstream create and perpetuate an unequal and "chilly climate" for faculty who teach from the margins as well as students who learn from the margins (Chilly Collective 1995). To illustrate my own chilly experiences in academia, I share the following personal vignettes.

My Life in Academia

Over twenty-five years ago, I started working as a social work professor. When I arrived on my first campus, as a new faculty member, I was full of excitement and energy, expecting to work in an environment that would be personally, professionally, and intellectually stimulating and rewarding. Instead, I found myself in a conservative bastion of straight white male over-advantage that produces and perpetuates attitudes and practices that discriminate against those of us who have been "othered." Strikingly, the term "a ton of feathers" has been used to describe women's and other marginalized groups' experiences of oppression and discrimination within these white masculine enclaves (Caplan 1993). Others describe such oppressive institutional practices as death by a thousand paper cuts. Consequently, I would like to share some of the feathers that have weighed me down.

A Ton of Feathers

Once when I was arguing a point in a faculty meeting, a male colleague told me to "shut the fuck up." At a different faculty meeting, when I was presenting a feminist perspective, another male colleague exclaimed that "all feminist theory is crap." This type of disrespect for women is not unusual; indeed, Keller and Moglen (1987, 26) found that "many women faculty experience . . . patronizing judgements made by scornful male teachers and colleagues."

I have also experienced a barrage of verbal, emotional, and sexual harassment. For instance, at another meeting, when I refused to support a male colleague's proposal, he came up to me at break time and physically shook me like I was a small child, in front of witnesses. When I complained, he treated his actions like they were a joke. I have also had a male faculty member march into my office, chastising and screaming at me and wagging his finger in my face, again like I was a small child. Another time, a male colleague attempted to shove his hand down the front of my skirt, making a joke about how "hot" I was, like that was a reasonable excuse for his actions.

Departmental Betrayal

Every time I attempted to stand up for myself, speak out, and resist these actions—as well as the overarching dominant-subordinate racist and heterosexist relations that govern faculty decision-making, communication, and power—I ended up paying a high price. I found myself socially ostracized and scapegoated, blocked from career advancement and graduate teaching, excluded from merit pay increases and sabbaticals, and having to increasingly defend my teaching, scholarship, and research (more so than my colleagues, who were often silent witnesses to these actions).

Indeed, not only was I guilty of naming my reality and demanding change, but I also failed to perform the appropriate passive femininity that my colleagues expected. For instance, I was once asked in a faculty meeting to bake cookies for a student fundraiser. When I laughed and refused to do this and pointed out the fact that no one expected or asked our male colleagues to bake, the female chair at the time responded, "Well, not all of us are altruistic as others." Similar statements were made to me and about me when I refused to volunteer for weekend work at high school career fairs. When I asked if the university was willing to pay for my day care and transportation for this "volunteer" work, as I was the only faculty member who was a lone parent, colleagues laughed at me. Consistent with Williams, Alon, and Bornstein's (2006) findings, the realities of managing lone-parent mothering and high academic workloads are rarely acknowledged in university settings. Instead, my reasonable refusal to volunteer was treated as evidence that I was not a "team player."

There you have it . . . I was not a martyr, nor was I maternal enough, sweet enough, or straight enough to satisfy their social constructs of womanhood. Significantly, my story is congruent with the research about women's experiences of discrimination in academia. Overall (1998) discusses the common sexist experiences and consequences for women in the academy, "ranging from the dangers of sexual assault and harassment and the contempt for feminist scholarship, to women's higher workload in student counselling and committees and the paucity of women who are full professors or hold significant administrative positions" (38). At the same time, female faculty "are expected be 'restrained and endlessly supportive' of colleagues while picking up extra secretarial work and to be 'softer' and more available to students than male colleagues" (Williams, Alon, and Bornstein 2006, 82). Similarly, I received backlash when I refused to mother or counsel students on personal issues, thus breaking existing "female" patterns and traditions in the workplace. This gendered expectation that women do what has been called emotional labor results in more of our work hours being spent dealing with students' academic and personal issues compared to our male colleagues (El-Alayli, Hansen-Brown, and Ceynar 2018). The time and energy spent on these tasks can also negatively impact female faculty members' research and tenure and promotion processes (Rinfrette et al. 2015). This is something male colleagues do not experience, or at least do not experience to the same extent (El-Alayli, Hansen-Brown, and Ceynar 2018; Williams, Alon, and Bornstein 2006). In a classic double bind, if we are indeed "supporting and nurturing, female instructors risk being perceived as less authoritative and knowledgeable than their male counterparts" (Mulhere 2014, 2).

Collegial Betrayal

Another example of the pressure to conform, in this case to a traditional standard of femininity, was the time a male boss called me into his office to talk because I "was not warm enough to my colleagues." I laughed out loud and responded that he would never have called in a male faculty member to have this type of discussion. I also challenged him as to why I should be warm to colleagues who had ostracized me and who had either participated in my discrimination or remained silent in the face of it.

Indeed, although anti-oppressive rhetoric abounds in the social work profession (Hillock 2011, 2016), what I have found to be most painful are the colleagues—some of whom share identities with me—who collude with the powers that be and stand by watching while those identified as "other" are being harmed. In order to survive, and succeed, they learn to side with power rather than speak to it or challenge it. In this ultimate betrayal, their silence, denial, and collusion underpin and support the racist, heterosexist dominant-subordinate relations that perpetuate oppression. These experiences can also lead to already marginalized faculty members experiencing loneliness, ostracism, and isolation in their workplaces (Overall 1998; Williams, Alon, and Bornstein 2006).

Betrayal by Students

I have also received a few vitriolic student complaints that I think are misogynist and biphobic, about content that I have taught (e.g., discussing an upcoming sex toy workshop in a feminist class, discussing sex and sexuality openly, supporting queer rights, etc.). However, despite the fact that the majority of students appreciate my content and methods, I have had to formally defend myself, more than once, to white, straight, male deans because a few conservative students dislike feminist/queer approaches. Intuitively, I know that the students' complaints were never about my content or methods, but were instead more about the fact that *I* dared to say controversial things out loud, as a female and as a queer-identified person.

Institutional Betrayal

Sadly, these are only a few examples of the history of sexist and homophobic discrimination and harassment that I have experienced in academia. To this day, in those particular institutional settings, I can safely bet that I am still viewed as the "problem." From the outside, people might find it shocking that this continues to happen within university settings, where we claim to hold values like respect, equality, and freedom of speech. Rebick (2009, 109) cites antiracist teacher Shakil Choudhury, who told her: "We have these fantastic theories, anti-racist theories, post-colonial theories. If our theories are so good, then shouldn't progressive organizations be the example of how to live in healthy relationship with one another? Shouldn't we be able to see that people are treating one another well and fairly and people are being treated equally and well in these organizations? . . . But often there is more dysfunction in these organizations than anywhere else."

For instance, when I have complained about the treatment that I was receiving to the individuals involved—chairs, directors, deans, and even union/association representatives—my experience has been minimized, invalidated, denied, and brushed off as "personality conflicts" and "misunderstandings." One *could* mistakenly make the assumption that these concerns and personal experiences are about organizational dynamics, personality conflicts, and individual hurts and inconveniences rather than oppression. However, this narrow view misses the point that our work, how it is constructed, and our individual experiences within these specific social and cultural institutions are also mediated, enhanced, and constrained by the same dominant-subordinate social relations that underlie all oppressions. Indeed, an individual experience of oppression or discrimination may seem as inconsequential and light as a feather, particularly when viewed from someone else's standpoint (often from a place of privilege), but over time from the view of oppressed persons, a "ton of feathers" can be overwhelming, exhausting, and debilitating (Caplan 1993).

Breaking the Silence

Unfortunately, but typically, no one in the administration of any of the institutions where I have worked has admitted that my professional struggles were related to discrimination and harassment, based on my gender and sexual orientation. Not surprisingly, there also seems to be little appetite to talk about the simultaneous privileging of male, white, heterosexual, and able-bodied faculty, even though research clearly demonstrates that they are over-rewarded compared to their counterparts (Acker and Armenti 2004; Corrice 2009). The chronic institutional denial of and refusal to define and frame the experiences of women, people of color, those living with disabilities, queer-identified individuals, and other marginalized people as directly related to systemic bias and discrimination betrays us all and "speaks to the heart of identity, belonging, and power" (Martínez and Casper 2020, para. 4). The clear message is "You are not enough and you do not belong."

The reality is that teaching from the margins is risky, especially as we try to implement new modes of teaching, create new landscapes of inquiry, and disrupt heteronormative and gender-conformist discourses and practices in traditional, conservative institutional settings. By daring to transgress, by even having the audacity to survive these institutions, our very presence continues to threaten dominant spaces and discourses. Disrupting norms is laudable, as it opens up possibilities for interesting and creative teaching/learning moments, but on the other hand, it can also be a risky business, especially for vulnerable instructors. For instance, based on intersectional social location and identity, some instructors will inevitably face more criticism, increased hostility, and possible job loss.

Correspondingly, for the serious crime of disrupting tradition (and making some people feel uncomfortable), those of us who resist have been sentenced to a lifetime of others trying to control what we say or do. Thus, we are continually at risk of receiving backlash from students, administrators, and/or colleagues (e.g., poor peer reviews; denials of promotion, tenure, and merit raises; bad course evaluations, etc.). In fact, research clearly demonstrates that course evaluations are "biased against female instructors by an amount that is large and statistically significant" (Boring, Ottoboni, and Stark 2016, 1), are "highly correlated with students' grade expectations," and measure gender, race, and physical attractiveness bias more than teaching effectiveness (Stark and Freishtat 2014, 13).

As a result, these institutional responses, from all parties mentioned above, perpetuate the status quo and operate like moral chastity belts: enforcing social norms, regulating our sexualities, silencing us, and keeping many of us in the closet. As a result, academics (particularly those who are female, queer, differently abled, and/or of color) are, in many ways, disembodied, metaphorically neutered, and therefore forced, in terms of our writing, teaching, and scholarship, to toe the line in terms of what we are *allowed* to say, as well as how we *should* behave.

Finally, from underneath the feathers, and standing with the survivors and supporters of the current Me Too, Idle No More, and Black Lives Matter movements, I share my story to quench my rage—but I am still left to ponder.* How many more studies and statistics about

---

* To learn more about these movements, see their respective websites: https://metoomvmt.org, https://idlenomore.ca, https://blacklivesmatter.com.

harassment, discrimination, and violence do we need before we finally act to make change? From a broader perspective, how many hours and tears, and how much energy, creativity, and productivity are wasted in this struggle? How many of us are forced to take "sick/stress" leaves, settle for teaching-stream positions instead of tenure-track jobs, or completely drop out of tenure-track positions because of the unrealistic expectations and demands placed upon us? How many of us are pushed out or choose to leave university life and careers, rather than continue the daily struggle for respect and equality?

Fortunately, there is one thing that gives me hope. I have come to believe that although these experiences are painful, they are actually a strong indicator that we are successfully disrupting traditional educational systems and methods (Neverson et al. 2013; Rinfrette et al. 2015). As such, we need to continue to work together to dismantle systemic inequality and to improve campus climates for everyone.

Works Cited

Acker, Sandra, and Carmen Armenti. 2004. "Sleepless in Academia." *Gender and Education* 16 (1): 3–24. https://doi.org/10.1080/0954025032000170309.

Boring, Anne, Kellie Ottoboni, and Philip B. Stark. 2016. "Student Evaluations of Teaching (Mostly) Do Not Measure Teaching Effectiveness." *Science Open Research*, 1–11. https://doi.org/10.14293/S2199-1006.1.SOR-EDU.AETBZC.v1.

Brown, Leslie, and Susan Strega. 2005. *Research as Resistance: Critical, Indigenous and Anti-Oppressive Approaches*. Toronto: Canadian Scholars Press.

Cain, Roy. 1996. "Heterosexism and Self-Disclosure in the Social Work Classroom." *Journal of Social Work Education* 32 (1): 65–76. https://doi.org/10.1080/10437797.1996.10672285.

Caplan, Paula J. 1993. *Lifting a Ton of Feathers: A Woman's Guide to Surviving in the Academic World*. Toronto: University of Toronto Press.

Corrice, April. 2009. "Unconscious Bias in Faculty and Leadership Recruitment: A Literature Review." *Analysis in Brief* 9, no. 2 (August): 1–4. https://www.aamc.org/data-reports/analysis-brief/report/unconscious-bias-faculty-and-leadership-recruitment-literature-review.

El-Alayli, Amani, Ashley A. Hansen-Brown, and Michelle Ceynar. 2018. "Dancing Backwards in High Heels: Female Professors Experience More Work Demands and Special Favor Requests, Particularly from Academically Entitled Students." *Sex Roles* 79 (August): 135–50. https://doi.org/10.1007/s11199-017-0872-6.

Fumia, Doreen, Camille Hernandez-Ramdwar, Amina Jamal, Melanie Knight, and Nicole Neverson. 2013. *Inhabiting Critical Spaces: Teaching and Learning from the Margins at Ryerson University*. Toronto: Learning and Teaching Office, Ryerson University.

Gutiérrez y Muhs, Gabriella, Yolanda Flores Niemann, Carmen G. González, and Angela P. Harris, eds. 2012. *Presumed Incompetent: The Intersections of Race and Class for Women in Academia*. Boulder: University Press of Colorado.

Hillock, Susan, and Nick J. Mulé. 2016. *Queering Social Work Education*. Vancouver: University of British Columbia Press.

Hillock, Susan. 2021. "Femagogy: Centreing Feminist Knowledge and Methods in Social Work Teaching." In *Teaching Social Work: Reflections on Pedagogy and Practice*, edited by Rick Csiernik and Susan Hillock, 39–55. Toronto: University of Toronto Press.

Hillock, Susan. 2011. "Conceptualizing Oppression: Resistance Narratives for Social Work." PhD diss., Memorial University of Newfoundland.

hooks, bell. 1994. *Teaching to Transgress: Education as a Practice of Freedom*. New York: Routledge.

Jeffery, Donna. 2007. "Radical Problems and Liberal Selves: Professional Subjectivity in the Anti-Oppressive Social Work Classroom." *Canadian Social Work Review* 24 (2): 125–139. https://www.jstor.org/stable/41669870.

Keller, Evelyn Fox, and Helene Moglen. 1987. "Competition: A Problem for Academic Women." In *Competition: A Feminist Taboo?*, edited by Valerie Miner and Helen E. Longino, 21–37. New York: Feminist Press.

Kirby, Sandra, and Kate McKenna. 1989. *Experience, Research, Social Change: Methods from the Margins*. Toronto: Garamond Press.

Levine, Helen. 1989. "The Personal Is Political: Feminism and the Helping Professions." In *Feminism: From Pressure to Politics*, edited by Angela Miles and Geraldine Finn, 233–67. Montreal: Black Rose Books.

Lund, Carole L. 2010. "The Nature of White Privilege in the Teaching and Training of Adults." *New Directions for Adult and Continuing Education* 2010 (125); 15–25. https://doi.org/10.1002/ace.359.

Martínez, Rebecca G., and Monica J. Casper. 2020. "Call for Submissions: Institutional Betrayal in Higher Education." *Who Belongs?* https://www.whobelongs.com/call.html?fbclid=IwAR1_GhedJ3uQrIv1FHUNPWtLcQeJCyzt29CS_z_d3uF8fr1V83ITDg-Aij0.

Matthew, Patricia A., ed. 2016. *Written/Unwritten: Diversity and the Hidden Truths of Tenure*. Chapel Hill: University of North Carolina Press.

Mulhere, Kaitlin. 2014. "Students Praise Male Professors." *Inside Higher Education*, December 9, 2014. https://www.insidehighered.com/news/2014/12/10/study-finds-gender-perception-affects-evaluations.

Niemann, Yolanda Flores, Gabriella Gutiérrez y Muhs, and Carmen G. González. 2020. *Presumed Incompetent II: Race, Class, Power, and Resistance of Women in Academia*. Logan: Utah State University Press.

Overall, Christine. 1998. *A Feminist 1: Reflections from Academia*. Toronto: Broadview Press.

Rebick, Judy. 2009. *Transforming Power: From the Personal to the Political*. Toronto: Penguin.

Redmond, Melissa. 2010. "Safe Space Oddity: Revisiting Critical Pedagogy." *Journal of Teaching in Social Work* 30 (1): 1–14. https://doi.org/10.1080/08841230903249729.

Rinfrette, Elaine S., Elain M. Maccio, James P. Coyle, Kelly F. Jackson, Robin M. Hartinger-Saunders, Christine M. Rine, and Lawrence Shulman. 2015. "Content and Process in a Teaching Workshop for Faculty and Doctoral Students." *Journal of Teaching in Social Work* 35 (1–2): 65–81. https://doi.org/10.1080/08841233.2014.990077.

Schick, Carol. 2005. "Keeping the Ivory Tower White: Discourses of Racial Discrimination." In *Inequality in Canada*, edited by Valerie Zawilski and Cynthia Levine-Rasky, 208–20. Oxford: Oxford University Press.

Stark, Philip B., and Richard Freishtat. 2014. "An Evaluation of Course Evaluations." *Science Open Research*, 1–26.

Superson, Anita M., and Ann Cudd. 2002. *Theorizing Backlash: Philosophical Reflections on the Resistance to Feminism*. Lanham, MD: Rowman & Littlefield.

The Chilly Collective. 1995. *Breaking Anonymity: The Chilly Climate for Women*. Kitchener-Waterloo, ON: Wilfred Laurier Press.

Williams, Joan C., Tamina Alon, and Stephanie Bornstein. 2006. "Beyond the 'Chilly Climate': Eliminating Bias Against Women and Fathers in Academe." *Thought and Action* (Fall): 79–96.

5

Vice-Chancellor Bliss-Simpson

Matthew Wills

Dr. Bliss-Simpson was awfully proud,
In his forty-fourth year, to put on the shroud
Of a vice-chancellorship on a campus quite near,
Bliss-Simpson had reached the bureaucratic top tier!

Now, Bliss-Simpson had come to feel some regret,
Toward his leadership talents—underutilized yet,
But, at last, sounded the calls of bureaucracy,
For Bliss-Simpson to join the campus plutocracy.

Take it from me, on this campus in question,
It pays to have ambition and give full attention
To matters "strategic" and "innovative"—teaching? Less so,
Keep your priorities clear and up, up you'll go!

Thus, when the big boss called for "dynamic innovation,"
And a new "thought leader" to guide said transformation,
Bliss-Simpson was ready, with ideas in hand,
Ready to lead us forward as planned.

"New visionary appointed!" the PR cried,
"Dynamic reform never before tried!"
VC Bliss-Simpson was the man of the hour,
Administrative culture's brightest new flower.

But, let me tell you, Bliss-Simpson was rather more keen
On cashing his paycheck than progress, it seems.
One grand per day to sit in on meetings,
To ramble on cue and make all the right bleatings.

Abstractness in vogue, stay away from detail,
"Our strategic plan is too good to fail!"
He met with the deans, ruled down from on high,
Thanked frontline workers, then sent them to die.

The thing is, VC, when disease hits the fan,
We do not need a "strategic" plan.
We don't need your "vision,"
We don't trust your word,
We don't want your platitudes
Nor your ideas absurd.

Amid a pandemic, how reassuring it is
To be managed by those for whom learning's a biz,
To suffer their perfidy and unquenched greed,
To see them ignore those truly in need.

Just like Bliss-Simpson, those who rise to the top
Self-interest drives them—no more, full stop.
We pay these "leaders" many thousands per year,
A cost of ambition now simply too dear.

Dedicated to all my friends at the University of California, San Diego

6

Dirty Money and Deliberate Indebtedness

Jasmine Banks

Six years after graduating, I have $215,000 in student loan debt. I am a working-poor mother of four living in Arkansas. I grew up in Oklahoma with a working-poor single mother. I remember my public education school years fondly, despite the hardships our family faced. My teachers took me to extracurricular activities, ensured that we had resources in order to eat, and often gave us shelter when we were houseless. I worked hard in school, not just to make the educators who'd become surrogate mothers to me proud but because I was routinely told that obtaining an education and making my way through college was the surest way to avoid homelessness, poverty, and suffering. I graduated with honors from high school, undergraduate school, and graduate school. I did exactly what I was supposed to. And now, six years after earning my master's degree, I live in a rental home with my family, paycheck to paycheck, and I'm $215,000 in student loan debt.

What no one told me was that in 2004, by the time I was leaving high school and headed to university, the institution of higher education had begun a horrific transformation into a corporate, capitalist model informed by neoliberal ideologies. No one explained that students and educators were becoming commodities for wealthy stakeholders to leverage their agendas through the administration's control. No one told me that the very school you choose could be a place that is captured to deepen structural and systemic inequity while ensuring that dark-money donors obtain their return on investment. Imagine my surprise when I applied for a part-time contractor gig with an organization called UnKoch My Campus and learned that the very conditions that underscored the betrayal I felt from higher education were strategic and intentional.

Now here I am, almost a quarter million dollars in debt due to pursuing a higher education, while billionaires continue to spread their money (made at the expense of marginalized people like me) around college campuses to benefit their corporate interests. Academic freedom—and so much more—hangs in the balance.

Billionaire Charles Koch and his broader network have been leveraging higher education for years with a sophisticated, strategic, and well-coordinated precision. Their aim? The "war of ideas." The Koch network set their sights on higher education, and educational institutions more broadly, because they understand that ideas, research, and narrative shape culture, policy, and law. They understand that quality education and the information produced through scholarly inquiry and academic freedom can be a public good used to transform communities or, if captured and controlled, to increase power. What you do with that power matters. Consider two examples of academic and institutional capture that reproduce structural inequity and betrayal.

George Mason University (GMU) in Virginia is considered Koch ground zero when it comes to undue donor influence in higher education. The GMU Foundation has received over $50 million from the Charles Koch Foundation (CKF) since 2005. More significantly, the university has also received additional funding from CKF for its think tanks: the Mercatus Center has received over $10 million and the Institute for Humane Studies (IHS) over $35 million. It is these centers that provide the Koch network the ability to exploit higher education institutions for their own benefit.

The Mercatus Center is an aggressive free-market think tank that studies markets and regulation. It was co-founded by Charles Koch, who remains a board member and central funder to this day. According to a memorandum of understanding between George Mason University and George Mason University Foundation, "regarding the use of funds contributing to the Koch Chair in International Economics Endowment Fund in the George Mason University Foundation, Inc.," Charles and his late brother David had control over committee seats that picked candidates for a professorship they funded (George Mason University Foundation 1990). They were also instrumental in selecting candidates for key economics appointments—ultimately choosing professors who had similar free-market values. Unfortunately, the Mercatus Center is not alone.

IHS awards scholarships, sponsors summer seminars, and provides career assistance to students interested in the study of "classical liberal ideas"—ideas rooted with intent to maintain white supremacy. It also provides reading and discussion materials to students and faculty who want to sponsor discussions about classical liberalism on campus. Beyond providing scholarly support and seminars, IHS faculty serve as recruiters to bring undergraduates and graduates into the Koch network.

Charles Koch has served as IHS's board chair for thirty-eight years. IHS is the driving engine behind Koch's "talent pipeline," training students and faculty and providing careers in Koch's "liberty movement." IHS explicitly teaches the Koch network's "Structure of Social Change," a set of policy documents, as part of a Careers in Public Policy framework. Along with Mercatus, IHS is a consistent feature of Koch's secretive donor summits. These campus programs are intended to groom a grassroots base of supporters aligned with the Kochs' policy agenda.

Thankfully, both students and faculty at GMU have rung the warning bell about undue donor influence for a while now, and they have pushed for change. In 2017, a student organization called Transparent GMU sued the school and the GMU Foundation for lack of transparency in donor agreements after GMU refused to disclose requested information surrounding dark-money private donors. In 2019, the lawsuit made it all the way to the Supreme Court of Virginia, where Transparent GMU ended up losing the case. Yet they were still able to secure a victory in the shape of two recent bills that passed in the Virginia General Assembly, which ensure that universities have to make donor agreements accessible under the Freedom of Information Act.

Nearby in Washington, D.C., students at the George Washington University (GW) have been facing similar struggles. One of around seventy research centers on campus, the Regulatory Studies Center (RSC) is "a leading source for applied scholarship in regulatory issues, and a training ground for anyone who wants to understand the effects of regulation and ensure that regulatory policies are designed in the public interest," according to the center's website. Dig a little deeper and it's clear that the Koch-funded center has a more frightening agenda.

A recent report on the RSC uncovered that the true purpose of the center is to "provide scholarly rationales against government regulation, focusing on measures that would affect the fossil fuel industry, such as those to reduce pollution or combat climate change" (Lincoln 2019). The antiregulatory views of the RSC's researchers fall right in line with those of one of the major donors, Charles Koch. With petrochemicals making up a large part of Koch Industries (which results in the company being one of the leading emitters of toxic waste and greenhouse gases in the country), it's unsurprising that Koch himself would funnel money into a center that provides data in support of laxer regulations.

It pays to look at who is employed by the RSC and follow those trails. Susan Dudley, who is a founder of the RSC and its current director, has been affiliated with eight different Koch-funded organizations in addition to the GW center, and she's not the only one. More than half of the RSC authors have also been affiliated with other Koch-funded organizations.

Thankfully, students at GW aren't stymied by this complex, interwoven relationship between dark-money donors and campus research centers. After successfully pressuring GW administration to divest the campus from fossil fuels in 2020—something the school promises to accomplish by 2025 (*GW Today* 2020)—they've set their sights on the RSC. Convincing campus administration to part from the millions of dollars the Koch network donates to the school will be a battle, but one that is necessary if GW students and faculty want to be a part of an institution that values learning over corporate interests.

Unfortunately, these two schools are not alone. Similar "pay for play" dark-money donations happen all across the country, from California and Arizona to Massachusetts, Florida, and New York. The Koch network supports and propagates institutional betrayal by exchanging money and control for the bastardization of academic freedom and integrity, making the work of students, faculty, and concerned community grassroots organizers all the more important. This is truly a story of David versus corporate-funded Goliath, with high stakes for those in and out of academia.

Academic institutions ask students from all walks of life to devote time and money—so much money—with the promise that they will receive a solid education, free from outside tampering, and with no hidden agendas. Unfortunately, we know this is not the case. Colleges and universities must work for the common good, not private interests. And yet, not only are so many of us—like me—in debt because of school, but we're also being unwittingly used as pawns in a game of institutional betrayal that will never benefit us.

Works Cited

George Mason University Foundation, Inc. 1990. Memorandum of understanding between George W. Johnson, president of George Mason University, and the George Mason University Foundation, Inc. https://shorturl.at/jLLZ2.

GW Today. 2020. "GW to Eliminate All Fossil Fuel Investments from Endowment." June 29, 2020. https://gwtoday.gwu.edu/gw-eliminate-all-fossil-fuel-investments-endowment.

Lincoln, Taylor. 2019. "A Key Cog in Charles Koch's Master Plan." *PublicCitizen*, June 3, 2019. https://www.citizen.org/article/Koch-cog-rsc/.

7

Teaching Up

How My Dream Job Became a Nightmare

Celeste Atkins

I love education. I truly believe that education is key to a better future, a better country, and a better citizenry. I was taught to believe that education is the path out of poverty. Unfortunately, I know better than that now. Sadly, research shows that for marginalized people, education just leads to a different kind of poverty. I am also what Patricia Hill Collins (2013) refers to as an intellectual activist in that I strive to both "speak the truth to power" as well as "speak truth directly to the people." In 2011, I was hired into my dream job: a community college instructor at Cochise College in rural southeastern Arizona. I wanted to teach specifically at the community college level because my life trajectory was completely changed by my first sociology class with Dr. Linda Rillorta at Mount San Antonio College.

Cochise College has two main campuses. The one on which I was based is in Sierra Vista, Arizona, which neighbors Fort Huachuca, a historic military site first established in 1877 to fight the Apache along the U.S.-Mexico border. It became an official fort in 1882, served as the base for the offense against Geronimo, and was one of the headquarters of the famous all–African American 10th Cavalry "Buffalo Soldiers." Currently, it is the headquarters for intelligence and technology work for the U.S. Army. The Sierra Vista community largely consists of military and retired military folks. It is rural, conservative, and predominantly Republican; however, it is also fairly diverse, as the military attracts many people of color.

This job was perfect. There was no need to publish, just to teach. I was full of enthusiasm, ideas, and passion. I was delighted to finally do the work I was meant to do. Even better, it turned out I was pretty damn good at it. It was extraordinarily rewarding. I was mentored by my dean, Chuck Hoyack, who taught me the importance of listening to and learning from students and to also know and defend my boundaries. I had exceptional students, who taught me more about the world than I taught them about sociology and who came back after taking my classes to share their knowledge and experience with other students. I was encouraged to try new things and to take risks. As a result, with a colleague I created a seminar series to encourage other faculty to share their interests and knowledge. I participated in learning communities with reading and English faculty to help students learn more holistically. I was promoted to department chair while still in my two-year probationary period. As chair, I was able to end a program that I felt wasn't helpful to students and to lead the movement to create the first meta degree: social sciences (combining sociology, anthropology, history, and political science). I was in my element and loving life.

Yet one aspect that challenged me was student feedback, which repeatedly referred to me as intimidating, aggressive, or domineering. These adjectives had followed me my whole life as a zaftig Black woman. Patricia Hill Collins (2009) refers to these stereotypes and expectations of Black women as controlling images. She explains, "as part of a generalized ideology of domination, stereotypical images of Black womanhood take on special meaning. Because the authority to define societal values is a major instrument of power, elite groups, in exercising power, manipulate ideas about Black womanhood" (76). For many students, I was not just their instructor—I was this big Black woman "playing the race card," as I taught well-established sociological theories of race, racism, and white privilege. Furthermore, my passion and enthusiasm were often perceived and interpreted as anger, which reinforced the controlling image of the "angry Black woman."

I had to carefully choose my words and always be aware of my mannerisms to not reinforce this idea of me.

Yet it was not just the students who challenged me. For most of my tenure at Cochise, I was the only Black woman faculty member. In my department of seven faculty, there was a white woman psychology instructor who started the same year I did. She made my life difficult in myriad ways. For example, at this time I had a master's degree and I was not well versed in the nuances of academic regalia. For my first graduation ceremony as a faculty member, I was excited to wear the crimson robes of the University of Southern California, my alma mater, but unknowingly rented PhD regalia instead of master's regalia. This instructor told multiple people around campus that I was a liar and lacked integrity because I wore PhD robes and only had a master's degree. Meanwhile, half the faculty were wearing associate of arts (AA) robes they rented from our bookstore.

Once I was promoted to department chair, the instructor's behavior worsened. Despite my strong reputation, she did not believe I had a chance at promotion, even stating, "If I actually thought you were going to be chair, I would have applied myself," implying she would have been promoted instead of me. Despite me going to bat for her as her department chair on several occasions, she began to wage a campaign to have me fired. For example, I had a welcome video in my class that stated I appreciated laughter at my dumb jokes and caramel macchiatos, and since some of my students worked at Starbucks, they would occasionally bring me coffee. She complained to the dean that I was taking "bribes" (in the form of four-dollar coffees) for grades, and I actually had to meet with him to address this.

Finally, we met with the vice provost and the dean to try to resolve this issue. She came in with a stack of papers at least eight inches high and accused me multiple times of "bullying" her. Exasperated, I stated, "Bullying is a very strong charge. Can you give examples of exactly how I bully you?" Her answer was that I had held a meeting with her without providing an agenda. The meeting with the vice provost and dean lasted more than two hours, with no resolution. In the end, she quit her job and blamed it on me. After she left, the dean admitted that she was actively working to get me fired. I worked for years to find a way to work with her, but nothing I did was successful. It is my belief that, as a white woman, she did not want to answer to a Black woman, particularly one who only had a master's degree when she held a PhD.

Overall, I really loved teaching and being department chair despite the microaggressions I faced. After all, workplace racism is widespread in the academy (Alleyne 2004; Griffin et al. 2011; Sue 2010). As a sociologist, I am also well aware of the structural racism inherent in our institutions. I thought I would spend the rest of my career at this college, but that idea began to change after my mentor and dean, Chuck Hoyack, died. Chuck had been at the college for decades and held a lot of sway. He protected us from much of the fallout from the university administration. Once he was gone, the administration began dismantling the department that I had worked to build for five years, infusing a sense of unity and recruiting wonderful instructors. To make matters worse, our new direct supervisor was a power-hungry, vendetta-loving dean who played favorites and actively undermined those she did not like. For example, she and I got along well until I had the audacity to disagree with her in public. After that, she decided to demote me from department chair, even though our department had a 100 percent compliance record and was functioning well. I had full classes and was a popular instructor with multiple students who took additional courses with me. Despite this, she tried to change how I taught. Instead of advocating fairly for me or mediating with students, she encouraged students to file formal complaints against me—which backfired when the student who claimed I was discriminating against them and did not like them because they were white earned an A. She was another white woman who found me unpalatable because I dared to have a voice and an opinion.

Although no one else in our department was interested in being chair, she placed a white woman in my spot who was grossly ineffective. The new chair actually advocated for me to have the job back along with the rest of the department once that dean had left; by then, however, the damage was done. I now had a "reputation" with the university's senior leadership—the same administration who had encouraged me to be part of the invitation-only President's Leadership Academy—as a troublemaker, because I openly disparaged the chair's decision to demote me. A former colleague-turned-dean explained to me that the chair position was for five years, and it was her call to make the change. However, there were department chairs who had been in the position for fifteen years or more. Furthermore, the administration in their never-ending reorganization hired a "super-dean," supervised only by the vice provost, to manage all the academic deans. This was a random position as part of the top-heavy bloat instituted by the upper administration. After they fired him, the position was eliminated. He knew nothing of my work, as he had come in from another school, and yet he refused to let me resume the chair position.

One of the changes we had made as a department was requiring that Sociology of Race be part of the Administration of Justice degree. This degree, often called criminal justice, was for aspiring police officers and border patrol agents. The addition of the class was spearheaded by our full-time Administration of Justice instructor because future officers and agents working at the U.S.-Mexico borderlands needed to understand race and racism. Unfortunately, a white male student complained to all the deans on campus, except my dean, that as an Administration of Justice student he should not be forced to take my Sociology of Race class. This belief was echoed by many of his peers because they felt that it was unnecessary and a "propaganda" class. After Trump took office, my student challenges increased.

For example, an online student wrote that Black, Latinx, and Native American people should be "grateful" to Europeans because we were all nothing but "savages and heathens" until we were "civilized" by Europe. I had a white woman use the N-word multiple times in an online discussion post and did not understand why I took issue with it. Another woman student was so incensed that I would not accept her racist rants (with no connection to sociology) as A papers that she and her husband scheduled a meeting with my dean, to which they wore MAGA gear from head to toe. My dean diplomatically suggested that another class might be better for her—sad, because she too was an Administration of Justice student. At this point, I began actively looking for another position, which both my dean and my department chair were aware of.

Then the pandemic hit, and with it, renewed outrage against police brutality and support of the Black Lives Matter movement. Protests were held across the nation, including colleges and universities; academic organizations, such as the American Sociological Association, began to speak out in solidarity. I waited for a statement from our college and when one was not forthcoming, I spoke to the dean about my concerns. She stated that the board of governors were the ones who had to make the statement, and so I began a letter-writing campaign to the board. Several letters were sent, and in response the president of the college issued a letter that stated, "We acknowledge that there are differences in how people of color are treated and call on every citizen to support equal justice under the law for all." As the only full-time Black faculty member, I was outraged. There are differences in how female athletes are treated compared to male athletes. Black and Brown folks were being MURDERED and this institution that I gave my heart to really could not have cared less.

To make things worse, planning was beginning for the fall semester and the administration was determined to have in-person, face-to-face learning. Other faculty members and I spoke out, albeit carefully, pushing for distance learning to keep teachers and students safe. I received permission to work remotely for personal reasons, but I was also warned that the administration thought it was a ruse because I also listed multiple reasons for working from home. As the summer wound down and the pandemic ramped up, I became concerned about my colleagues who were afraid to return to work for valid reasons, such as being a cancer survivor or having other risk factors around COVID-19, and I felt guilty for being safe. I carefully crafted a letter to the administration sharing my concerns. I felt safe to do so because I had accepted a full-time job elsewhere and was no longer in fear of being fired.

Instead of listening to my concerns, the president himself responded to my letter dissecting every section in red writing, as if I were a student. When I shared, "While I acknowledge that there are colleagues of mine who are willing and eager to come back to face-to-face teaching, in my conversations with other faculty and staff they have explicitly stated that they are afraid to speak for fear of repercussions, including losing their jobs." His response was "The fear is self-generated and not based in reality in my experience." However, from my perspective, the high turnover, retirement, and resignation rates indicated that while people may not have been fired, many were pushed out or encouraged to leave.

I began my new position, and although I had planned to leave Cochise, I did not want to add to my department chair's stress by resigning so close to the beginning of the fall term. I had planned to work virtually until I tendered my resignation in October. I had shared this plan with my department chair but not yet with the dean, as we had a new person coming in whom I had never met. Somehow the Cochise College administration found out that I had accepted a job at the University of Arizona and instead of reaching out directly to their employee of *nine years*, the president of the college called my new supervisor to ask her if I would be working for her—thereby risking my new position. Once they had spoken, a human resources representative at Cochise called me and without asking for any explanation, asked for my resignation. When I stated that I was not resigning and asked if they were firing me, he was stumped and indicated we would speak again. Meanwhile, my new supervisor at the University of Arizona reached out directly to me and explained that I would not be able to work full time for both positions because I would be "double-dipping" in benefits and retirement from the state. I spoke with my department chair and advised her that I would teach three classes and that she was free to share my prepared class with another adjunct to teach. I indicated that I would be willing to teach four classes, if necessary, as an adjunct. Meanwhile, the HR office prepared to try to fire me for "ethical reasons" even though, technically, I was off contract until August. I spoke with the provost and the vice president of human resources, who had worked with me for years, and explained the situation to them. Finally, I handed in my resignation with the understanding that I would continue to teach as an adjunct.

The summer ended and the fall semester began, and things were fine until I received word that I had been removed from the spring schedule at Cochise College. I was removed not only from the face-to-face class but also from the online classes that I had been scheduled to teach. This was not the decision of my department chair as my direct supervisor who oversaw the schedule. It seemed to me that I was being blacklisted. But instead of slinking away, I reached out to the new dean to ask why I was removed from the schedule. He just referred me to HR. I reached out again to the vice president, who claimed that I was not being blacklisted; however, when I spoke to the department chair, she had given away the classes that I had originally been scheduled to teach and had no more classes left for me. I advised the dean and vice president that I felt that I was being discriminated against and that I was going to explore my options for a discrimination complaint. Reflecting back, I am not sure why I wanted to stay at Cochise College at all, as the issues with students had continued.

A student from my fall intensive writing class was dropped (according to my policy) because she had four zeros and an 11 percent score in the class. That complaint was elevated, and I was asked to meet with HR and the dean. The HR rep suggested that I take a "civility" class but had no issue with how I dropped the student according to policy. The student complaint read as follows: "The instructor needs to be more respectful. I had informed the instructor that I was having trouble [getting into the learning management system] and she was very rude back to me saying that she is not technical support. The instructor's attitude towards the student was very rude. The instructor never talked with the student about her papers. The instructor is very insensitive. The instructor set up the student to fail—because the student said she was 'Mormon.'" Anyone who has taught a class will recognize sour grapes when they see it, and yet I was expected to respond to these allegations in writing. The HR rep also resurfaced a complaint that was six months old from an Administration of Justice student who felt that he should not have to take Sociology of Race because the "professor and the course materials are blatantly biased against conservatives and whites" and were an "attempted indoctrination of the liberal agenda." Although this complaint had been handled and the student went on to complete the course with a passing grade, I was instructed to "please explain further how to respond to students who make this or similar complaint, using a civil or sensitive tone."

This attempt to "civilize" marginalized people is not new. Tracey Owens Patton asserts that the idea of "civility" is used in higher education to allow the proliferation of racism and sexism. In fact, she asserts, "hegemonic civility is so ingrained that it shows up everywhere" (2004, 62). Allison Hawn uses the term "civility cudgel," sharing her keen insight at how often the ideas of "civility" are used "as a genteel cudgel, wrapped in the American flag, guarded by privileged academics, and adopted by those of the populace that the word unwaveringly serves" (2020, 219). Báez and Ore state that demands for civilizing discourse are actually "a call to insulate white fragility through appeals to language and scholarship that protects whites from racial discomfort . . . includ[ing] calls for more gracious and less 'angry' speech that don't offend white sensibilities" (2018, 331). My directness and firm boundaries aggravated my students, colleagues, and senior leadership. I believe this was because they felt I did not know my place. A white male colleague and I had several conversations about how our approach to teaching was similar—we were direct, had high standards, and did not take much guff from students. However, I was inundated with student complaints, while he had very few.

At this point, incensed by the expectation to justify the curriculum that was created by the department, I had had enough and responded in a letter. "Perhaps what is needed is cultural sensitivity on your part to help you understand the biases I face as a Black woman teaching about race and gender, especially since I am the ONLY ONE in the entire college. . . . Moreover, your directive to rewrite my words reeks of cultural insensitivity. I am a doctoral student with an excellent grasp of the English language who has been published multiple times in peer-reviewed texts and journals. I do not need help with expressing myself, nor am I going to change the way I speak and write because it's not the way you would do it. . . . I say what needs to be said directly. That's not rude, it's efficient."

As I write this chapter, I am in a much better place. I have completed my doctorate and hold a position as director of student engagement and recruitment in the Graduate College at the University of Arizona. I facilitate and create programming that makes a vital difference in the lives of underrepresented graduate students, and I have an associate dean and a dean who both appreciate and respect what I have to offer and who have my back. I have not returned to Cochise College since 2020. It was traumatizing and extremely painful to leave my beloved college because I had colleagues and students whom I adored. However, I could no longer fight for my humanity and justify my existence in a place that refused to honor both. In summation, Leslie Lokko's words about her resignation from a deanship resonate with me and beautifully express my outlook on this experience: "I suppose I'd say in the end that my resignation was a profound act of self-preservation" (Flaherty 2020).

Works Cited

Alleyne, Aileen. 2004. "Black Identity and Workplace Oppression." *Counselling and Psychotherapy Research* 4, no. 1 (July): 4–8. http://dx.doi.org/10.1080/14733140412331384008.

Báez, Kristiana L., and Ersula Ore. 2018. "The Moral Imperative of Race for Rhetorical Studies: On Civility and Walking-in-White in Academe." *Communication and Critical/Cultural Studies* 15 (4): 331–36. https://doi.org/10.1080/14791420.2018.1533989.

Collins, Patricia Hill. 1990. *Black Feminist Thought: Knowledge, Consciousness, and the Politics of Empowerment*. Boston: Unwin Hyman.

Collins, Patricia Hill. 2013. "Truth-Telling and Intellectual Activism." *Contexts* 12, no. 1 (Winter): 36–39. http://dx.doi.org.10.1177/1536504213476244.

Flaherty, Colleen. 2022. "A Profound Act of Self-Preservation." *Inside Higher Ed*, October 12, 2020. https://www.insidehighered.com/news/2022/03/25/professor-accuses-linfield-u-silencing-faculty-members.

Griffin, Kimberly A., Meghan J. Pifer, Jordan R. Humphrey, and Ashley M Hazelwood. 2011. "(Re)defining Departure: Exploring Black Professors' Experiences with and Responses to Racism and Racial Climate." *American Journal of Education* 117, no. 4 (August): 495–526. https://doi.org/10.1086/660756.

Hawn, Allison. 2020. "The Civility Cudgel: The Myth of Civility in Communication." *Howard Journal of Communications* 31 (2): 218–30. https://doi.org.10.1080/10646175.2020.1731882.

Patton, Tracey Owens. 2004. "In the Guise of Civility: The Complicitous Maintenance of Inferential Forms of Sexism and Racism in Higher Education." *Women's Studies in Communication* 27 (1): 60–87. https://doi.org.10.1080/07491409.2004.10162466.

Sue, Derald Wing. 2010. *Microaggressions in Everyday Life: Race, Gender, and Sexual Orientation*. Hoboken, NJ: Wiley.

8

Institutional Betrayal and the Role of Male Allies in Supporting Women in Higher Education

Meg A. Warren and Samit D. Bordoloi

Women faculty in North America, particularly in male-dominated disciplines, such as STEM, have historically faced challenges to success across the career life cycle—from hiring (Glass and Minnotte 2010) to promotion (Bonawitz and Andel 2009; Van Miegroet et al. 2019) to earning prestigious administrative and leadership appointments (Daldrup-Link 2017; Hart 2016; Qamar et al. 2020). As such, there is a large body of research, funding, and practice on women faculty advocating for greater equity and inclusion in higher education. In response, institutions have been developing diversity, equity, and inclusion strategic goals (Williams 2013), creating diversity and inclusion statements (Wilson, Meyer, and McNeal 2012), and otherwise signaling inclusiveness via recruitment materials, brochures, websites, and other avenues (Ford and Patterson 2019). Yet women, particularly in male-dominated disciplines of academia, continue to experience institutional betrayal. Women faculty of color and those with other intersectional identities are particularly vulnerable. They are more likely to encounter "the quadruple threat of racism, sexism, homophobia, and class-based subordination . . . [a] combination of 'isms' [that] can be lethal to their careers, bodies, and spirits" (Niemann 2012, 446).

Institutional Betrayal

Institutional betrayal is described as "wrongdoings perpetrated by an institution upon individuals dependent on that institution, including failure to prevent or respond supportively to wrongdoings by individuals committed within the context of the institution" (Freyd, n.d.; Smith and Freyd 2014). In academic institutions, betrayal may occur via various agents, such as administrators and colleagues who act on behalf of the institution, whose acts of betrayal are protected by the institution. Women faculty who are dependent on the institution expect that they will be treated equitably because institutions routinely make these claims in diversity and inclusion statements. Failure to prevent inequity constitutes institutional betrayal. It is even more egregious when, after a transgression, a victim reports an incident to the authorities, trusting that the institution will support them and mete out justice, but the institution betrays this trust by failing to respond or inadequately responding to the transgression. As one potential solution, Smith and Freyd (2014) call for research on protecting institutional members from betrayal. We move this work forward by considering the role of allies as agents who can (1) prevent institutional betrayal by intervening *before* the potential victim is involved (e.g., by working to change hiring practices) and (2) interrupt institutional betrayal by intervening *during* or *after* a transgression has occurred (e.g., through wrongful denial of tenure and promotion) and push the institution to adequately correct course or repair the betrayal. We explore these dynamics by considering the stories of allies.

Men as Allies

Washington and Evans (1991, 195) describe an ally as "a member of the 'dominant' or 'majority' group who works to end oppression in his or her personal and professional life through support of, and as an advocate for, the oppressed population." We approach issues of inequitable treatment of women in male-dominated disciplines of academia in North America by considering the role of male allyship. In this chapter, male allies are identified as those men who advocate for women by leveraging their power and privilege (Erskine and Bilimoria 2019) and who engage in "intentional action to interrupt sexism or gender injustice" (Madsen, Townsend, and Scribner 2020, 4). Research has shown that there are significant benefits of male allyship (Warren, Bordoloi, and Warren 2021), as calling out objectionable behavior is more effective when it is done by men than when done by women (Cihangir, Barreto, and Ellemers 2014), and other men hear male allies differently than they do women because of systemic patriarchy (Berkowitz 2004). Given that men continue to be the numeric majority in a number of STEM and other academic disciplines, male allies can be powerful resources in bringing about changes in gender dynamics and androcentric structures within academic institutions (Warren et al. 2019). As such, in this chapter we examine stories by male allies to unpack the consequences of men interrupting institutional betrayal toward women faculty. Of note, substantial past scholarship on gender equality and institutional betrayal has examined both actions and failures at the structural level (Pyke 2018; Smith and Freyd 2014). Yet the role that male allies can play at the individual and interpersonal levels in interrupting institutional betrayal remains relatively unknown. In this chapter, we extend past work by focusing on the role of male allies in contributing to gender equality through individual and interpersonal actions and on the consequences that accrue from these behaviors.

Method

Data were collected, through an open-ended online survey, from 101 male faculty in male-dominated disciplines of STEM, philosophy, religion, business, and law in 64 elite research-intensive universities in the United States and Canada. Men were asked to respond to the following prompt: "Please write about an incident at work that stands out in your memory as a time when you went out of your way to support, empower, or advocate for a female colleague. Perhaps, you did something when she was being treated unfairly, or you stood up for her, or you did something that was supportive of her. Please think about the incident and describe it in vivid terms. Please share exactly what happened. Who was involved? What were your thoughts and feelings? Why is this significant for you?" We selected stories that aligned with the concept of institutional betrayal. Using thematic analysis, we identified patterns and themes that we describe below.

Findings

Overall, the stories suggest that institutional betrayal may occur on multiple levels, constituting betrayal not only of women but also of the male allies who seek to support women.

Levels of Betrayal

Institutions fail to prevent harm toward women, and male allies can intervene where women are not present to advocate for themselves.

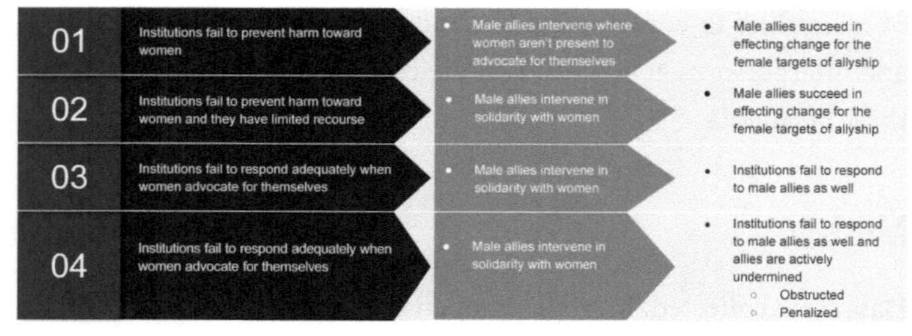

Levels of Betrayal. Graphic by Meg A. Warren and Samit D. Bordoloi.

The failure of institutions to secure the interests of women faculty in processes such as hiring and promotion were areas where male allies had to intervene to prevent harm. Within academia, where hiring and tenure/promotion decisions are often made by a small group of faculty members who carry disproportionately high levels of power, women faculty are placed in circumstances wherein, due to the structural processes that are inherently male dominated, the full extent of institutional betrayal is not visible to them.

AB* shared an experience where a woman candidate for a mathematics position "was being trashed by a small but influential group of senior colleagues. They harassed her in meetings during her interview, asked nasty and dismissive 'questions' during her job talk, and one even sent an email to faculty—all questioning her intelligence." Even though the ally worked in a completely different area of mathematics, he "wrote a long letter praising the potential applications of her work and sent it to [the] department head," which was instrumental in her hiring.

BC shared how the promotion case for a female colleague was being undermined, necessitating his intervention: "Student comments in question were not appropriate and should have been dismissed, yet several faculty members raised concern and continued discussion when it was not appropriate." Moreover, some faculty members wanted to count the faculty candidates' maternity leave against her: "I also made it quite clear the time allotted for maternity leave should NOT be considered in the time to tenure, as explicitly stated in our university's policy."

Institutions fail to prevent harm and women have limited recourse; when male allies step up in solidarity, they may have more success due to their relative privilege. Men's role as allies matters because women

---

* Initials and/or pseudonyms are being used throughout to protect the identities of our informants.

often face a double bind within institutions: if they do not attempt to speak up, they are penalized for not appearing agentic; if they do advocate for themselves, they face backlash that silences them (Bosak et al. 2018). "Doing their part" toward gender equity and inclusion means that men must step up as allies at the interpersonal level as well. Allyship intervention is necessary so that women do not have to suffer continued betrayal and be burdened with combating that betrayal alone.

CD shared a story of a woman staff member "who was administratively involved but not responsible" for a human subjects review document. She was "being bullied on email by a male professor who is both powerful and well liked" but had a history of treating female staff poorly. He sent her "a nasty email in all caps describing in many awful words his frustrations with the feedback he had received. He attacked her personally." CD noted that the staff member "had little recourse because the faculty member is well liked and also good friends with the staff member's boss," and it compelled him to intervene via "a little chat with the faculty member, calling him out on his lack of professionalism and his being an $@#%$@#. . . . he apologized to the staff member, and the staff member certainly appreciated it."

Another male faculty member, DE, shared how a female colleague found her application for promotion to full professor being challenged within her department due to an administratively ordained change in campus departments: "Her field of research changed when she moved . . . and her current department head 'just did not know what to do with her' and told her she could not see a way to get her promoted." DE became actively involved in ensuring that this situation was rectified: "I worked to get her tenure home moved to my department, worked with her to prepare her dossier (including putting her up for a major award which she won and helped her case), and shepherded her case through the process. . . . She was indeed promoted."

Institutions betray women and also often fail to respond to their allies. In this category, we consider the experiences of allies who intervened when they discovered women colleagues faced institutional betrayal but found that their own efforts were thwarted.

EF shared how a female colleague "was denied midterm continuation in a Tenure Track faculty position." He advocated for her at multiple levels and hired her as a research associate while she looked for employment. He noted that unfair gender expectations played a part in the decision process: "The bar was being moved with regards to necessary requirements. . . . Others were not held to the same standard."

Similarly, FG shared a story of how a woman colleague was denied promotion to full professor due to failed and unjust administrative processes at multiple levels: "[an] external letter solicited by the department head from a close colleague that was needlessly negative . . . errors in interpretation by the university [promotion and tenure] committee . . . factual errors in reporting funding amounts by the dean." He attempted to intervene by meeting the provost and president and expressing his displeasure at the situation. He noted that institutional betrayal did not just involve administrative failures but went against the very rhetoric of equality and inclusion employed by the institution: "[It's] not okay given all of the talk from many of the same individuals on empowering women in STEM!"

Institutions not only betray women but also actively undermine male allies. In this last category, we consider the narratives of allies who faced significant obstruction or were penalized for their actions when they attempted to intervene. GH was the chair of a search committee and shared that some members of the search committee, when they found that two of the top candidates were married to each other, "soured on inviting the two of them." He said that they could not consider their marital status when selecting candidates to interview and was particularly concerned that such a rule was discriminatory toward female candidates. He noted that "among the pool of applicants who were married to each other, 50% of them were women, compared to the overall pool, which was 10–15% women." However, he found himself in conflict with a few senior faculty and the chair of the department. He pointed out that "if we discriminated based on being married to another applicant, we'd be making a decision that had nothing to do with their ability to do the job . . . [and it] was prohibited by the Civil Rights Act of 1964." Due to his stand, the search committee eventually interviewed both candidates and subsequently "the faculty as a whole voted to offer them two positions." However, GH was penalized for his actions as he "was never asked to be on a hiring committee again."

HI intervened when two doctoral students sought his counsel about egregious behavior at an orientation program, where "two male faculty members teaching the class used an extended (half hour) metaphor about how being good at Computer Science research required 'big, hairy balls.'" In response to the complaint, HI "sent an email to the faculty members, and to their school chairs (their bosses). I told them that it was inappropriate, that it made the female students uncomfortable, and that the instructors should apologize." Rather than supporting HI, the administration penalized him: "The Dean and the Dean's Cabinet determined that I denied these two faculty due process. . . . they considered firing me, but decided that it wasn't a case that could revoke my tenure. I was reprimanded by the Dean, and had to apologize (in person and in writing) to the two instructors."

For allies, the pervasive nature of such systemic biases often results in a realization that sustaining institutional change is difficult. IJ, who attempted to help a faculty colleague with a pay disparity, noted one quickly realizes that an individual's "power and influence is small and insufficient in the massive academic machine."

Discussion

Research shows that institutional betrayal is widespread in higher education (Pyke 2018; Stader and Williams-Cunningham 2017). We draw from stories of male allies in male-dominated disciplines in higher education to offer a nuanced picture, highlighting the value of male allyship in protecting against institutional betrayal of women but also identifying its limits. The stories show that although allies serve an important role in protecting victims or potential victims from institutional betrayal, allyship is not a foolproof measure. First, allies find that there are limits to how effective their efforts are in protecting victims against institutional betrayal (e.g., feelings of helplessness). Further, even the most successful interventions by allies are limited to individual circumstances and are unlikely to result in structural changes. In the long term, individual allyship is also unlikely to be sustainable without changes to the androcentric structures within academia. Allies recognize that the institutional betrayal women experience is sustained by a male conceptualization of academic value that is willing to excuse egregious behaviors if the individual in question is valuable to the institution. As CD shared, "nothing's essentially changed. He's still an oblivious and aggressive SOB who's protected because he's a 'good researcher' and 'doesn't really mean all that stuff—he's just a dramatic guy.' My perception is that 'we' enable this crap so long as the person involved is doing something useful for the school."

Second, allies themselves are subject to institutional betrayal, wherein they find their efforts to seek justice are obstructed or, worse, they find themselves punished. When institutions betray allies, they also undermine future work on equity and allyship. Our findings demonstrate that while allyship makes a useful contribution, institutions cannot rely on individual allies to serve as the sole protecting mechanism against institutional betrayal. If academic institutions are truly willing to engage in institutional courage, that is, "seek the truth and engage in moral action, despite unpleasantness, risk, and short-term cost" (Freyd, n.d.), they not only need to actively promote and boost male allyship but also focus on disrupting the many structural barriers that women academics face. As male allies are willing to advocate for women by leveraging their power and privilege, they are the ideal candidates to resist institutional betrayal, demand transparency, and hold academic institutions accountable for their actions.

Works Cited

Berkowitz, Alan D. 2004. "Working with Men to Prevent Violence Against Women: An Overview (Part One)." National Electronic Network on Violence Against Women, October 2004. http://www.alanberkowitz.com/articles/VAWNET.pdf.

Bonawitz, Mary, and Nicole Andel. 2009. "The Glass Ceiling Is Made of Concrete: The Barriers to Promotion and Tenure of Women in American Academia." *Forum on Public Policy Online* 2009, no. 2 (January): 1–16. https://files.eric.ed.gov/fulltext/EJ870462.pdf.

Bosak, Janine, Clara Kulich, Laurie A. Rudman, and Mary Kinahan. 2018. "Be an Advocate for Others, Unless You Are a Man: Backlash Against Gender-Atypical Male Job Candidates." 2018. *Psychology of Men & Masculinities* 19 (1): 156–65. https://doi.org/10.1037/men0000085.

Cihangir, Sezgin, Manuela Barreto, and Naomi Ellemers. 2014. "Men as Allies Against Sexism: The Positive Effects of a Suggestion of Sexism by Male (vs. Female) Sources." 2014. *Sage Open* 4, no. 2 (Aril–June): 1–12. https://doi.org/10.1177/2158244014539168.

Daldrup-Link, Heike E. 2017. "The Fermi Paradox in STEM—Where Are the Women Leaders?" *Molecular Imaging and Biology* 19, no. 6 (September): 807–9. https://doi.org/10.1007/s11307-017-1124-4.

Erskine, Samantha E., and Diana Bilimoria 2019. "White Allyship of Afro-Diasporic Women in the Workplace: A Transformative Strategy for Organizational Change." *Journal of Leadership & Organizational Studies* 26, no. 3 (August): 319–38. https://doi.org/10.1177/1548051819848993.

Ford, Karly Sarita, and Ashley N. Patterson. 2019. "'Cosmetic Diversity': University Websites and the Transformation of Race Categories." *Journal of Diversity in Higher Education* 12 (2): 99–114. https://doi.org/10.1037/dhe0000092.

Freyd, Jennifer J. n.d. "Institutional Betrayal and Institutional Courage." Freyd Dynamics Lab. Last modified March 10, 2024. https://dynamic.uoregon.edu/jjf/institutionalbetrayal/index.html.

Glass, Christy, and Krista Lynn Minnotte. 2010. "Recruiting and Hiring Women in STEM Fields." *Journal of Diversity in Higher Education* 3 (4): 218–29. https://doi.org/10.1037/a0020581.

Hart, Jeni. 2016. "Dissecting a Gendered Organization: Implications for Career Trajectories for Mid-career Faculty Women in STEM." 2016. *Journal of Higher Education* 87 (5): 605–34. https://doi.org/10.1080/00221546.2016.11777416.

Madsen, Susan R., April Townsend, and Robbyn T. Scribner. 2020. "Strategies That Male Allies Use to Advance Women in the Workplace." *Journal of Men's Studies* 28, no. 3 (October): 239–59. https://doi.org/10.1177/1060826519883239.

Niemann, Yolanda Flores. 2012. "Lessons from the Experiences of Women of Color Working in Academia." In *Presumed Incompetent: The Intersections of Race and Class for Women in Academia*, edited by Gabriella Gutiérrez y Muhs, Yolanda Flores Niemann, Carmen G. González, and Angela P. Harris, 446–99. Boulder: University Press of Colorado.

Pyke, Karen D. 2018. "Institutional Betrayal: Inequity, Discrimination, Bullying, and Retaliation in Academia." *Sociological Perspectives* 61, no. 1 (February): 5–13. https://www.jstor.org/stable/26580552.

Qamar, Sadia Raheez, Kiran Khurshid, Sabeena Jalal, Matthew D. F. McInnes, Linda Probyn, Karen Finlay, Cameron J. Hague, et al. 2020. "Gender Disparity Among Leaders of Canadian Academic Radiology Departments." *American Journal of Roentgenology* 214, no. 1 (January): 3–9. https://doi.org/10.2214/ajr.18.20992.

Smith, Carly P., and Jennifer J. Freyd. 2014. "Institutional Betrayal." *American Psychologist* 69 (6): 575–87. https://doi.org/10.1037/a0037564.

Stader, David L., and Jodi L. Williams-Cunningham. 2017. "Campus Sexual Assault, Institutional Betrayal, and Title IX." *The Clearing House: A Journal of Educational Strategies, Issues and Ideas* 90 (5–6): 198–202.

Van Miegroet, Helga, Christy Glass, Ronda Roberts Callister, and Kimberly Sullivan. 2019. "Unclogging the Pipeline: Advancement to Full Professor in Academic STEM." *Equality, Diversity and Inclusion: An International Journal* 28 (2): 246–64. https://doi.org/10.1108/EDI-09-2017-0180.

Warren, Meg A., Samit D. Bordoloi, and Michael T. Warren. 2021. "Good for the Goose and Good for the Gander: Examining Positive Psychological Benefits of Male Allyship for Men and Women." *Psychology of Men & Masculinities* 22 (4): 723–31. https://doi.org/10.1037/men0000355.

Warren, Meg A., Scott I. Donaldson, Joo Young Lee, and Stewart I. Donaldson. 2019. "Reinvigorating Research on Gender in the Workplace Using a Positive Work and Organizations Perspective." *International Journal of Management Reviews* 21 (4): 498–518. https://doi.org/10.1111/ijmr.12206.

Washington, Jamie, and Evans, Nancy J. 1991. "Becoming an Ally." In *Beyond Tolerance: Gays, Lesbians, and Bisexuals on Campus*, edited by Nancy J. Evans and Vernon A. Wall, 195–204. Alexandria, VA: American Association for Counseling and Development.

Williams, Damon A. 2013. *Strategic Diversity Leadership: Activating Change and Transformation in Higher Education*. Stylus Publishing.

Wilson, Jeffery L., Katrina A. Meyer, and Larry McNeal, L. 2012. "Mission and Diversity Statements: What They Do and Do Not Say." *Innovative Higher Education* 37 (2): 125–39. https://doi.org/10.1007/s10755-011-9194-8.

Part II

Gender-Based Violence, Sexual Assault, and Title IX

When I Naïvely Thought a Guilty Finding Meant We Won

Title IX and Institutional Betrayal in a PhD Program

Alanna Gillis

I was sexually harassed by one of my graduate school professors and served as a witness in an official complaint brought against him by one of my peers. We'll call the offender Prof X. He touched me, manipulated me, and gaslighted me, and did this to several other women. But that is not what this essay is about. Instead, this is a story about how a sociology department responded un-sociologically to the clear evidence of gender inequality in their department, how the faculty in positions of authority denied their ability to hold anyone accountable for their actions, how a mentor turned against me during the time of crisis, and how I ultimately learned that an academic institution will always choose to protect itself. In other words, I show how my institution betrayed me in multiple ways.

I will start with what I assumed was the good news, the triumph that most sexual harassment victims can only hope for. In the case my peer brought forward, Prof X was found guilty: "After carefully considering the record as a whole, including but not limited to the interview summaries of all participants and documentary evidence submitted, the Administrative Reviewer determines that the preponderance of the evidence (i.e., more likely than not), demonstrates that [Prof X] engaged in sexual harassment of [graduate student] as defined under the Policy."

I felt proud to have played a role in that decision, using the testimony of my experience of harassment to provide evidence for her case, so that it was not simply her word against his. As stated in the report, "[Prof X] denied ever touching [student]'s inner thigh; however, there is sufficient evidence to support a pattern of behavior and propensity by [Prof X] to engage in conduct with female students when working side-by-side with them, particularly physical contact of various degrees, which made them feel uncomfortable. The evidence makes it more likely than not, that [student]'s version of the events should be considered as true."

Up until this point in the story, it might seem as if this is a case study of challenging institutional betrayal. After all, the reviewer followed the policy and came to the only reasonable conclusion: it was sexual harassment. However, that would overlook the crucial fact that I was Prof X's teaching assistant in the semester in which the investigation and appeal occurred. Despite giving my first statement before the semester even began, I was not given an option to maintain my stipend without staying in this subordinate position, the first act of institutional betrayal. I was thus required to have extensive conversations, email exchanges, and meetings with Prof X even after he knew that I had testified against him. For instance, one time he used his position as my boss to require an in-person meeting with him for almost two hours, in which he tried to manipulate and pressure me into testifying on his behalf. I cried for days afterward, but I needed the money so I couldn't quit my teaching assistant position. Perhaps I should have taken that as a sign of what was to come.

The next semester, I met with my department chair for what I hoped would be a sympathetic chat. I tried to take an approach that would make me seem "reasonable" in requesting some individual accommodations and departmental changes after Prof X was found guilty. Instead, the chair told me that he could not confirm or deny any such case even existed, as it was part of the confidential personnel file.

Thus, he could not discuss anything associated with it, even though he knew I was a key witness. These confidential protections are not a coincidence, but instead serve their purpose well to protect the university administrators from having to sufficiently hold themselves accountable for their employee's actions. Additionally, even if he was unable to confirm the case existed, he still could have taken my discomfort seriously and addressed that regardless of the reason. This was the second act of institutional betrayal.

The year after my testimony, I began preparations for my first comprehensive exam. Prof X was one of my assigned committee members. As a student who testified about his sexual harassment of me, I should have easily been entitled to an academic accommodation that removed him from my committee. There was no good reason for this man to have a deciding vote in whether I passed or failed. Instead, the department chair assured me that the grading of the exam was anonymous, so I was protected—despite me pointing out that I was the only student taking the exam that semester. Institutional actors hide behind seemingly fair processes like anonymity to excuse themselves from taking real action necessary to support an equitable environment. In this case, it was obviously untrue that an exam taken by only one student could be anonymous. It had never occurred to me that my chair would deny my request, and I was stunned by the excuse given, making it institutional betrayal number three.

After talking to my department chair, I then built up the courage to talk to the Title IX office, the office legally responsible for enforcing gender equality on my college campus. This was the office that investigated the case and found Prof X to have violated the policy. Surely the people in this office would be my allies? After all, there are pages on the office's website dedicated to stark language about taking sexual harassment seriously and providing accommodations for students who need them. A specific accommodation example on the website was that a student can switch classes to avoid someone who sexually harassed or assaulted them. I naïvely assumed that my situation clearly fell under this purview. Instead, the Title IX official talked with my department chair and then reassured me that my department had a good plan in place to protect my confidentiality in taking the exam, so I did not need an accommodation. Their response was institutional betrayal four.

Finally, as a last resort, I asked my therapist to write a letter on my behalf. Her letter read, in part,

> Ever since Ms. Gillis was told he would remain on the Committee her symptoms she presented with at the beginning of therapy have returned. She is anxious and more tearful. She is having a hard time focusing and her appetite has decreased. Her nightmares have returned and she feels a general sense of being unsafe. The recurrence of these symptoms is not surprising to me. . . . I believe this forced interaction of him being on her Committee could create further psychological distress. I also believe that the work she would be able to produce under this stress would not be a representation of her abilities.

As my therapist notes, my psychological distress was exactly what someone would predict, something that a sociology department and an office specializing in gender inequality in higher education knows. However, they have the institutional protections to ignore the inevitable harm to students. This was especially infuriating given that Prof X was not needed on the committee: most committees in my department had only three faculty members and he made number six on mine, the largest of all committees. Removing him would not have caused any additional work requirements for other faculty.

After six months of fighting, I finally got the university to reverse their decision and remove him from the committee. Given the toll on my mental health, calling it a victory would be a lie.

The next semester, I prepared to take my second comprehensive exam and faced my fifth case of institutional betrayal. One of the committee members, let's call her Prof Y, had been an ally of Prof X ever since the case began. She told numerous other students that the students filing complaints were overreacting. She made it clear to her advisees that they should not engage in departmental activism attempting to hold Prof X accountable. She was successful: several of my good friends told me that while they absolutely supported me trying to get accountability, they could not personally be involved, for fear of Prof Y finding out. They couldn't risk losing her mentorship, no matter how badly she abused her position of power. I understood this problem firsthand. Prof Y had been my mentor since my first semester of graduate school. Prior to this case, she used to make me feel like I belonged when I doubted myself. However, after the case broke, she began to blatantly ignore my presence in departmental social events. The only exception in that year was one time to loudly criticize my hair for being unkempt. She said this directly to me, at the beginning of a research talk with more than fifty faculty members and graduate students in attendance. Needless to say, her lack of support at the time I most needed it in my graduate career was crushing.

Prof Y was on my second comprehensive exam committee, and I knew it would be impossible to get her removed, considering I barely succeeded in getting Prof X off the first committee. I feared that she would take her grudge out on me in this exam, but friends and mentors repeatedly told me that I was being paranoid. I started to let my guard down and hoped that perhaps this nightmare was finally ending. Instead, less than two months before the exam, another student told me that Prof Y bragged to the student that she was intentionally writing far more difficult questions than normal for my exam. Begrudgingly, I knew I had to try again to make my department protect me, and so I took my concerns to a different administrator in the department, the director of graduate studies. I had a stronger relationship with him than with the chair. I was hoping for a more sympathetic response. This was a pretty blatant case of abuse of power, and surely he, the person in charge of overseeing all comprehensive exams, could use his position to ensure my exam was fair? But of course he didn't. I was somehow still too naïve to predict the depths of institutional betrayal that a department will take to protect its existing structures.

Instead, the director told me that while he could talk to Prof Y about what I reported, he didn't recommend that I request that he do so. He stated that she would likely bully me even worse afterward. Instead, I could take comfort in remembering that she was one of several committee members and I only had to answer four out of the six questions—I could just skip hers! In other words, his suggested solution was for him to do nothing. Institutional betrayal number six. He could have put in place a mechanism to ensure fairness for my exam, such as an outside member. But he simply turned it back on me as my problem to study harder and have fewer question options available to me.

I left that meeting with my thoughts reeling. I felt pretty confident in my ability to pass the exam. Because I had feared this reaction from Prof Y (despite being told I was being paranoid), I had studied far beyond the typical preparation levels. I felt fairly confident that I would produce sufficient quality work.

But what if I had been a student with less privilege?

What if I did not speak English as my first language? What if I had not attended such a rigorous undergraduate program to prepare me well to pass this exam? What if I had a physical or learning disability that made it more difficult to perform at a satisfactory level to pass? What if I had children to care for and could not spend forty hours per week for eight weeks preparing for this exam, while also teaching my first course as instructor of record that semester? I did pass both exams, on my first try, despite the roadblocks, but that was far from an inevitable outcome.

Eventually Prof X did leave the department, but it had nothing to do with sexual harassment. He was a tenure-track faculty member and scheduled to go up for tenure the year after he was found guilty. The chair of the department told me that the sexual harassment case, if there was one (don't forget, he couldn't comment on it), would not be considered as a factor in Prof X's tenure review. This was institutional betrayal number seven. From the department gossip threads, it was clear that everyone believed Prof X had not published nearly enough to get tenure at a research university. Thus, my ally professors explained to me, the university likely sought to ensure that there were no grounds for Prof X to claim wrongful denial of tenure if the sexual harassment case was included as part of the decision. (Though never forget, he was found guilty, despite his appeal.) Instead, the department was likely acting in accordance with university counsel to make sure that Prof X could not sue the university. This process facilitated Prof X's ability to move on easily to a new workplace—as is often the case with serial sexual harassers.

Everyone knew that due to the horrendous impact it would have had on my job prospects and the huge financial costs, there was no way I would sue, despite the blatant disregard for federal law demanding gender equality in higher education. They were right. I did not seriously consider suing.

Prof X was given an extra year in the department after he declined to go up for tenure. I was told the extra year was normal protocol for anyone who does not go up for tenure, to allow the person to search for a new job. Institutional betrayal number eight: using the rules of being "fair" to justify perpetuating an inequitable learning environment for all of us victims for yet another year. One more year of feeling anxious going to department research talks, going to department social events, and walking the hallway past his office to meet with other professors.

So here I am, three years later, finishing the first semester of my new job as an assistant professor, finally with the job security to think that perhaps I will not suffer another round of institutional betrayal for speaking my truth. To any graduate students or contingent faculty without that power, be warned that the institution will always act to protect itself. Your small efforts to push back will likely be punished. Build allies and resist if you can, but you should know that the structures are built to tear you down.

To other faculty members, do not naïvely believe that this could never happen in your department. Sociology is a discipline that studies institutional inequality and power dynamics, and yet my experience is far from the only such reaction from a sociology department.

Most importantly, to those of us in increasing positions of power, we can and must do better. Institutional policies and decisions are made by people—let's be the people who make structural changes for good. We must hold other faculty members accountable, even if they are our friends. We must advocate for policies that protect students, even if they inconvenience us as faculty, such as making disciplinary records of faculty public record. We must create tenure and promotion regulations that hold faculty accountable for their disciplinary history at each stage. Without intentional collective action taken to dismantle these current structures, institutional betrayal will continue to occur.

•

May we never lose our passion or naïve optimism that helps us believe that we can change institutions, so that maybe one day we actually do.

10

#MeTooUC

An Autoethnographic Account of the University of California's Response to Sexual Violence and Sexual Harassment

Cierra Raine Sorin

Every day, the University of California (UC) remains woefully underprepared to protect its community from sexual violence, let alone appropriately respond to violations. Taking a stance to the contrary demonstrates lack of familiarity with sexual violence policy across the UC system for the last six years and/or blatantly ignores the enduring student activism that has flooded our campuses over the last decade. As a student activist, a feminist sociologist dedicated to the study and abolition of sexual violence for nearly a decade, and a domestic violence survivor, I am deeply committed to systemic change. This is my brief autoethnography of being a sexual violence / sexual harassment (SVSH) researcher and activist at UC Santa Barbara (UCSB) since 2015, alongside an analysis of UC-wide SVSH policy. Change will come only with prioritizing survivor voices and adequately responding to their needs. Focusing specifically on graduate students, I offer a list of policy changes, informed by student survivors, that are imperative to bettering academia for survivors.*

* These policies are influenced from data I helped collect for two studies. The first, UC Speaks Up, is a 2019 qualitative study of SVSH on three UC campuses, which in-

Enduring Institutional Betrayal: An Autoethnographic Account of Antiviolence Activism at UCSB

My work on SVSH started in community college and continued after I transferred to UC San Diego to complete my BA. My post-admission visit to UCSB, where I would be attending graduate school, coincided with a protest by antiviolence student activists—nearly all undergraduates—denouncing the university's handling of SVSH. This demonstration imprinted on me, and after beginning my PhD program, I joined nowUCsb, the group behind the protests. Organized primarily by undergraduate women of color, nowUCsb intended to pressure the university to be more accountable to SVSH survivors. We expended a significant amount of effort fighting for policy change and increased resources. We ran campus teach-ins crashed by far-right rape apologists, posted flyers with annotated excerpts of the UC SVSH policy* to bring awareness to our peers, and held sit-ins in the chancellor's office. We screened the documentary *The Hunting Ground*—a film so deeply cutting that when I stumbled upon a crying colleague in the bathroom after the showing, I held her in my arms as she sobbed. Despite all else, our experiences of gendered violence bonded us. Yet nowUCsb endured every institutional strategy UCSB administrators threw at us.

---

cluded both undergraduate and graduate students, staff, faculty, administrators, and community members. I only draw from graduate student interviews and focus groups for comments herein. The second, #metoogradschool, is an ongoing digital survey project I am conducting to examine graduate students' experiences with SVSH during their programs. Some of these also come from conversations with fellow graduate and undergraduate activists over the last five years, most of whom are also survivors themselves.

* See more in the following section for an unpacking of the problems with the 2015–16 incarnation of the policy.

Higher ed's top favorite ways to stall and defuse student activist efforts/demands:

1. Listening sessions
2. Instituting a Special Task Force
3. Hiring Chief Diversity Officers
4. Climate Surveys

11:32 AM · Jun 8, 2020 · Twitter Web App

Unsurprisingly, these tactics worked. Our monthly "listening sessions" were scheduled at inconvenient times for students, almost never with our input, and timed so that many administrators had to leave before we finished. We asked for minor changes with potentially huge impacts: update the required SVSH online trainings for faculty and staff, post graduate student–specific antiviolence flyers in graduate housing, and hire a graduate specialist in CARE.[†] These requests were routinely met with condescending messages about the budget, as if there is not always money when the university has a priority funding need. We recognized SVSH was not a priority, contrary to what administrators wanted us to believe.

More institutionalized mechanisms for change seemed designed to stall. Campus committees formed to respond to issues from the 2012 UC climate survey[‡]—including an SVSH subcommittee I served on—and spent the 2015–16 year discussing the results, deriving plans

† CARE stands for Campus Advocacy, Resources & Education; it is the campus sexual violence resource center, with an office on each UC campus.

‡ The survey is dated as approved in 2012 and the final report was released in March 2014 (Rankin & Associates, Consulting 2014).

for improvements, and writing memos to the chancellor. There was no further engagement with the survey data, nor further outcomes. In a meeting with the Graduate Student Association (GSA) in my third year, a campus dean suggested we pursue a climate survey. This appeared to be another performative action meant to assuage us; it was unclear if they were aware of the past climate survey or that the work afterward went nowhere. Three years later, a different SVSH committee, not affiliated with nowUCsb, petitioned for *another* climate survey. Our most significant recommendation to the chancellor was to prioritize hiring a vice chancellor of diversity, equity, and inclusion to shift this work to them. When all the university does is write reports and bounce SVSH efforts between administrators, the lack of institutional memory ensures the status quo.

Eventually, the undergraduates graduated and only three graduate students were left; nowUCsb dissolved. As graduate student activists, we barely had time for our own work, but the institutional betrayal (Smith and Freyd 2014) we faced—minimization of our experiences as activists and survivors, poor responses to reporting our traumas, and refusal to implement necessary improvements—fueled our desire for change.

"The Third Rape": Bad UC Policy Changes and Worse Implementations

In feminist discussions of SVSH, the reporting process is colloquially referred to as the "second rape," where trauma survivors endure another wave of victimization when seeking social services post-assault (Schulz 2000). Equally detrimental is what I call the "third rape": institutional policies put in place seemingly to protect survivors but that actually shield institutions and offenders from litigation when SVSH cases are brought forward. The original SVSH policy issued by the UC Office of the President (UCOP) in December 2015, which went into effect in January 2016, exemplifies this. As much as we centered our efforts on campus issues, nowUCsb took issue with the policy as soon as it was released; the policy also greatly affected how our work continued after nowUCsb's dissolution.

"Sexual violence," per the 2015 incarnation,* was defined as "without the consent of the Complainant, penetration, no matter how slight, of the vagina, anus, or mouth by a penis; or the vagina or anus by any body part or object."† This heteronormative definition excludes many kinds of interpersonal violence. Findings from the 2010 National Intimate Partner and Sexual Violence Survey (NISVS) illustrate how lesbian, gay, and bisexual individuals experience higher rates of interpersonal and sexual violence than do their heterosexual counterparts (Chen et al. 2023); an oversight of this nature was infuriating, especially for the many queer students like me doing SVSH work.

The definition of "relationship violence," separated into "dating violence" and "domestic violence," only counted "bodily injury to the Complainant or [violence that] places the Complainant in reasonable fear of serious bodily injury."‡ As SVSH prevention specialists, counselors, and researchers all attest, much interpersonal violence is not physical. This version of the policy did not include emotional, psychological, or financial abuse, all of which are common.

Survivors could be asked by the university to keep the outcomes of their cases confidential: "The Complainant can be advised of the confidential and sensitive nature of personnel and student disciplinary

* "University of California Sexual Violence and Sexual Harassment." 2015. https://ucnet.universityofcalifornia.edu/wp-content/uploads/tools-and-services/administrators/policies/proposed/shsv.pdf.

† *Complainant* refers to the survivor/victim, while *respondent* refers to the accused/perpetrator.

‡ "University of California Sexual Violence and Sexual Harassment." 2015. https://ucnet.universityofcalifornia.edu/wp-content/uploads/tools-and-services/administrators/policies/proposed/shsv.pdf.

matters that arise under this Policy, and in appropriate circumstances, such as in connection with a settlement of a matter, may be asked not to further disclose it."* It should be immediately self-evident why this was problematic.

The UC policy on immunity was left sufficiently vague for campuses to punish students reporting SVSH if they were violating other university policies simultaneously:

> To encourage reporting, neither a Complainant nor witness in an investigation of sexual violence will be subject to disciplinary sanctions for a violation of the relevant University conduct policy at or near the time of the incident, unless the violation placed the health or safety of another at risk; involved plagiarism, cheating, or academic dishonesty; or was otherwise egregious. Because alcohol, drugs, and other intoxicants are often involved, Complainants may be afraid to report Prohibited Conduct where they have also engaged in an activity that violated University policy or State law, such as a person under age 21 drinking alcohol. UC encourages the reporting of Prohibited Conduct and therefore *generally* does not hold Complainants and/or witnesses accountable for alcohol or drug-related student violations that may have occurred at the time of the Prohibited Conduct. (emphasis mine)

In a meeting nowUCsb had with the Sexual Violence and Sexual Assault Task Force—composed of upper administrators and staff—in February 2016,† administrators confirmed they interpreted "generally" to mean UCSB could discipline complainants or witnesses with

* "University of California Sexual Violence and Sexual Harassment." 2015. https://ucnet.universityofcalifornia.edu/wp-content/uploads/tools-and-services/administrators/policies/proposed/shsv.pdf.

† I attended this task force meeting and also have records of this confirmation from other UCSB students in attendance. That said, the administrator who confirmed this

violations in these cases. While the policy was likely intended to protect students, it was instead weaponized to harm those needing other forms of support.

Another shortcoming of the policy was that although it defined domestic violence, *nothing* in it specifically addressed how to handle domestic violence cases, an especially critical oversight regarding graduate students, who are more likely to be in long-term relationships and thus more likely to endure domestic violence. Moreover, domestic violence for graduate student survivors affects all other aspects of life, including housing, health care, financial security, and education. With no oversight on how to respond to domestic violence, UCOP left it to each campus to devise policies for survivors living in university-owned housing, needing day care provisions, and so on. At UCSB, at the time of this writing, there are still neither specific nor well-advertised policies for helping students in these situations.

Finally, the policy did not include a clear and accessible process for implementing sanctions for faculty-on-student SVSH, though it allegedly addressed this dynamic. This was most harmful for graduate students, who are more likely than undergraduates to experience harassment or assault from faculty members (Carapezza 2019). Student activists across the system concluded this policy was directed predominantly toward student-on-student SVSH, specifically between undergraduates. Graduate student needs and interests were eclipsed, despite those students comprising nearly 20 percent of the overall student population across the UC.‡

In response to student outcry, a systemwide Title IX Student Advisory Board (TIX SAB) formed in November 2017 and began meeting in early 2018. The board consisted of one undergraduate and one graduate

for us has since retired, and I would be unsurprised if this was not recorded in minutes by staff, as it was an especially contentious topic of discussion.

‡ Using fall 2019 enrollment data, there were 58,945 graduate students out of a total population of 285,216 students in the UC system (University of California, n.d.).

student from each campus.* Our graduate representative for UCSB was the same nowUCsb friend who agreed to run with me for student government leadership. With our background in SVSH activism—and the majority of GSA candidates being women that year—we ran on a platform of addressing SVSH issues, thinking our connection to the TIX SAB might further our goals at UCSB and across the UC. Instead, beginning in October 2018, we confronted institutional betrayal coming directly from UCOP, which ultimately resulted in our graduate student representative being removed / resigning from her position on the board and a boycott of the TIX SAB by the UCSB GSA.

The TIX SAB was formed by UCOP in response to student disgust and frustration over the narrow, exclusionary policy, which also did not capture many graduate students' experiences with SVSH. The TIX SAB was to work with officials from UCOP on policy revisions. In this capacity, our student advisory board representative presented suggested changes to the policy at a General Assembly meeting of the GSA and at an Associated Students Senate meeting for the undergraduates, as we were without an undergraduate representative. The changes—some of which beneficially reflected general student concerns, many more of which were detrimental—were reported in the *Daily Nexus* (Berkness 2018). Soon administrators at UCOP demanded the paper retract the article, citing inaccuracies with the presentation.† Ultimately, our representative was unceremoniously removed from her position and told not to attend the next meeting of the TIX SAB at UC Irvine. With no members from UCSB slated to attend with less than twenty-four hours' notice, we elected to send her anyway. She experienced bullying and attempted shaming from the UCOP officials running the meeting, leading to her resignation from the board. Her full testimony of this experience—including

* UC San Francisco has no undergraduate students and thus has two graduate student representatives.

† For those interested, a complete breakdown of the issues UCOP had with the presentation can be found in Verna and Kamidi 2018.

emails with UCOP officials—can be read in her public resignation letter (Selvidge 2018). The GSA General Assembly voted unanimously to boycott the TIX SAB altogether until some attempt at reparations was made. As of this writing, we are one of the only campus bodies without a graduate representative. It remains clear our participation is only a performance meant to placate students, not an opportunity to meaningfully critique and improve upon the policies directly impacting *our* lives. Of course, as graduate students usually left out of policy conversations, this is no surprise.

Making Amends: Necessary Policy Changes Informed by Graduate Student Survivors

Graduate students occupy a precarious position on campus, as students and as lab workers, research assistants, or instructors. Many graduate students are wholly dependent on faculty advisers for funding, letters of recommendation, and other professional acts of service necessary for success in academia or in industry, a dynamic that can lead to abuse from faculty. As graduate students are essential to keeping campuses functioning, it is imperative they are properly supported in their varied roles. Drawing from recommendations of graduate students in multiple studies, the scant literature on graduate students' experiences with SVSH, and my own informal observations and discussions with other graduates, below are several changes that must happen.

Gender-based violence scholars and practitioners have argued that online SVSH trainings alone are neither effective nor efficient, especially for certain student groups and in certain disciplines. Unfortunately, there have been few studies addressing this. Online trainings must be appropriately geared toward graduate students, with development and regular review that incorporate graduate student input. Additional in-person trainings must be required for all departments, with staff, faculty, and graduates participating together as a community.

Graduate student experiences of SVSH do not directly match those of undergraduates, and our liminal positions within the university necessitate at least one on-campus advocate specifically trained in understanding and working with graduate survivors. There must be at least one counselor on every campus whose specialization and time is solely dedicated to graduate students and SVSH, housed in a sexual assault resource center or a related center.

Restorative justice approaches to SVSH are more important than ever. These emphasize examining who has been harmed and what the best steps forward are for them and can include "circles, victim-offender dialogues, victim impact panels, sentencing circles, and conferencing" (Coker 2017). At least one person on campus must be formally trained in restorative justice approaches to handling SVSH cases (Keys 2019).

SVSH work is handled primarily by women and femmes—on the administration side, usually white women. But SVSH affects every single one of us. We must be more intentionally mindful of how SVSH affects different communities and more inclusive of who participates in policymaking, resource design, and survivor care. That necessitates calling in men and masculine folks on our campuses, who also experience SVSH and must be actively involved in efforts to prevent and respond to it. It also necessitates recognizing that SVSH is experienced differently by people of color, people with disabilities, and queer individuals. Taking an intersectional approach to SVSH prevention and response is not just pivotal—it is the only way forward.

Graduate students must be involved in the design and revision of university SVSH policies. We must develop interdisciplinary campus community boards bringing together SVSH experts with tenure-track and adjunct faculty within and outside of the department(s) in question, graduate and undergraduate students, and staff. Team case evaluations will more fairly account for power dynamics across campus, making it more likely for survivors to receive adequate support.

Many graduate students leave their programs for others, or leave academia altogether, because of their experiences with SVSH. This is not well documented, but ought to be. (It is also the case that there is very little data on undergraduate student retention and experiences of sexual assault and harassment.) Exit surveys of graduate students must inquire about SVSH and provide resources regardless of students' answers.

SVSH is related to other forms of violence. A recent report on sexual harassment in academia (Benya, Widnall, and Johnson 2018) demonstrates that acceptance of bullying, racism, xenophobia, and other inappropriate social behaviors turns the academy into a breeding ground for other violence, which most directly impacts women of color, queer women, and trans and nonbinary students. To address SVSH on campus means holding our academic communities and institutions accountable, not just the individuals who perpetrate violence. SVSH is preventable, but this requires communal buy-in and participation. Without concerted efforts to include graduate students, especially survivors, these kinds of violences will continue to occur.

We can do better—and we must.

Works Cited

Benya, Frazier F., Sheila E. Widnall, and Paula A. Johnson, editors. 2018. *Sexual Harassment of Women: Climate, Culture, and Consequences in Academic Sciences, Engineering, and Medicine*. National Academies of Sciences, Engineering, and Medicine; Policy and Global Affairs; Committee on Women in Science, Engineering, and Medicine; Committee on the Impacts of Sexual Harassment in Academia. Washington, D.C.: National Academies Press. https://doi.org/10.17226/24994.

Berkness, Aaron. 2018. "Title IX Policy Changes Explained By Student Advisory Board Representative." *Daily Nexus*, October 11, 2018. https://dailynexus.com/2018-10-11/title-ix-policy-changes-explained-by-student-advisory-board-representative/.

Carapezza, Kirk. 2019. "'Opportunity and Power': Graduate Students Face Higher Rates of Sexual Harassment.'" GBH, December 19, 2019. https://www.wgbh.org/news/education-news/2019-12-19/opportunity-and-power-graduate-students-face-higher-rates-of-sexual-harassment.

Chen, Jieru, Srijana Khatiwada, May S. Chen, Sharon G. Smith, Ruth W. Leemis, Norah W. Friar, Kathleen C. Basile, and Marcie-jo Kresnow. 2023. *The National Intimate Partner and Sexual Violence Survey 2016/2017: Report on Victimization by Sexual Identity*. Atlanta: National Center for Injury Prevention and Control, Division of Violence Prevention. https://www.cdc.gov/https://www.cdc.gov/nisvs/documentation/nisvsReportonSexualIdentity.pdf.

Coker, Donna. 2017. "Crime Logic, Campus Sexual Assault, and Restorative Justice." *Teas Tech Law Review* 49 (147): 147–210. https://ssrn.com/abstract=2932481.

Keys, Domale Dube. 2019. "Restorative Justice for Curbing Campus Sexual Violence." *Center for the Study of Women Policy Brief Series: Rethinking Policy on Gender, Sexuality, and Women's Issues*: Policy Brief 27, 9–11. https://csw.ucla.edu/wp-content/uploads/2019/06/Policy-Brief-Series-2019_FINAL.pdf.

Rankin & Associates, Consulting. 2014. *University of California System: Campus Climate Project Final Report*. https://campusclimate.ucop.edu/_common/files/pdf-climate/ucsystem-full-report.pdf.

Schulz, Priscilla. 2000. Review of "Secondary Victimization of Rape Victims: Insights from Mental Health Professionals Who Treat Survivors of Violence" by Rebecca Campbell and Sheela Raja, *Violence and Victims* 14, no. 3 (1999). https://mainweb-v.musc.edu/vawprevention/research/victimrape.shtml.

Selvidge, Jennifer. 2018. "Formal Notice of Resignation." https://dailynexus.s3-us-west-1.amazonaws.com/dailynexus/wp-content/uploads/2018/11/Selvidge-Title-IX-Student-Advisory-Boar . . . signation-Letter-11-2-18-Google-Docs.pdf.

Smith, Carly P., and Jennifer Freyd. 2014. "Institutional Betrayal." *American Psychologist* 69 (6): 575–87. https://doi.org/10.1037/a0037564.

University of California. n.d. "Fall Enrollment at a Glance." Last modified January 19, 2024. https://www.universityofcalifornia.edu/infocenter/fall-enrollment-glance.

Verma, Simren, and Sanya Kamidi. 2018. "UCSB Graduate Rep. Resigns from Title IX Student Advisory Board." *Daily Nexus*, November 8, 2018. https://dailynexus.com/2018-11-08/ucsb-graduate-rep-resigns-from-title-ix-student-advisory-board/.

11

What We Did with Institutional Betrayal

The Open Secrets Project on Faculty Sexual Violence in Canada

Connor Spencer, Chantelle Spicer, and Emily Rosser (Students for Consent Culture Canada)

There are those who these institutions were built for and by, and those who they weren't. This shows a lot in who is given the benefit of the doubt, who is given second chances, and who is believed. When high levels of leadership don't reflect the diversity of the university community, and those who share identity with leaders are not held accountable, that sends a strong message about who matters.

—Student survey participant

I'm so tired of this bullshit. So goddamn tired. I hate that these men . . . will hold on to their jobs while raping students, while the rest of us non-rapists struggle to find work. I am tired of university administrations' lack of loyalty and accountability to students.

—Student survey participant

In October 2017, a group of student survivors and advocates from across the nation of Canada worked together to form the National Our Turn Committee, which produced *OurTurn: A National Action Plan to End Campus Sexual Violence* (Salvino, Gilchrist, and Cooligan-Pang 2017). This document facilitated, for many of us, our first connections with other students pushing for similar radical accountability for sexual violence on their campuses. Shortly after publication of the action plan, the #MeToo movement took off, and we saw many of our institutions change their rhetorical strategies. Instead of the liberal argument that sexual violence occurs because of the actions of individuals and that the institution plays no role in why or how this violence occurs, we started hearing administrators mention "rape culture" and acknowledge that violence could happen at school-sanctioned events, such as orientation week, and within Greek life. Committees and task forces were formed, and we suddenly found ourselves valuable to institutions across the country looking to our resources for creating or updating sexual violence policies. Our collective knowledge—which, to be clear, was recorded for other student activists, not for postsecondary administrators—was suddenly able to enter into spaces that previously had been barred to us. It seemed the document was more palatable to university leaders than our lived experiences of harm or our collective expertise. Student consultation with no students present—an institutional dream!

Watching this unfold, we decided we needed a formal group that was clearly *by* and *for* student survivors, where the memories, experiences, and skills produced directly from experiences of institutional harm were taken seriously and valued. From a network born out of institutional betrayal, we created Students for Consent Culture Canada (SFCC),* a strong national organization with a reach that far exceeds its limited resources. One of the best parts of building a national network is being able to quickly detect patterns across institutions. As postsecondary institutions began to slowly acknowledge sexual violence perpetrated by students against students, there was another kind of violence that they were (and continue to be) unwilling to speak about: sexual violence perpetrated by academic faculty against students. Many of us found the doors that had slowly creaked open for us due to the sociocultural impact of #MeToo were slammed shut when we tried to speak about the actions of sexually violent and

* Learn more about SFCC at https://www.sfcccanada.org/.

harassing professors on our campuses. This is unsurprising, given this problem is where institutions would most have to confront how structures inherent in the academy uphold and perpetuate issues of power imbalance, hierarchy, and coercion (Armstrong, Gleckman-Krut, and Johnson 2018; Henry and Tator 2009; Bellas and Gosset 2001).

From our networks, we were hearing that when faculty engaged in sexually inappropriate or harassing behavior, students were experiencing serious negative impacts. Some of the impacts were similar to the experiences of sexual violence committed by fellow students, but others were unique. With this in mind, we embarked on a research project with the intent of creating a set of resources, similar to our original Our Turn action plan. These tool kits offer student survivor-activists data, support, and ideas to help hold their institutions accountable.

Guiding Principles

Our methodological approach draws on a larger feminist inquiry into ethical research on power, violence, and intersectionality (Harris and Linder 2017; Cho, Crenshaw, and McCall 2013; Guntarik 2009; Lazar 2007; Crenshaw 1991). Further, our own experiences within various institutions have informed the guiding principles that underpin our methodological decisions in this project. These guiding principles and practices exist in direct contradiction to the capitalist hyper-individualism, ableism, patriarchy, and white supremacy of the academy.

Amplify survivors' voices and experiences. We are not reducible to statistics. We are not objects to be studied or tokens to be invited to the table, expected to remain silent. We have our own voices and analyses.

Work in intersectional and trauma-informed ways, throughout the entire research process. Antiracist and anticolonial frameworks structure SFCC's work. We are a grassroots organization that is accountable first to students and survivors and driven by the need to interrogate how power operates to uphold injustice for those most marginalized by institutions.

Create/contribute to a baseline of research on the topic in Canada. As in other areas related to violence, the relative absence of comprehensive data on the prevalence and impacts of faculty perpetration of sexual violence allows university and college administrators to underestimate and downplay its existence and impact.

Do research that meets conventional standards of ethics and study design. Student activists are accustomed to having our collective experience dismissed as "anecdotal." This study is one effort to speak to this form of dismissal.

Do research that meets our own standards of ethics as part of broader movements for social justice.

Address concerns that are not often priorities in policy research. First and foremost, this means to recognize, name, further theorize, and eventually dismantle rape culture.

Carry out an ambitious project uncompromised by institutional restrictions. We conducted the research without affiliation with any university or college. This position does not equate non-affiliation with "objectivity." We recognize and honor the fact that this work is deeply subjective, with our varied positionality and shared commitment to equity guiding us in all stages of this work.

Work in ways that prioritize community care and do not retraumatize for the sake of expediency. This principle has always been important in our work. It was especially crucial during the COVID-19 pandemic and on research teams that included survivors. Working with community care as a focus has its foundations in the ways that we came together, and it draws from the long-term advocacy of antiracist, queer, and disability justice activists (Haga 2020; Spade 2020; Piepzna-Samarasinha 2018; Adams and Rojas-Caroll 2015).

Mapping Institutional Betrayal and Rape Culture

The Open Secrets Project* is one of the first comprehensive attempts to explore the scale and impact of sexual violence and harassment perpetrated by professors. With this project, we are consolidating existing data and developing a better baseline for SFCC and other student survivor–led groups to inform and support mobilization on their campuses. We are working to gain accountability from postsecondary institutions for the behavior itself *and* to change the culture that supported it. At the heart of the project are the experiences of those who came forward with their stories, who have previously been disbelieved, marginalized, and ignored by administrators.

Between January and July 2020, we collected data from current and former students and faculty across Canadian postsecondary campuses through an online anonymous survey and semi-structured interviews. We also conducted literature reviews in four areas: contemporary news and online media (such as blog posts), academic research, federal and provincial privacy and sexual violence legislation, and campus sexual violence policies. We paid particular attention to Canadian data, emerging questions that consider intersecting forms of violence and oppression, and grassroots advocacy, which—with some notable exceptions—are often neglected in mainstream press coverage and academic literature on campus sexual violence.

Our final survey data set includes 225 student responses and 57 faculty responses. Participants could opt out of any question and withdraw at any time before completion. Though our sampling was not random or large scale, the responses showed that a diverse range of students and faculty across many colleges and universities are looking for support, change, and spaces to be heard. Here, we focus on student experiences: all quotes below are from the student surveys.

* Learn more about the project and accompanying reports at https://www.sfcccanada.org/open-secrets-report.

Many respondents took the opportunity to disclose specific experiences with professors. Students at many levels of study detailed inappropriate comments, behaviors, sexual assaults, and coercion in the context of lectures, office hours, travel, field research, and teaching assistant and research assistant roles.

> *My professor asked me out via email while I was in his class. He was the department head. Not only was this around midterms, I still had a year left in my degree and our faculty was small. I'd have to take more classes from him. I was terrified about what to do.*

> *The professor made residential school jokes while pressuring me for oral sex in exchange for a passing grade on an assignment I'd missed due to a depressive episode. He knew I was Indigenous. . . . It sickened me that he was steeped in knowledge of historical atrocities and weaponizing my own intergenerational trauma and the effect of the class subject matter on my mental health in order to solicit sexual favours.*

> *I was sexually assaulted by my professor during a field course abroad. It was the worst experience of my life. I wasn't believed and the professor still continues to teach and mentor students on field courses.*

> *My PhD supervisor liked to tell me sexual things about himself before he was finally accused of rape by another student (and confessed to it) and I dropped him. He still holds his emeritus status and can supervise students.*

Participants shared many experiences that we could broadly term "institutional betrayal," as defined by Smith and Freyd (2013). Universities and colleges will generally direct potential complainants to file an official report, while scholars and survivors of violence continue to highlight gaps between formal policy or law, and what is practiced on the ground (Gotell 2010). For those in our study who experienced harassment and sexual violence from faculty members, reporting it to the institution often did not seem like a realistic option.

I stopped trying to bring it up when other faculty laughed it off.

I know [reporting] won't be taken seriously because people tend not to believe Black people. So there's better chances if someone else reports it.

When I first reached out to student affairs about this incident I was asked if I had previously flirted with this professor, and if I had any mental health conditions. I was encouraged to not proceed with any formal statements and to work out my differences with this professor independently.

Respondents underlined the contrast between institutional claims to care about sexual violence and their responses to specific situations. Many also showed a degree of resignation about these realities.

The senior admin do not truly care about survivors with any real commitment. So much of what they care about is simply public relations. I recently worked on a consent education video with the sexual violence office and the PR staffer would not approve it until we changed the prof-student scene to be more ambiguous—they said they were open to showing the power of authority figures, just did not want to draw attention and make it seem like there are issues with the profs at our university.

Even if I reported and he was punished or fired, I'm convinced that school reputation and fundraising would be the reasons the school takes action—not genuine concern for students.

I felt absolutely gutted that the consequences put upon the professor who harassed me were reversed within two years, and that he still has access to students. I found out he is still drinking with students on a regular basis.

The survey responses help us trace the contours of a culture within academia that tolerates the grooming of young and potentially vulnerable students by older faculty and teaching staff in mentorship positions. Respondents repeatedly describe the sense that faculty members feel untouchable and underscore the power they have over students both academically and psychologically (see also Hodgetts et al. 2020; Page, Bull, and Chapman 2019; Steiner 2019; Bellas and Gosset 2001).

The professor that offended against me was white, male, straight, nondisabled, and at the height of his career. His status had everything to do with why I trusted him, why he could talk me into it for so long, and why I never told anyone.

The professor did not use threats but emotional manipulation to entangle me. Even though I was an adult, I was so impressionable and naïve. At every turn, every new level of sexual engagement, I doubted my fear and hesitation. It was a slow process of him pushing me to consent—very much like grooming children for sexual abuse—so that I would feel like it was all my fault.

The professor said "I'm tenured, so I can do whatever and say whatever I want."

Many who had secondhand knowledge of such situations felt doubtful that reporting would make a difference. In response, systems of open secrets have a long history on many campuses, passed through whisper networks from older (most often women and nonbinary) students and faculty to younger or newer students (Cole 2019; Fusco 2019).

These systems work to relay information about which professors are "creepy," who students should avoid being alone with, and who actively pursues intimate relationships with students.

Participants acknowledged the contrast they felt between mutual support among students through such informal systems and the absence of support on the part of administrators:

> *The way that women and trans students share info through grassroots texts and convos in order to protect each other is amazing. We continue to find ways to protect each other because we know we are all we have. I would trust another student I have never met before more than admin at my school.*

> *My fellow students do more than the admin do.*

Such statements speak to the betrayal students are feeling within postsecondary institutions, their understanding of how systems of power are upheld and reproduced, and the expertise needed to build something different.

New Visions

As well as asking participants to share what happened to them and their impression of how faculty sexual violence is addressed on their campus, we made sure to ask visioning questions. This moves the research past documentation and allows participants to dream beyond where we are now. What does that future look like?

> *Transparency. The school does far too much on the down-low where profs are just "let go" quietly and not punished publicly. They are predators. We should know who they are.*

> *Any accountability measures should be equity-informed and accessible (e.g., it should be designed to meet the needs of the most disadvantaged/marginalized students).*
>
> *[The sexually inappropriate faculty member] holds a Canada Research Chair. We need to interrupt the cycle of academic power accrual for faculty who are exploiting those around them.*
>
> *We must begin to refuse to participate and disrupt these systems that were designed to control what "student" input looks and sounds like.*
>
> *There needs to be more resources available for both students and professors to safely report inappropriate actions. I know for a fact, some professors feel scared that if they stop known behaviour, or try to, they fear they will lose their job. There must be security, and validation.*

We have been inspired by the brilliance of our participants and fellow student organizers. It is exciting being able to document these ideas and present them as legitimate contributions from people with the expertise of lived experience. In the face of incredible adversity at neoliberal institutions, they continue to show up with compassion, excellent research, and well-articulated arguments. Yet it is heartbreaking that this labor is still so crucial. It is not only the work of students. Our survey responses from faculty frequently refer to struggles with the compounded impacts of inappropriate sexist, racist, and otherwise violent behaviors over twenty, thirty, or more years of lived experience in academic spaces. This showcases the need for our visioning and strategic action to be collaborative and multifaceted. The betrayals we experience are intimately tied to the collectives we create together, but we won't give the universities credit for that. If change is going to occur—and it must—it will not be the institutions who lead it.

Our work has been punctuated by the COVID-19 pandemic and by global antiracist uprisings. As we document student and faculty visions of how and what our postsecondary institutions could be, we are also engaging in parallel processes of visioning in our own communities about how our world could be. These things are not unrelated. We have been betrayed by the institutions and systems that have been supposedly set up to support and nourish us. Powerful figures and institutions can no longer pay lip service to taking oppression and violence seriously. The façade is falling, and all around us the betrayed rise up—full of ideas for new systems and care, never settling for less than we deserve.

Acknowledgments

Open Secrets, Power, and Professors: A Study on Rape Culture and Accountability at Canadian Post-Secondary Institutions Final Report and Toolkit will be published in 2025. *A Preliminary Summary and Recommendations* was released by SFCC in 2021. We are very proud of this work and all those who entrusted us with their experiences. We did this research with no core funding, "off the side of our desks" as we worked in precarious jobs, studied, experienced a global pandemic, and supported each other and our communities in calls for justice of all kinds. We want to thank all our co-researchers, the larger SFCC team, and everyone who participated in the research or helped to support the project (and us). The Open Secrets Project received ethics approval from the Community Research Ethics Office in Waterloo, Ontario, in August 2019.

Works Cited

Adams, Chanelle, and Rojas-Carroll, Irene. 2015. "Care Under Conditions of Capitalism & White Supremacy: An Interview with Mia Mingus." *Blue Stockings Magazine*, April 21, 2015.

Ahmed, Sara. 2017. *Living a Feminist Life*. Durham, NC: Duke University Press.

Armstrong, Elizabeth A., Miriam Gleckman-Krut, and Lanora Johnson. 2018. "Silence, Power, and Inequality: An Intersectional Approach to Sexual Violence." *Annual Review of Sociology* 44, no 1 (July): 99–122. https://doi.org/10.1146/annurev-soc-073117-041410.

Bay-Cheng, Laina Y., and Rebecca K. Eliseo-Arras. 2008. "The Making of Unwanted Sex: Gendered and Neoliberal Norms in College Women's Unwanted Sexual Experiences." *Journal of Sex Research*, 45 (4): 386–97. https://doi.org/10.1080/00224490802398381.

Bellas, Marcia L., and Jennifer L. Gossett. 2001. "Love or the 'Lecherous Professor': Consensual Sexual Relationships Between Professors and Students." *Sociology Quarterly* 42 (4): 529–58. http://dx.doi.org/10.1111/j.1533-8525.2001.tb01779.x.

Cho, Sumi, Kimberlé Williams Crenshaw, and Leslie McCall. 2013. "Toward a Field of Intersectionality Studies: Theory, Applications, and Praxis." *Signs: Journal of Women in Culture and Society*, 38, no. 4 (Summer): 785–810. https://doi.org/10.1086/669608.

Cole, Violet. 2019. "When Women Whisper: Rumor and Gossip as Transcripts of Resistance." Senior capstone project, Vassar College. https://digitallibrary.vassar.edu/collections/institutional-repository/671ce5dd-9b4b-4c66-9b0e-6c93d61444a9.

Crenshaw, Kimberlé. 1991. "Mapping the Margins: Intersectionality, Identity Politics, and Violence Against Women of Color." *Stanford Law Review* 43, no. 6 (July): 1241–99. https://doi.org/10.2307/1229039.

Fusco, Katherine. 2019. "Feminist (Dis)Pleasure and Anita Loos's Whisper Networks" *Feminist Modernist Studies* 2 (3): 340–47. https://doi.org/10.1080/24692921.2019.1669863.

Gotell, Lise. 2010. "Canadian Sexual Assault Law: Neoliberalism and the Erosion of Feminist Inspired Law Reform." In *Rethinking Rape Law: International and Comparative Perspectives*, edited by Clare McGlynn and Vanessa E. Munro, 209–23. London: Routledge.

Guntarik, Olivia. 2009. "Resistance Narratives: A Comparative Account of Indigenous Sites of Dissent." *Narrative Inquiry* 19 (2): 306–27. http://dx.doi.org/10.1075/ni.19.2.06gun.

Haga, Kazu. 2020. *Healing Resistance: A Radically Different Response to Harm*. Berkeley: Parallax Press.

Harris, Jessica C., and Chris Linder, eds. 2017. *Intersections of Identity and Sexual Violence on Campus: Centering Minoritized Students' Experiences*. Sterling, VA: Stylus Publishing.

Henry, Frances, and Carol Tator, eds. 2009. *Racism in the Canadian University: Demanding Social Justice, Inclusion, and Equity*. Toronto: University of Toronto Press.

Hodgetts, Lisa, Kisha Supernant, Natasha Lyons, and John R. Welch. 2020. "Broadening #MeToo: Tracking Dynamics in Canadian Archaeology Through a Survey on Experiences Within the Discipline." *Canadian Journal of Archaeology / Journal Canadien d'Archéologie* 44 (1): 20–47. https://canadianarchaeology.com/caa/file/7056/download?token=grCJ7He4.

Lazar, Michelle M. 2007. "Feminist Critical Discourse Analysis: Articulating a Feminist Discourse Praxis." *Critical Discourse Studies* 4 (2): 141–64. https://doi.org/10.1080/17405900701464816.

Page, Tiffany, Anna Bull, and Emma Chapman. 2019. "Making Power Visible: 'Slow Activism' to Address Staff Sexual Misconduct in Higher Education." *Violence Against Women* 25, no. 11 (September): 1309–30. http://dx.doi.org/10.1177/1077801219844606.

Piepzna-Samarasinha, Leah Lakshmi. 2018. *Care Work: Dreaming Disability Justice*. Vancouver: Arsenal Pulp Press.

Pyke, Sandra W. 1996. "Sexual Harassment and Sexual Intimacy in Learning Environments." *Canadian Psychology* 37 (1): 13–22. https://doi.org/10.1037/0708-5591.37.1.13.

Smith, Carly Parnitzke, and Jennifer J. Freyd. 2013. "Dangerous Safe Havens: Institutional Betrayal Exacerbates Sexual Trauma." *Journal of Traumatic Stress* 26, no. 1 (February): 119–24: 123. https://doi.org/10.1002/jts.21778.

Salvino, Caitlin, Kelsey Gilcrhsit, and Jade Cooligan-Pang. 2017. *OurTurn: A National Action Plan to End Campus Sexual Violence*. Montreal: Student's Society of McGill University.

Spade, Dean. 2020. "Solidarity, Not Charity: Mutual Aid for Mobilization and Survival." *Social Text* 38, no. 1: 131–51. https://doi.org/10.1215/01642472-7971139.

Steiner, Linda. 2019. "Addressing Sexual Harassment in Journalism Education." *Journalism* 20 (1): 118–21. https://doi.org/10.1177%2F1464884918809272.

Students for Consent Culture Canada. 2021. *Open Secrets, Power, and Professors: A Study on Rape Culture and Accountability at Canadian Post-Secondary Institutions; Preliminary Summary and Recommendations*. https://www.sfcccanada.org/open-secrets-report.

Part III

Belonging

12

The Story of Ping

Wang Ping

For my mother and all the teachers

The river foams like mad from last night's storm.*

I scull along the sandstone cliffs, the only gorge for the entire Mississippi.

Every dawn, I row ten thousand meters through the Twin Cities, my daily meditation with eagles, turtles, foxes, sky and water, along the national park.

The river runs fast. Driftwood floats by, bottles, cans, plastic bags, cushions . . .

My blade hits something. The handle jumps out of my hand. My boat tips to the right, and suddenly I'm in the river.

The current is fast, rushing toward the Ford Dam. I have three minutes to flip the boat over, get my ass back on, and row away from the falloff, all the while treading the river.

No one is around. It's almost impossible to get back to a single scull, alone.

My other option is to swim and push the boat to the shore.

I hang on to the bow. "Never ever let go your boat. It's your lifeline!" is the first thing my coach barked at me. Rowers can't row wearing life

---

* This poem was originally published in the Michigan Quarterly Review (https://sites.lsa.umich.edu/mqr/2021/02/the-story-of-ping-living-through-mao-trump/). It is reprinted with the permission of the author.

jackets. When they flip, they're on their own saving themselves, unless there's a coach boat nearby.

My boat spins. Something hits the stern, big and weighty, then hits my temple, sharp. I turn. A giant carp, belly up, fins stretching like paddles, its stench choking my breath . . . I almost lose my grip on the boat. In its open jaw, a hook deep in its throat, fish line entangled around its teeth, its body tattered like a battle flag, its white eyes staring at me.

I try to get away from the death stare and stink. But the fish is lodged between my boat and oar. We're locked together, spinning in the whirlpool of the Mississippi.

I have only three minutes to swim and push the boat to the shore. But I'm frozen.

The stench flashfloods my memory of the Cultural Revolution.

A rotting fish hung around my mother's neck and mine.

We were on a truck, being paraded through the cobblestone streets on the island of East China Sea. Our hair was freshly cut in yin-yang style 阴阳头, half-white from a clean shave, half-black with hair. This public shaming was the most "severe disciplinary action" for those who refused to obey the order from the Red Guards, those who read "poison weeds"—books other than Mao's Little Red Book.

The fish banged on the cardboards around our necks: Big Beauty Snake (my mother was the island's beauty queen), Little Poison Weed (eight-year-old ugly me). Our hair and clothes were covered with spit, our faces bruised by rocks from the crowd.

My mother looked more dead than the fish around her neck. Her eyes closed shut, her ashen face blackened with ink. The girl Red Guards had written slogans on her cheeks with brushes, but sweat and tears had washed away the ugly words. Her knees bent. She would have collapsed on the truck bed if not for the two girls popping her up.

As a pianist, singer, dancer, and music teacher, my mother took great pride in her image, especially in public. Now shame and death were carved on her face.

I was too shocked to cry, too guilty to look at my mother. This was all my fault.

Sixteen months ago, I unearthed a box of banned books Mother had buried under the chicken coop. I formed an underground book club with the treasure, secretly exchanging books with members. Mother caught me and burned them, but I still had a few books hidden away. Finally I got caught while reading *Dead Souls* in the woods. It led them to my other books: *Romeo and Juliet*, *The Call of the Wild*, *Dream of the Red Chamber* . . . all of them had Mother's signature. The Red Guards arrested us.

Everything had been a blur after that. I remember the sleepless night on the concrete floor of the school where Mother taught music and dance, listening to her weeping over mosquito buzzing in the corner. I remember the dawn breaking into the barbed window, then the Red Guards dragging us onto the truck, the midsummer sun scorching my half-shaven scalp, setting my brain on fire. I remember the noises—jeering laughing shouting drumming exploding . . . A girl lit a red string of firecrackers and threw it at me. I dodged. It exploded at my ear. Suddenly everything became mute, and my hearing and sense of direction were no longer the same.

The two girls were kicking my mother to make her stand taller. I grabbed them to make them stop. They looked up and my mouth dropped. They were Mother's adoring students, had come to our house once a week to study accordion and piano with her. I remember being jealous, because I had been longing to learn those instruments, any instrument, to make beautiful sounds . . . Mother was so pleased with their progress, told me to make dinner for them every time they came: yellow croaker soup with pickles, dumplings, eggs, all the precious, rationed food that took me hours standing in line to purchase on the market. I remember how they enjoyed every morsel, and how pretty and grateful they looked as they sang while Mother played accordion, or vice versa. Now their eyes gleamed with a vicious light as they grabbed Mother's hair and lifted her face to show the cheering crowd . . .

I remember asking why this was happening, why the girls beat her up like this, when we were back to the school prison. Have they forgotten the Chinese saying? Once a teacher, forever your parent. How are they going to face Mother again, ever?

I remember silence. Mother's face turned to the wall as she lay on the concrete, death written all over her back.

I remember the terror of losing her forever. So many teachers, scholars, poets and artists hung themselves, jumped off buildings or drowned in the sea, since the madness began. I remember searching every corner of the room, making sure there was no rope, no sharp object . . . I remember keeping myself awake to watch her through the long nights . . .

No, I don't remember. I have buried them, all these years, except for my heart, beating like crazy every time I hear a firecracker, my breathing ceased from the inaudible shouting and scolding every time I see a crowd, every time I attend the all-faculty meetings at noon on Tuesday. I hate meetings. I hate crowds. But I couldn't tell the provost why. I have no words to explain myself.

"You want a promotion, show up at the damn meetings," she said.

"Why are you here?" I ask the carp.

The fish looks me in the eyes, its mouth wide open as if laughing, the hook so deep in the throat it's impossible to untangle.

Despite its tattered body, I recognize her: 草鱼. Grass carp, the most treasured symbol in China for five thousand years, as good luck, perseverance, beauty, bravery, power, persistence. It offers its body as the abundance and delicacy. It offers its beauty as koi, a golden fish. It offers its dragon spirit by jumping over the impossible cliffs, waterfalls. Yet, in America, she's vilified in every possible way. The only words for her are *invasion*, *problem*, *take-over*, *undesirable*, *inedible*, *ugly* . . . The government spends billions of dollars to eradicate her, kill her, electrify her, hunt her, trap her, mass murder her, feed her to dogs and cats . . .

Since January 2019, I've been this fish, trapped, lured, hunted down . . . lead hooks deep in my mouth, lungs, heart, liver, hands squeezing around my throat as knife cuts along the spine, flaying the meat, smiling blue eyes watch me drown, dry drowning, my lungs gasping for oxygen, but only rumor, poison, lies and false allegations pouring in, as alveoli collapse sac by sac, as my body thrashes in agony . . . in the lily hand that writes dozens of "thank you for saving my life for making me a good poet a good writer" notes, and the bloody hand that records how much time I spend workshopping each student's poem as evidence how I play favoritism how I manipulate their emotion with poetry to feed the Machine that just wants to crush, eradicate, kill at any cost . . .

My friends ask: "Why can't you at least pretend being quiet, obedient, beautiful, like a koi? Why can't you say, 'I'll do whatever you want' to your colleagues and admins, even if you don't mean it?"

But I can't be a koi or a golden fish. I can't be a pet fish, kept in a tank or pond. It's a death sentence.

My son came home with fires in his eyes. "How could they smear you like this, after you fed them, taught them, cared for them since I was born? I was jealous that you gave them more time than me . . . how dare they do this?"

I heard my own voice asking my mother the same questions. I heard myself telling my son, "Would it make you feel better if I tell you that none of them actually took my class?"

A student called me on my birthday, wailing: "You're going to die, Ping, and it's not fair you give us your flesh and blood, and we were escorted to tell lies to kill you. Not fair you have to be removed because you can't be controlled. You're the only woman of color teaching poetry at your rank in the nation. You're the only one who makes people like us feel welcome. Not fair they treat you like a criminal, an animal . . . this is worse than the Cultural Revolution . . ."

I had to hang up, gently. I had no words to appease him. I wanted to laugh, but didn't know how. I'm proud of being called "animal," because that is who I am, a stubborn, untamable carp, a duck that forgets to come home from exploration and gets a whack in the butt. But why does my heart race like mad when an email arrives from the admins?

Until now, face-to-face with this carp, hook in its mouth, horror from the interior.

I asked Mother the same question: "How could they shame you like this, after you gave them everything you had? What am I going to do if you die?" I wanted to tell her about my jealousy, about my wish to learn the things she had taught those students who were beating spitting stomping on her . . .

After a long silence, Mother said, "I would have done the same again, if I had a choice. No, I don't have a choice. Teaching is a calling. You go in and give your whole being, no matter what. If you can't, then you do something else."

She looked at me with her bleeding eyes. "You'll do the same thing, child. You'll bring out light from people. You'll be whacked and knocked down, but you'll stand up and do it all over again. You're Ping. This is your story, the story of Ping."

So Mother knows. So Heart knows. So Body knows, even though Mind is confused about the wild heartbeat, this sudden weak knee, this sinking stomach . . .

I'm so close to the dam. Another minute, it'll be all over, this dry drowning, this agony, this smearing campaign. Sinking is easy. Let go. Just let go. It'll be over in one minute, but my hands grip.

A giant piece of deadwood rams into the boat, knocking the bow out of my fingers. I sink. My feet touch something sharp. Pain shoots through the soles to the apex of my head. I jolt, leap, swim. My head knocks into the boat. The boat rocks the oar. The oar hits the fish. The fish jumps as if coming alive, spitting out the hook, the pus, the worms from inside. It untangles itself out of the snare and flows toward the dam, its white eyes saying good-bye and thank you, its mouth laughing.

Suddenly I'm free from the spinning eddy.

I grab my boat, climb onto it, and paddle with my arms and legs like mad, upriver.

"Never swim with the current, but against it, the only way to reach the shore," said the coach.

I reach the bank just in time and flip the boat over. The dam is a hundred feet away. I hear its roar as it drops off laughing like a wild animal.

The carp is gone. Did it swim across the oceans, jump through dams and cliffs . . .

Just to live?

I left China thirty-three years ago, to answer the yearning for freedom. I knew I'd not survive dictatorship with my love for thinking and speaking truth. I found freedom in America, in academia, I thought . . .

But this is what I learned: all crows are black; all hooks catch lies and truths.

The carp showed up to teach me life through death. The deadwood showed up to teach me how to let go. Only by sinking to the bottom could I untangle from the snare and leap into the light.

I don't have a choice. I do have a choice, as a living witness of Mao and Trump eras, to tell the truth. Truth is the hook in my mouth, the knife that flays my flesh that also flays the tormentors' souls. Truth reveals the rotting interior, before beauty is born.

The sun comes up, shining into my eyes. I start laughing. Minnehaha. Laughing river.

An eagle flies over my head, dropping its tail feather in my boat.

The wind blows, pushing me upstream.

A carp leaps out of the water, its tail splashing the Mississippi, water splashing the sky, making a rainbow over the dam that turns the silver carp into a golden dragon.

So this is the legend of 鲤鱼跳龙门: carp jumping over the dragon gate.

So there is life after the dam.

"There's life outside academia, Ping, and it's just as beautiful and exciting, if not more," a friend told me during the Moth performance, on the stage of Lincoln Center.

Keep going, Ping. There's a purpose for all the sufferings. Pain is a boat that carries you to the shore, against the current, across the chasm. You chose to live on the edge of running water, to be a poet. So live like one.

I pick up my oar handles, slide, blades running parallel with the current, three inches above, wings in the sky, drop blades in, catch the river, drive, and the entire Mississippi runs with me, smooth like a carp, fierce like a carp, fast and powerful like a carp.

This is my life: live through Mao's Cultural Revolution, live through Trump's academia, as a witness, as a storyteller, as a poet, as a carp, as a duck, so the memory lives on, so we don't forget, so we may get off from the wheel of karma, avoid flipping the same boat in the same river, over and over.

This is the story of a grass carp, no, the story of Ping, a wild duck from the Yangtze, no longer afraid to be whacked on the butt or head, to bring peace and love to the Mississippi, to all the rivers and mountains on earth.

13

Tracking the Academy

Experiencing My Projects of Belonging

Aparajita De

As I reflect on the trajectory of my academic life in the United States, I fall back on some incidents that have stayed with me. Nearly twenty years ago, I just knew that what was happening was not right and later learned to work through it. It was the time when the foundational concepts we use now to discuss hostile work environments and the tools that help categorize experiences of BIPOC were not as mainstream, and were therefore deemed inscrutable. Nonetheless, they are intense sites to revisit emotionally; however, intellectually, they keep me engaged when I realize how much still needs to get done, not by BIPOC, but this time around by our well-meaning allies. Before I discuss allyship, my experiences of bullying and academic hostilities spring to mind, not only because they are painful but also because we can grow only from memory. Revisiting them enabled me to recognize and condition my mind to register the complicities and the silences of "allies," to eventually identify the murky spaces of personal and professional intent and its intersections (or otherwise) with institutional intentionality.

I know that my experiences as a South Asian woman are not unique, but they were unfamiliar at the time they occurred, and parts of my mind have not healed. Over time, my education and visibility as a postcolonialist cultural studies faculty member in majority-serving institutional spaces created a frustrating existence for me and those who perceived me differently. My difference outed me as an exclusive Cultural Other. It helped reinforce that I will remain a perennial academic pariah in the closely guarded, normatively coded spaces. The spaces remain exclusively heteropatriarchal and Eurocentric, without inclusive conversation.

When I started as an international teaching assistant, undergraduate student evaluations often called me out as the *nonnative* English speaker instead of the English speaker *who knew what she was doing*. Students claimed they could not learn anything from a teacher who they felt had zero credibility. Despite a graduate degree and skills within my subject matter, I was not deserving of any individual attention (or respect); students felt that they could, somehow, convincingly argue that I was not enough. I wasn't who they wanted in their classroom. These assessors, evaluators, and key opinion makers were undergraduate students who did not have any accountability to anyone, let alone have a college degree. Notwithstanding, they felt I needed an evaluation whose parameters they'd decide. And that somehow those parameters were correct and credible. When annual evaluation reports were shared with my advisers and coordinators (all white folx), the resulting silences indicated there would be no gestures of talking to me or of hearing me. I was told that expecting any conversation was unreal and that this was not how things were done here. So, anger, humiliation, and a passive (and active) acceptance of apathy got internalized. It has stayed there. This feeling of never being enough or the consequent anxious energy of overworking and overpreparing has helped me in my academic journey, but it has come at the cost of low self-esteem and self-confidence.

Institutional accountability, I was soon to realize, intertwined with institutional courage, which I could not expect as an international graduate teaching assistant, and eventually, not from anyone who took me to be an outsider to the academy. None in my department at the time felt anything amiss in those smug and racist evaluations. I was told that my international student status made me vulnerable and that these things were a small price to pay in exchange for the "American dream"—I was promised delivery afterward! By implication, my on-campus "advocates" were telling me that international students were dispensable entities, and their right to complain or resist, or expect any conversation, were factors that would eventually impact their "promised" entry into the American Dream space! My cross-cultural presence and experience across continents were not of enough value to demand accountability against prejudice. During those years, my younger self pondered whether or not I was knowledgeable *enough*. I became doubtful of my intellectual abilities and lost some of my faith in academic rigor, not absorbing the normality of structural racism.

Did a faculty status make it any better? It seemed that being reasonably intelligent wasn't enough and that academic credibility was *relevantly connected* to the color of my skin and my biological gender. All of this was, of course, optics and sonics dependent; the extent of melanin and the speech accent made it plausible for people to *know* that I wasn't good enough, and others stood by them and legitimized them. And, no, these were not bystanders, as they later became my peers and colleagues. Even if I were to remain a cultural outsider, I wondered if I was going to *forever* remain outside of the classroom. Would a faculty role help me become academically credible? Would the label of "in American higher ed" help? Maybe one needed an exceptional affiliation to a network to claim space as an educator, despite academic integrity and skillset?

Well.

When I entered the adjunct tier after graduate school, my professional integrity and credibility were challenged by a white male staff member. This person thought he needed to get me disciplined for something unremarkable! In this instance, and on the rare occasion of having left my photocopies for class at his desk, I had told him that I would pick up the copies after my class (on the other end of campus).

Mindful of my class time, I had avoided placing the photocopies on my shared desk on another floor. The staff member heard me and then reported me to the chair of the department, alleging that I had "irresponsibly" left my class copies at his desk and that he did not know what to do with them (how very self-righteous, you'd say, right?). So I was given a dressing down by the department chair, a white woman. Denied the opportunity to explain what was going on, I was told that I was "confusing" and that people did not know what I was doing! I figured out that this time, my students were NOT those people. One white man's testimony of me being confusing made all the difference to another white person. Without weighing in on my explanation, armed with the presumably honorable testimony of a person not directly (or indirectly) benefiting from my duties as a teacher, the chair took my classes away. I was moved to a satellite campus and allowed an hour to commute between the flagship and the satellite. In other words, I was made dispensable, since a white man was more credible than a woman faculty of color. I was simply *more* punishable and needed to be disciplined before being purged from the system. My vulnerability and lack of being considered a colleague in the workplace I held sacred scarred me and helped me realize that this would be an unequal place at the least and a hostile one at best.

This college campus had other singular-minded office staff as well. Another staff member discouraged me from filing a complaint against a student who had openly uttered profanities against me and shown his "rightful" anger for a grade in front of the class. When I complained, the department's secretary, a woman of color, called me on my cell phone asking me to drop the complaint and stop "overreacting." I was not surprised, but I felt that I had erred on the side of assuming that because she was a woman of color, she might be an ally. In my case, the institutional establishment was greater than any imaginary alliance I sought. It was the same department with the same set of people who refrained from making any performative gestures when I experienced a miscarriage during a later semester. Despite knowing my condition (it happened on campus), I never received *one* supportive phone call. As a person who was labeled expendable by the system and who, as an adjunct lecturer, was also the most vulnerable member of the faculty body, I was denied a gesture of common humanity. In the life of the institution, our emotional health and well-being did not matter. What mattered were our labor and subservience. What mattered the most were the institution's values and how they intersected with those of its gatekeepers and maintained the status quo. Unsurprisingly, when this institution started lowering its employee salaries, somehow adjuncts and lecturers also became subject to pay cuts. Even if our emotional well-being did not matter, the institution felt that our financial sacrifices mattered for its well-being.

Soon after I resigned and sifted through the local higher education job landscape, I got hired in a nontenured visiting position. The well-meaning white men (and a few white women) at the table confirmed my hiring decision a day later. It all happened so fast, but I was also sixty miles away. Because of the distance, I asked if I might be accommodated with a later-in-the-day class. I was not. Despite voicing the inconveniences, I was given an 8 a.m. class, sixty miles away. No, I should never complain, my colleagues told me, after all, I was "given" the job! The other candidates who got hired at the same time as me in tenure-track positions relocated locally and did not know that I had requested a late-morning/afternoon class. A semester later, weighing ten pounds less, I had my first book publication out. At the same time, my tenure-track white woman colleague created the department's social media page on Facebook. While my published work remained "unmentionable" in the department's newsletter, her social media *innovation* received wide approbation and visibility across campus. Indeed, spaces of conversation and interaction meant that I was to serve while remaining invisible. I was given courses that I redesigned, incorporating issues of the intersectional ties among race, class, gender, sexuality, and colonialism. Ironically, these topics remained largely out of the active conversation in the spaces around me in my institution. Or perhaps I was being too critical and needed to learn that "these" things needed to be conveniently glossed over in practice while being widely publicized for purposes of tenure and related publications? The shallowness of institutional intentionality to incorporate conversation, practice, and policies of inclusive spaces has often been debated (if at all actively acknowledged) but never steered by the people who could identify with these experiences. The presence of Black, Brown, Queer, and Indigenous people in academia hinges on our identification as token womyn (see Rich 1986), and our concerns about issues of representation remain unaddressed and largely dissonant in intersecting with institutional structure and practice.

Nonetheless, after that year, I moved into my tenure-track position. At this campus, students did not know that a woman of color could be a source of comfort, credibility, and control. They liked me. Some even came out of class or from a regular office meeting teary eyed, eventually telling me that my presence in the classroom was inspiring. That my being there mattered for them. I felt that my being there could be a powerfully charged moment for undergraduate students of color. People looking for a place under the sun had found me, among others, who could positively influence them. If I was still looking for validation, it came from my students. It felt tremendously satisfying and rejuvenating for me. My colleagues, however, remained interested in other aspects of my identity: how did *I* speak the language *so well*, or, what were the pathways that brought me to the humanities instead of the sciences? I was exhausted trying to define and, to some extent, justify my presence by discounting the easy stereotype based on my ethnic origin. I was a sore thumb, so to say, a misfit in the campus space where faculty sometimes noted that by my build and gait, I was somehow *more* acceptable as a student but not quite as faculty. Not yet!

While at the same institution, another colleague singled me out and said that in her part of the world, English was done differently (paraphrased). The exclusivity in that statement was the code for "outsider," immediately dismissing me from the imaginary fold that I was still trying to belong to. Eventually, I moved forward with a report to the school's chief diversity officer, pointing out that such incidents were damaging enough for me, a faculty member of color, and that this attitude, in general, could be hostile for students of color on campus. The chief diversity officer eventually mentioned how this faculty member already had several incidents registered and that my complaint won't be enough for any administrative reprimands. Soon afterward, I was discouraged from pursuing the matter, the diversity office posted a vacancy, and the campus was left without an officer for a while. Litigation over a hostile work environment and the gamut of actions that I *should* have taken seemed expensive and time consuming, going far beyond the demands of the tenure clock. In other words, the tediousness of the process ensured that repeat offenders were protected. My publications were coming out, which was good for my career, but they demanded more time from me. According to the mid-tenure review, I was way ahead, but this process also signaled, in its aggressive competitiveness, that I couldn't afford to slow down. And I did not.

In the meantime, my students knew that I was on their side. Conversations during scheduled office appointments often transpired into moments when students needed more than course curriculum help. Some teared up and shared stories of abuse; some talked about how they had been suddenly compelled into responsibilities that were hindering their academic endeavors; someone else thought I would be able to get them through school. I had unknowingly created a space where students felt safe, confident, and supported. My emotional labor and acceptance by minority students steered me through some of the most difficult periods as I struggled to gain acceptance into the institution by my peers and colleagues. My faculty colleagues often thought I would not know any better after they had already reduced me to a category of their creation. In this category, I was powerless, unimpressive, and there did not seem to be any relative value to the work I was doing. My work in mentoring, supporting, and listening to vulnerable students, my advocacy for them in maintaining enrollment, in building communities of empathy, remained invisible in my service record. My cultural taxation (Padilla 1994) as a minority professor supporting enrollment and academic continuity of minority students on campus did not seem worthy of a mention in faculty meetings, evaluations, and assessment conversations. I resigned without tenure to take full-time care of my family in another state.

When I moved back to my home state, I joined a minority-serving institution. I felt I could be me here, outside of the majority-serving institutions I had worked in. But, really, no such place *already* exists for minority women of color unless we actively *work* on these spaces. My new colleagues wondered if I went to the same church, asking if I had the right religion, and if it was not Christianity, did I fast? Someone commented on my petite appearance, wondering aloud where I kept my brains, and others wanted to know why I did not have children. Then there is the ongoing chorus of surprise that I am still at this minority-serving institution when I could easily find a position at a bigger university elsewhere. I have no answers. But the questions never cease, sometimes reducing me to a "colored woman," to an unpronounceable name, sometimes to a speaker with an accent, and at other times, as a misfit. My intelligence, body of work, integrity, and academic record fall short of answering these questions.

The conversation becomes more complicated when we think about the shifting parameters of tenure and promotion. Whereas some faculty colleagues have been tenured with nothing commendable in their portfolios or continue with consistent ratings of distinction, I was told by the administration of my new school that I needed nine (you read that right) publications before filing for tenure. At the time, I had eight that were peer reviewed. When I asked for criteria under tenure guidelines of the college, or if this went beyond Research 1 institutional tenure guidelines (I wasn't working in an R1), the mid-level white male administrator remained silent and maintained the department's stance. The paths of tenure, I soon read in Patricia Matthew, were capricious, and for people of color, based on a standard of opaque judgment that routinely masqueraded as "objective evaluations" (Matthew 2016a, xiv). More scrutiny and less support from the institution were the gold standard and had little to nothing in connection with minority-serving or majority-serving institutions. Unsurprisingly, the administrative rungs in this minority-serving institution were homogeneously populated by a segment that shifted standards or adhered to an unwritten code that would always keep people of color out of positions of power and responsibility (Matthew 2016b, 3). Eventually, I got tenure with a portfolio whose standards went over the ones mentioned in the college guidelines. As a woman of color, evaluated by faculty administrators who were mostly cisgender white males in a minority institution, it remained a matter of anticipation that my work and entry into the institutional domain of knowledge hierarchy through tenure would be doubly scrutinized and interrogated in the high standards of "objectivity" that tenure approval committees supposedly uphold.

In the ongoing battle to recognize that academic cronyism and structural racism exist, there is a gap in diversity practices that actively and overtly work to exclude us. I believe that regardless of our intentional and intellectual labors of questioning the establishment for inclusion, parity, and fairness, the establishment will keep reinventing itself to keep us out. Interrogating and resisting, writing and noticing, standing up instead of sitting down, and organizing instead of fighting it alone seem to be the best strategies for bringing these gatekeepers of supremacist behaviors to answer. It has been a long process since I started seeking validation from the institution to realize much later that I can be me despite *the system*. As for fairness and parity, that system needs to be recalibrated and made more inclusive by allowing more evaluators who have been on a similar receiving end like mine. In navigating the murky networks of academic and institutional structures that are designed to keep us out, those of us on the margins can help redefine institutional intent by holding stakeholders accountable. By making these gatekeepers of the system also understand that for a diverse workplace, practices of embracing diversity and equity matter. Sara Ahmed had long written about "bodies [that] stick out when they are out of place" (2012, 42), and, in reflecting on my experiences of being cast in out-of-placeness within academia, my choosing to stand up and stick out has made me precarious and more vulnerable.

My robust advocacy for change has helped me create a pathway that embodies my space and creates more spaces for others like me. As a midcareer faculty member in higher education, my experiences have taught me that we must continually renew these spaces. Hiring practices can be less hostile; our allies need to be identified and reeducated to advocate for a less hostile space. Perhaps equity adviser positions could be created in departments and programs so that there is a midlevel check that prevents the perpetuation of these hostile environments. International faculty can serve as mentors for international graduate students and help support these vulnerable populations; faculty bodies can create local solidarity networks within their programs and departments that help them identify these inhospitable environments. Then academe can become the space for collaborative innovation that it ideally is supposed to be, where I can grow along with the rest, without having to combat and feel bristly about sticking out or becoming invisible to fit in.

Works Cited

Ahmed, Sara. 2012. *On Being Included: Racism and Diversity in Institutional Life*. Durham, NC: Duke University Press.

Matthew, Patricia A., ed. 2016. *Written/Unwritten: Diversity and the Hidden Truths of Tenure*. Chapel Hill: University of North Carolina Press.

Matthew, Patricia A., ed. 2016b. "Preface." *Written/Unwritten: Diversity and the Hidden Truths of Tenure*, xi–xvii. Chapel Hill: University of North Carolina Press.

Matthew, Patricia A., ed. 2016b. "Introduction: Written/Unwritten; The Gap Between Theory and Practice." *Written/Unwritten: Diversity and the Hidden Truths of Tenure*, 1–25. Chapel Hill: University of North Carolina Press.

Padilla, Amado M. 1994. "Ethnic Minority Scholars, Research, and Mentoring: Current and Future Issues." *Educational Researcher* 23, no. 4 (May): 24–27. https://doi.org/10.2307/1176259.

Rich, Adrienne. 1986. "What Does a Woman Need to Know?" *Blood, Bread, and Poetry: Selected Prose 1979–1985*. New York: W. W. Norton.

14

Xenophobia in the Academy

Who Gets a Seat at the Campus Roundtable?

Rashna Batliwala Singh

Academic institutions are envisioned as spaces where free speech flows easily, discourse is unrestricted, and all perspectives and points of view are welcome if they do not impinge on the freedom of others or amount to hate speech. Yet, as we have become increasingly aware in recent years, such freedoms can be curbed in less apparent ways, for example through monitoring by various watchdog sites. Many academics who introduce issues of race, class, and gender into their curricula and/or classrooms are deemed radical and may find themselves on one or another media watch list. However, when foreign-born faculty speak on political issues in the United States, they are often silenced by xenophobic and/or nativist attacks from within the institution by U.S.-born colleagues, even those of a liberal bent, and including, at times, those of color.

In her book *On Being Included: Racism and Diversity in Institutional Life*, Sara Ahmed asks "how some and not others become strangers; how emotions of fear and hatred stick to certain bodies; how some bodies become understood as the rightful occupants of certain spaces" (2012, 2). In this essay, I examine how "the stranger" inhabits space in the academy and how "the stranger" is perceived. From my subjective experiences, and from the experiences of colleagues, I look at how xenophobia in the academy is so often a matter of space and place, a matter of who belongs or is permitted to belong within that space and place.

Steven Salaita says at the outset of his book *Uncivil Rites*, "This book is partly about me, but only as I have been actualized by various communities" (2015, ix). Even though Salaita is American born, he was seen as speaking far too forthrightly about the oppression of Palestinians by Israel, and that made him seem threatening, even to many on the left. Speaking out about the plight of Palestinians is especially problematic and risky, and this was the original context of Edward Said's phrase "permission to narrate" (1984, 27). Salaita's perceived "foreignness" did not afford him the permission to narrate. How are foreign faculty actualized by the academic communities in which they teach? That they are often actualized, whether openly articulated as such or not, as interlopers, even intruders, is precisely because of their foreignness.

The fate of Professor Steven Salaita is well known in U.S. academic circles. Salaita had been a professor of English at Virginia Tech and was offered a tenured faculty appointment at the University of Illinois Urbana-Champaign in the American Indian Studies program. However, a series of tweets about Israel's war of aggression on the Palestinian people in 2014 resulted in major backlash, and the chancellor made the decision not to forward Salaita's appointment to the board of trustees. Salaita was left without income and insurance. He subsequently accepted a position at the American University of Beirut, from which he was later ousted, allegedly due to pressure from U.S. senators and university donors. He now drives a school bus. His recently published book, *An Honest Living: A Memoir of Peculiar Itineraries* (2024), relates these experiences.

•

Since October 2023, speaking out about the plight of Palestinians and the actions of Israel in Gaza has become a form of academic suicide for many professors, even American Jewish professors. Professor Maura Finkelstein, for instance, has been placed on administrative leave at Muhlenberg College (where she is an associate professor of anthropology) for calling Israel's actions genocide and condemning them in no uncertain terms. Similarly, Professor Raz Segal of Stockton University, who is a scholar of the Holocaust and both Israeli and Jewish, saw his job offer to lead the University of Minnesota's Center for Holocaust and Genocide Studies rescinded over his comments characterizing the Israeli assault on Gaza as "a textbook case of genocide." These are only two instances of a slew of disciplinary actions leading to suspension and even job loss, at times in contravention of due process, as in the case of Professor Jairo I. Fúnez-Flores, an assistant professor of curriculum studies and teacher education at Texas Tech University. Punitive actions have been taken not only for views expressed in publications or public talks but also in extramural spaces such as social media. Often these administrative actions are the result of pressure from boards of trustees, who are responding to the demands of big donors.

Said's phrase "permission to narrate" refers to who can speak, when, and how. Only too often, this permission is denied to perceived outsiders in the academy: foreign faculty of Asian, Middle Eastern, or African origin, and sometimes, though less frequently, those of European origin. Race, ethnicity, nationality, and gender remain operative in who can speak and, perhaps more importantly, who is heard. Xenophobia, like racism, involves a form of "othering," but there are differences, the main one being that of belonging. Foreign-born faculty are often seen as people who are on the borders of belonging, metaphorically speaking, or beyond the borders and thus pushed to the periphery of campus conversations about racism. Foreign policy is seen through the prism of party politics rather than as a transnational matter of interest and importance to all, a matter of human rights. As a result, many self-censor, or they are effectively censored by the extreme reactions they elicit when they do speak.

When foreign faculty keep their heads down and stay silent, there is less resistance to their "foreignness." It is, after all, that foreignness itself that is threatening. The melting pot was not only about cultural and social norms but also about conformative and normalized patterns and pathways of thinking. Louis Yako, who obtained his PhD in cultural anthropology from Duke University and is originally from Iraq, shared the following with me in an email: "From my experience, the imperial university embraces and totally supports foreign faculty (and other professionals) whose work contributes to vilifying the very places from which they come. In other words, ironically, the only way for our viewpoints to be palatable is to affirm our interlocutors' gaze when it is directed at you and the place from which you come." Ahmed says something similar when she discusses the functioning of the multicultural nation and how it is a hospitable and even loving space only conditionally: would-be citizens are expected to return this hospitality by integrating or identifying with the nation (2012, 43).

The subject of xenophobia and nativism, however, remains neglected in campus discussions or roundtables. While a recent Netflix series called *The Chair* has sparked many op-eds and conversations on social media about the racial and gender issues in academia that the series excavates, Professor Ji-Yoon Kim's perceived "foreignness" remains something of a subtext. Even though she is Korean American, Asian Americans have long had to battle the "forever foreigner" or "perpetual foreigner" stereotype. It was a good touch to have Kim teach Emily Dickinson, rather than pigeonhole her in Asian American literature, but the latent xenophobia in her colleagues' treatment of her is not really allowed to surface. In fact, the show's producers play it safe by having Professor Kim be of South Korean descent rather than, say, Iranian descent, since the United States has friendly relations with South Korea. It also keeps it safe by having the students protest something crude and clearly inappropriate: a professor who allegedly performed a Sieg heil! salute in class while discussing Nazism, rather than something more akin to Salaita's critical commentary.

Discussions of racial disparities and of physical and epistemic violence against communities of color within the United States seem to generate less resistance among faculty of all races than discussions of U.S. imperialism, even though U.S. imperialism can be seen as the larger, more global manifestation of domestic white supremacy. At the very least, white supremacy and imperialism participate in an interlocking relationship expressed in the rhetoric of exceptionalism. Quasi-military police forces become domestic enforcers, while the U.S. armed services are the enforcers of U.S. might abroad. Police violence and military violence are closely linked: The military is, in a sense, the international arm of the police, and the police the domestic arm of the military, even to the point of receiving some of their older equipment. Police brutality at home manifests the same forces that operate overseas. Many veterans participate in right-wing militias, which recruit heavily from their ranks. And many random mass shootings have been committed by veterans who served in Iraq and Afghanistan and suffer from severe PTSD.

These well-documented connections seldom enter campus discussions of police brutality and racism. Discussions of transnational issues, such as imperial wars of aggression and regime change, are often pushed to the side or met with resistance, sometimes even hostility, when they are brought up in campus conversations about domestic racism. The intersectionality of racial violence against people of color in the "homeland" and imperialist violence against people of color beyond these borders are the dots that many fail (or refuse) to connect. Xenophobia kicks in most noticeably at times of national tensions, such as 9/11 and the critical 2016 election. Just as President Obama had to establish his legitimacy by producing a birth certificate, foreign-born faculty must metaphorically produce their citizenship papers to establish their right to participate in conversations about U.S. hegemony and domination. Natural-born citizenship then becomes its own form of privilege and works to confer legitimacy in conversations that concern the United States. And even natural-born citizens are often seen as outsiders if they are first generation and bear "foreign"-sounding names. The algebra of citizenship and legitimized belonging is complicated and contingent.

People feel more empowered to fight racial discrimination and oppression at home and see the ballot box as one way in which they can make their voices heard. They feel more powerless when it comes to "foreign policy"; the very term sanitizes and even softens the brutal bombings and occupations the United States carries out in the name of spreading democracy. Creating a binary between domestic and foreign policy is another way in which the latter is elided, allowing for the erasure of the constitutive relations between the two. It is no coincidence that Derek Chauvin, the police officer most directly responsible for the death of George Floyd, began his career as a military police officer at Fort Benning. The base is home to the notorious School of the Americas, now called the Western Hemisphere Institute for Security Cooperation, where the U.S. Army has trained people who have gone on to become cruel dictators and has fostered death squads, assassins, and torturers.

Xenophobia and nativism can be exhibited by people of all racial and ethnic groups in the United States, and this may also be a factor in why such subjects create a sense of discomfort in campus discussions and roundtables. Diversity initiatives seldom address xenophobia, remaining focused principally on racism. Foreign students are not a large or powerful enough constituency to force a discussion of their experiences, which are often subsumed into discussions of racism. When foreign-born academics attempt to contribute to campus conversations about race beyond anecdotal and experiential accounts, and reference U.S. foreign policies and actions as racist and imperialist, they are often shut down or positioned outside the national conversation, because this is considered "foreign policy," which is seen as a discrete issue.

When they feel implicated in the dangerous and destructive actions of their country, many faculty of color may assume highly defensive nationalistic positions that are then personalized and weaponized in xenophobic and nativist rhetoric. For example, in an online discussion, a reminder to liberal commentators that Fiona Hill's testimony against Trump at the first impeachment proceedings doesn't constitute her a feminist hero, especially given that she was an assistant to arch war hawk John Bolton, resulted in an attack on the foreign-born faculty making that intervention, who were then reproached for being privileged international faculty. The truth is that foreign-born faculty, especially those without citizenship, do not enjoy some sort of privilege as "international faculty," but are more typically either contingent faculty, graduate labor, or employed to teach large lecture classes in subjects such as engineering or computer science. Sometimes they are asked to teach their native language rather than the subject in which they obtained a PhD. However, positioning foreign-born faculty as outsiders, or at least as insider-outsiders, serves to deflect or defang their critiques of U.S. imperialism.

Criticism from people of foreign origin, even if they are just sharing alternative perspectives and points of view, can threaten Americans' sense of themselves and their place in the world and provoke defensive and/or nativist responses. The threat is to their agency and autonomy, to a received history and narrative, and perhaps to pride and patriotism. Such criticism and exposés are far more easily received from those not perceived as foreign. There is a taxonomy of difference and a taxonomy of belonging.

Discussions of U.S. imperialism also compel Americans of color to recognize and acknowledge their participation in the imperial project, most visibly through membership in the armed forces, where people of color serve at a much higher proportion than their percentage of the population, but also in other ways. The U.S. armed services function as a de facto job program, forcing many people of color and disadvantaged white people to enlist. Foreign-born faculty are insiders when they share racist experiences as fellow people of color, and outsiders when they bring up issues that implicate all Americans, such as wars of aggression or even the less onerous issue of passport privilege. The American *mission civilisatrice* is exposed as a lie. American exceptionalism also encompasses Americans of color who are privileged above the Brown and Black people of other countries. The fort is always defended from within.

In addition, the suggestion that a U.S. person of color partakes of any type of American privilege simply by virtue of being American meets with resistance and even anger. While both foreign-born and U.S.-born communities of color can speak with relative impunity in liberal academic circles about racial discrimination, police violence, climate change, health care, and similar concerns, the foreign born may meet resistance when they criticize or even reference the racism and Islamophobia of the U.S. empire or the actions of the military. The military commands a great deal of respect as an institution in the United States, and any criticism of it is seen as close to treasonable. While faculty colleagues are usually too politically correct to indulge in the usual retort of "If you don't like it here, go back to where you came from," they do find creative ways of saying just that. For instance, they may ask what brought you here in the first place, or point out that xenophobia is much more vicious in many other countries, or remind you of instances of prejudice and discrimination in your own country of origin, all of which deflect from the issue at hand.

Nativist instincts kick in, and native-born faculty, both white and those of color, may be found rallying round the flag. That racism is a safer, more legitimized, and openly debated topic in academia than xenophobia may be ironic, but it is not surprising. White liberal guilt and an insular focus on domestic matters may be factors. The connections between racism and a white supremacist foreign policy are seldom established. That race factors into geopolitics becomes evident when we note that since World War II, with one exception, only African, Asian, and Latin American countries have been singled out for regime change, bombing, or wars of aggression. As Gurminder K. Bhambra et al. write in the journal *Foreign Policy*, "Matters of race are usually addressed as domestic issues—that is, as questions of *identity* or in terms of *stratification* (the differential distribution of rewards and resources within a country). While both of these categories of analysis are of fundamental importance, they often neglect the international processes through which race and racial differences have also been *produced*" (2020). While the relationships and interactions between these categories of analysis may be acknowledged in academic publications, transnational feminist critiques among them, they do not figure as frequently in campus conversations about the politics of race, which are often campus related, experiential, or anecdotal.

After referencing the "imperial privilege" of Americans of all races and ethnicity in a co-authored article published in *Common Dreams*, I was informed in castigatory terms on a college listserve by a colleague of color that "as a member of another country's electorate" I had no right to comment or opine on the U.S. election. Never mind that a U.S. election has far-reaching and often devastating consequences for other countries, as we saw in 2000 as well as in many other instances, of course. "People of colour in white organizations are treated as guests, temporary residents in someone else's home," Ahmed says (2012, 43). I was treated as a guest, an unwelcome one at that, and "home" was only for Americans, of whatever race or ethnicity, not for those seen as intruders. In this case, referencing our article informationally on the listserve was seen as an intrusion on our campus home as embodied in the listserve. It was very telling that most of the blowback was directed at me and not at my white American coauthor. Ultimately, it is the case of an ungrateful guest: "The woman of colour should be grateful, as she lives in our democracy. We have given her the right and the freedom to speak" (Ahmed 2012, 162), and so should be the woman who came here from another country. That "we" then is fluid and can become contingent and contextual, no longer referring to white people only, but, in this case, to Americans of all races who are native to the soil.

In this article, my co-author and I write:

> Imperial privilege allows Americans (black, brown, and white) to focus only on the "homeland" and ignore the consequences of their political choices for any other country. There is a disturbing moral disconnect here. Voters who support a candidate that recognizes black lives matter nevertheless avert their gaze in good conscience from the thousands who are killed as a direct result of that same candidate's interventionist policies. Voters scandalized when a child's life is jeopardized during a domestic police confrontation regard the slaughter of large numbers of children in other countries as regrettable but inevitable "collateral damage." They call for context. But what context justifies the taking of innocent lives? "Collateral" and "context" then become part of the lexicon of imperial privilege. (Singh and Wright 2016)

The offended colleague ascribed the article to my elitism and privilege, which, again, is a way of deflecting attention away from the article and toward the author. Ironically, to be able to ignore or set aside interventions, regime change, and wars as important election issues and focus only on the domestic—affirmative action, women's rights, the Supreme Court, etc.—is itself a form of privilege, an insulation from the harsh realities and intense suffering experienced by those on the receiving end of bombs and occupations. This is certainly not to suggest that domestic issues are not important, but they are placed higher in the hierarchy, and foreign policy and actions abroad are strategically distanced.

In addition, the strain of witnessing the destruction, degradation, and destabilization of their countries is a traumatic experience for foreign-born faculty whose family members are directly affected. Often, this trauma is unseen and unacknowledged by fellow faculty members. That trauma, rather than the accent reduction programs sometimes required of foreign-born faculty or learning to adapt to the different teaching styles and classroom environments of an American university, is the most difficult to deal with. They see life going on as usual, and people talking about the "war being over," whether in Iraq or Afghanistan or elsewhere, when their missives from home speak of the decimation of people's lives.

Creating a binary division between "foreign policy" and "domestic policy" then becomes a "head fake" to deflect attention from the actions carried out in the countries of the Global South, actions that serve the geopolitical interests of the United States of America. That does not change, no matter which party is currently in power. It also allows campus conversations to be reduced to the duopoly, where one party is seen as working against the interests of people of color and the less advantaged, and the other is seen as working in their interests. This not only leads to reductive discussions but centers the experiences of U.S. people of color. Support for and solidarity with the Black Lives Matter movement is widespread in liberal academia, but ask the question "Do Black lives matter equally everywhere?" and an uncomfortable silence often follows.

Some colleagues were furious that I had posted on social media negative articles about Hillary Clinton's hawkishness and regime change proclivities. I was supposed to put all that aside and support this putative feminist, even though wars adversely affect women in other lands. A few of them lashed out at me on Facebook, saying, tauntingly, that I must be happy about Trump's election. One of them was a white man in a position of power over me, my department chair, who gave me a dressing down for posting anything negative about

Hillary Clinton. His inference was that my posts helped to get Trump elected, which was comical given that I have no power nationally or globally, and my posts were for my Facebook friends only and not public. In a formal letter addressed to him and read out to him by me before our Title IX officer, with whom I had registered an official complaint, I said, "In your U.S.-centric white man anger you lash out at the nearest Brown foreign female and lay the blame at her door. White people elected Trump, including a majority of white women. Why are you lashing out at a Brown woman?"

I also asked him why he felt that he could talk to me in the way he did, and whether he had ever spoken to any of our other colleagues in that manner. I asked him to consider the position of power and privilege that he felt comfortable speaking from. "Is it because I am a woman, a woman of color, a foreign woman, or because I am only disposable contingent faculty?" I asked. I informed him that among my friends and colleagues of South Asian or Middle Eastern backgrounds, my views were far from unusual and reminded him that "we foreign women of color do not need white knights to rescue us or save us, because the same white knights turn on us when we speak for ourselves and stand up for ourselves." Ironically, these white colleagues were far less at risk of hate crimes than my family was under a Trump administration. Their attacks, both personal and public, were rancorous. What helped me cope is that so many of my students jumped in to speak on my behalf, saying that I had taught them how to think critically and to speak truth to power, and I was simply modeling that in my political posts.

Some years ago, at the University of Colorado Colorado Springs (UCCS), where I taught part time, Newt Gingrich had been invited to speak, and a discussion ensued on a faculty listserve. Many faculty members raised objections to the invitation, and I was among them. A white male colleague admonished me for my objections to the invitation and for "using the faculty mailing system, or its computers, for promoting [my] liberal agenda" (Rory Lewis, email to author, 2009), but he felt free to use the same to launch a vicious attack on me, saying, in an email addressed to me but sent to the entire listserve, "It is perfectly acceptable for you to be a terrorist loving, anti-American, whining liberal with no backbone or understanding of colonialism or the Constitution because this is indeed the land of the free" (Rory Lewis, email to UCCS faculty listserve, 2009).

In the very same sentence where he extended me license to speak, he simultaneously attempted to silence me with his demeaning and derogatory language. He suggested that I have lunch with a hard-right conservative colleague, also a white male, who would, he said, set me straight on my errant liberalism. He called me on my "vitriol" against Gingrich, a public figure, but remained blissfully oblivious of his own against me, an actual colleague. Another faculty member told me that I am like Chávez, Castro, and Ahmadinejad, all rolled into one, and reminded me that America is "a shining city on a hill" (Alexander Soifer, email to UCCS faculty listserve, 2009), something he seemed sure this benighted foreigner would not have known. Other faculty on that same discussion board also objected to the Gingrich invitation, and in much stronger and harsher terms than I did, but they were not castigated. Only I, the perceived foreigner, was denied the right to contribute my thoughts to the discussion without repercussion. It all harks back to the politics of what Sara Ahmed has called "stranger making" (2012, 3).

Without independent institutions such as the NAACP to offer legal support and help, foreign faculty often flounder when they experience injustice in the tenure or promotion process and must rely on personal lawyers for the most part. Xenophobia is not as verifiable or demonstrable when actual slurs or direct affronts are not involved. A colleague of Bangladeshi origin recently emailed me to tell me that her promotion to full professor was unanimously voted on by her department. Instead of feeling joy and relief, however, she described feeling "heartbroken and furious," adding that the department also voted to send forward the file of a woman more than a decade her junior who also went up for full. She felt that her file was solid even five years ago, but she was denied. She referenced "fear, discrimination and gaslighting tactics" and said that her promotion came at a really high cost to her health (unnamed sender, email to author, 2021).

Sensitivity to criticism of one's country is not unique to the United States—but the United States has more foreign-born faculty than perhaps any other country. For them to feel safe and secure, their voices must be listened to respectfully, with an open mind, and truly heard. Their perspectives and lived experiences must not only be accommodated but solicited. They must become part of the national conversation without punitive consequences. Otherwise, academic freedom, a vaunted benefit of tenure, becomes merely academic. The answer to the question "Who belongs?" is predicated on the person who asks and the person who answers the question: the subject position of the person who gets to ask and the person who feels free to answer. It is also predicated on whether the subject of the conversation is sanctioned. The subject of Palestine is clearly not. As Stuart Hall writes, "identities are the names we give to the different ways we are positioned by, and position ourselves within, the narratives of the past" (2003, 225). The question insinuates place, the place from which we speak, but also space: the space within which someone is accommodated or excluded.

Works Cited

Ahmed, Sara. 2012. *On Being Included: Racism and Diversity in Institutional Life*. Durham, NC: Duke University Press.

Bhambra, Gurminder K., Yolande Bouka, Randolph B. Persaud, Olivia U. Rutazibwa, Vineet Thakur, Duncan Bell, Karen Smith, Toni Haastrup, and Seifudein Adem. 2020. "Why Is Mainstream International Relations Blind to Racism?" *Foreign Policy*, July 3, 2020. https://foreignpolicy.com/2020/07/03/why-is-mainstream-international-relations-ir-blind-to-racism-colonialism/.

Hall, Stuart. 2003. "Cultural Identity and Diaspora." In *Theorizing Diaspora*, edited by Jana Evans Braziel and Anita Mannur, 233–46. Malden, MA: Blackwell.

Said, Edward. "Permission to Narrate." 1984. *Journal of Palestinian Studies* 13 (3): 27–48. https://doi.org/10.2307/2536688.

Salaita, Steven. 2015. *Uncivil Rites: Palestine and the Limits of Academic Freedom*. Chicago: Haymarket Books.

Salaita, Steven. 2024. *An Honest Living: A Memoir of Peculiar Itineraries*. New York: Fordham University Press.

Singh, Rashna B., and Peter Wright. 2016. "Imperial Privilege: On War and Violence Near and Far." *Common Dreams*, October 14, 2016. https://www.commondreams.org/views/2016/10/14/imperial-privilege-war-and-violence-near-and-far/.

15

Who Belongs in Women's, Gender, and Sexuality Studies?

Kristina Gupta

Writing about my personal experience of institutional betrayal is painful but necessary. Painful because it requires me to relive the trauma of the past and the continuing absence of justice in the present. Necessary because this is what we do in feminism—we share our personal experiences because our silence will not protect us, because the personal is political, and because shared experience can become collective knowledge about the ways injustice operates and collective action to transform the world for the better.

A senior colleague in my department published an op-ed. In the op-ed, they argued that liberals should reconsider their opposition to Trump's Muslim ban because Muslims are less likely to support women's rights and gay rights. Not surprisingly, this article upset many people, including me. Students organized a rally and, later, a petition. Many of us asked our department to respond. After more than a month, the department still had not responded. Another member of the department, a queer woman of color, told me she was planning to resign from the department due to the op-ed and the department's failure to address anti-Muslim racism and white supremacy. I criticized the op-ed, both privately to the author and in a campus publication (Gupta and Ramachandran 2017). I criticized the department's delayed response to the op-ed during a department meeting. In the face of defensiveness, I became angry and my words harsh. In Sara Ahmed's terms, I snapped (2016).

Although I am a biracial woman of color, my light skin and socioeconomic privilege often protect me from individual and institutional violence. But in this case, the blowback was immediate. I was told I was not acting like a feminist—as if critiquing anti-Muslim racism and white supremacy and unjust systems of power is not a feminist project. I was told that maybe I was no longer fitting into the department's culture. If the culture was about tolerating anti-Muslim racism and white supremacy, then I didn't want to fit in.

Even so, considering my record of teaching, research, and service, I was floored when I learned the department had voted not to renew my contract after my fourth-year review, citing lack of collegiality as a primary reason. The departmental letter explaining this decision included distortions and lies while omitting important information. I received a termination letter from the Dean's Office, just before winter break. Words cannot convey how miserable I was during the break. I had trouble sleeping. My stomach ached constantly, tied into knots of anxiety. I love being a professor—teaching, research, service, all of it. I love the field of women's, gender, and sexuality studies (WGSS)—at that point, I had already devoted fifteen years of my life to academic feminism. I believe in the field as a transformational project. During that winter break, I thought my career—which feels like a calling—was over.

I informed the Dean's Office that I thought the decision to not renew my contract was an act of bias and retaliation. To this day, I don't know whether my claim was investigated at that time. I certainly felt the Dean's Office did not take my claim seriously. Indeed, it seemed that the very fact I had alleged bias and retaliation had confirmed, in their eyes, my lack of collegiality. Maybe, in their minds, collegial people don't accuse their colleagues of bias and retaliation? Or maybe, in their minds, collegial people aren't retaliated against by their colleagues?

In describing the figure of the feminist killjoy, Ahmed writes, "for those who do not have a sense of the racism or sexism you are talking about, to bring them up is to bring them into existence. . . . However she speaks, the one who speaks as a feminist is usually heard as the cause of the argument . . . she is getting in the way of something, the achievement or accomplishment of the family or of some *we* or another, which is created by what is not said. . . . We become a problem when we describe a problem" (2016, 36–39). My experiences conform closely to Ahmed's description of the feminist killjoy—in speaking up about anti-Muslim racism, I got in the way of the "we" of the department, the "we" of the university. Rather than anti-Muslim racism being recognized as the problem, I became the problem.

Eventually, the Dean's Office overturned the department's decision and I was sent back, with a provisional contract, to the department that had voted to end my employment. That spring semester was torturous. With summer, the Dean's Office brought in an outside chair and restructured the department, yet some of my senior colleagues remained. They were allowed to sit on my tenure committee; they were allowed to vote on my tenure; they are allowed to vote on the tenure of others. They will be allowed to vote if I ever seek promotion to full professor. The department culture remained hostile. Just entering the space was enough to make my stomach clench with anxiety. The department is a site of ongoing trauma for me. I am expected to sit with those I feel victimized by in department meetings, and I am expected to be "collegial"—which seems to mean acting as if my colleagues had not tried to end my career in retaliation for my interruption of their "we." I'm not very good at it, but I keep trying because I'm not ready to give up my job—my calling.

A key takeaway from my story is that even WGSS, if not explicitly committed to antiracist practices and feminist policies and procedures, is a site of institutional violence. Of this, Ahmed writes, "To talk about racism within feminism is to get in the way of feminist happiness. If talking about racism within feminism gets in the way of feminist happiness, we need to get in the way of feminist happiness" (2016, 177). What stood out to me during this experience was that a number of senior faculty who identified as feminist scholars seemed unable to perform even the most basic structural analysis of the situation. Rather than interpreting my critique as one aimed at the Islamophobic argument of the op-ed and the culture of anti-Muslim racism perpetuated by the department's failure to respond to the op-ed, senior members of the department interpreted my critique as a personal attack. While some were capable of discussing concepts such as white fragility, tone policing, and white feminism in the abstract, they seemed unable to apply them to their own behavior.

In an earlier publication, I argued that PhD programs in WGSS must put into place clear policies and procedures for the protection of graduate students, who are institutionally vulnerable (Gupta 2018). Based on my experiences of disavowal and isolation as an assistant professor in a WGSS department, I believe it is essential that these departments put into place such policies for assistant professors and contingent faculty as well, a point that is expanded on below.

Another key takeaway of this story is that broader institutions can engage in willful ignorance when it comes to acts of bias and retaliation, and they use practices of confidentiality to maintain their ignorance. I still do not know if my claim of retaliation was seriously investigated at the time. It certainly felt as if I was positioned as the problem, and in overturning the department's decision, the Dean's Office gave me a chance to "correct" my willfulness. Yet, where does the refusal to see bias and retaliation come from? Acknowledging bias and retaliation can undermine institutional legitimacy—is it really the meritocracy it presents itself as? Is it really as committed to "diversity and inclusion" as it claims?

In her work on ignorance, Nancy Tuana writes, "Willful ignorance is a systematic process of self-deception, a willful embrace of ignorance that infects those who are in positions of privilege, an active ignoring of the oppression of others and one's role in that exploitation"

(2006, 11). According to Tuana, willful ignorance involves a desire for claims to be false, "coupled by a fear that they are not, but where the consequences of their being true are so high, *it is better to cultivate ignorance*" (2006, 11; emphasis in original). This kind of willful ignorance was illustrated to me during a recent meeting with a high-level administrator. This person acknowledged there was no identified person at our university to whom faculty could report allegations of racial bias. Later, in the same conversation, this administrator remarked, seemingly with no irony, that fortunately these "types of situations" are rare at our university. The (to me) obvious possibility—that these types of situations are not rare but underreported—was not obvious to this administrator.

A final key takeaway of my story is that a strong network of supporters can protect, to a certain extent, against institutional violence. A number of colleagues, of different genders and races, advocated on my behalf when I appealed my department's decision to not renew my contract. From then until now, I have been supported openly and behind the scenes by colleagues, friends, and family members, who comforted me during bouts of anxiety and depression. At low points, I wondered if I was, in fact, the problem. But this extensive support network has consistently affirmed that although I had been positioned as the problem, the real problem is the patriarchal whiteness of the institution. It is only because of this support that I have been able to remain in the institution thus far and that I have been able to continue killing joy by speaking out against injustice.

In closing, I want to offer a perspective on mitigating institutional betrayal in the academy. After the majority of this article was written, the university recruited a senior scholar from another institution to chair the department and contracted a consulting firm to help improve departmental culture. These are important developments. And yet these developments themselves do not ensure that what happened to me will not be repeated. What policies could be put into place to assure that promotion and tenure processes—and careers—are not derailed by senior faculty with hidden (or not-so-hidden) agendas? In terms of immediate practical steps to take, I think that WGSS departments need to develop their own codes of conduct that outline just labor practices (particularly related to contingent faculty and staff) and clearly identify bias, discrimination, and retaliation as misconduct. In addition, WGSS departments need to conduct audits of their own universities to find out whether they have a robust system in place for receiving, investigating, and responding to reports of bias, discrimination, and retaliation. If the answer is no—as was the case at my university—department members should advocate for the creation of such systems.

At the same time, departments must recognize that even if universities do have or put these systems in place, as the institutions in which we work are saturated with sexism, racism, classism, heterosexism, ableism, colonialism, etc., these systems do not guarantee just outcomes—other contributions to this volume provide ample evidence of this. WGSS departments should not limit themselves to working within the university as institution—for example, departments could commit to a policy stating that if a faculty or staff member believes they have been treated unfairly or unjustly in an employment decision, the department will go through a conflict resolution process with a facilitator or group who has expertise in transformative justice. In general, WGSS department faculty should commit ourselves to engaging in ongoing conversations about what it means to live a feminist life as a feminist academic, in terms of our responsibilities as scholars and teachers, and as program managers, supervisors, and colleagues.

Works Cited

Ahmed, Sara. 2016. *Living a Feminist Life*. Durham, NC: Duke University Press.
Gupta, Kristina. 2018. "The Structural Vulnerability of Doctoral Students: A Political and Ethical Issue for Doctoral Programs in Women's/Gender/Sex-

uality/Feminist Studies." *Feminist Studies* 44 (2): 409–23. https://doi.org/10.15767/feministstudies.44.2.0409.

Gupta, Kristina, and Tanisha Ramachandra. 2017. "Staff Members Reject Religious Intolerance." *Old Gold & Black*, February 24, 2017. https://wfuogb.com/3351/opinion/staff-members-reject-religious-intolerance/.

Tuana, Nancy. 2006. "The Speculum of Ignorance: The Women's Health Movement and Epistemologies of Ignorance." *Hypatia* 21 (3): 1–19. https://doi.org/10.1111/j.1527-2001.2006.tb01110.x.

16

Teaching While Brown

Understanding Latina Faculty Experiences in Higher Education

Mercedes Valadez and Alma Itzé Flores

Academia is a hierarchical structure where institutional racism and sexism persist. The lack of racial/ethnic representation among tenure-track faculty has long plagued academia. Research focused on exploring racial and ethnic bias and negative stereotypes generally highlights the challenges encountered by Black and white faculty only. The literature has yet to fully explore the challenges and barriers that Latinx faculty face as they navigate the tenure and promotion process (Anderson and Smith 2005). Latinas are one of the most underrepresented groups among tenure-track faculty (Nuñez and Murakami-Ramalho 2012). As a result, some students may go through their entire college experience without ever being taught by a Latina instructor. Lack of representation impacts student beliefs and expectations about faculty. Latina faculty fight against a host of gendered and racial/ethnic stereotypes, including the "diversity hire" or the "token," and as such confront questions about competency and qualifications. These stereotypes can seep into the classroom and impact faculty-student dynamics, leading to negative teaching evaluations, which then impact the tenure and promotion process.

This essay draws on personal experiences from two Latina tenure-track assistant professors about student-faculty dynamics. First, Dr. Mercedes Valadez discusses her experiences when faced with students who question her qualifications and role in the classroom. Next, Dr. Alma Itzé Flores shares her experiences when confronted with racial-gendered microaggressions directed at her in the classroom. Both narratives address how the authors navigate situations where their students challenge their presence and position in the classroom, making assumptions that they do not belong in the role of instructor.

"Do You Actually Have a PhD?" Addressing Questions About Qualifications, Dr. Mercedes Valadez

Latina professors battle against gendered and racial/ethnic stereotypes centered around the misconception that they possess lower competence, skills, and qualifications, relative to those of their racial/ethnic counterparts. Students often employ both subtle and overt bias when faced with a Latina instructor. They are not accustomed to seeing a Latina in a position of power or leadership in the classroom and will often resist by challenging their presence and position.

On the first day of the semester, I usually get questions one might expect about extra credit or attendance expectations. However, it never fails that at least one student will ask my age and whether I really earned a PhD. While I do not find it relevant to discuss my age, I do go over my educational background. It seems that in some ways this information helps some students feel more comfortable with my role as their instructor. However, I have encountered several instances where students continue to challenge my role and qualifications.

In one example, a white student interrupted a class activity to ask me, as she rolled her eyes, "Do I have to call you 'Doctor'?" In response, I said, "No, you may call me 'Doctor' or 'Professor.'" This was a student who consistently interrupted lectures and made several biased comments about racial/ethnic minorities during class time. I addressed her comments and used them as a teachable moment to disrupt misconceptions and negative stereotypes. My presence in the classroom possibly challenged her gendered or racialized/ethnic assumptions about professors and women of color. My field and discipline, criminal justice, is predominantly white and male dominated. While most students in my department self-identify as Latinx, I am the first Latina tenure-track faculty in my department. I understand that some colleagues may not have a preference in terms of how they are addressed in the classroom, but I request that students not call me by my first name, "Miss," or "Mrs." Today, there is still some debate about whether a doctorate is worthy of the title of "Doctor" or if using that title without a medical degree is fraudulent. Yet, this issue only came to national attention when it was a woman being scrutinized for her degree (First Lady Dr. Jill Biden). The public was shocked and angered by the disrespect Dr. Biden experienced. Yet, women of color have been continually mocked and scrutinized about their credentials in higher education for years.

Given that so few tenure-track faculty are Latina, it is no wonder that it seems like an anomaly when students are faced with a Latina college instructor. This violates whatever norms and preconceived notions they have about college professors, particularly in fields dominated by white men. Discussions about connecting with students are often framed around the idea that white faculty have a difficult time connecting and reaching out to nonwhite students. However, one area that is seldom addressed is that Latinx faculty bear the struggle of overcoming negative stereotypes and biases from students, particularly white students.

"Where Is the Professor?" Racial Microaggressions in Academia, Dr. Alma Itzé Flores

I started my academic career at the age of twenty-eight, when I accepted a visiting assistant professor position. Shortly after this, I started my current tenure-track position. Being a young, petite Chicana has made me both hypervisible and invisible in academia. During my very first class as a freshly minted Doctor Flores, I arrived at my classroom early and started setting up my technology. Students began to trickle in and take their seats. As the start of class neared, I heard a student ask, "Where is the professor?" I saw heads turning, scanning the classroom looking for "the professor." I smiled, hoping they would catch my face. Soon after, I heard another student add, "I think after five minutes we can leave if he doesn't show up." At that point, I immediately blurted out, "Good morning, everyone, I am Professor Flores." Students looked at me both embarrassed and confused. This was the start of my career as a professor.

Unfortunately, this would not be the first or last time something like this would happen to me. The reality is that most college students expect an older white man as their professor, maybe a white woman, but most definitely not someone like me. The questioning of my position as faculty not only comes from students but by colleagues as well. While making copies for class, a white woman in my department yelled from outside the copy room, "Students are not allowed in here!" I turned around to correct her, saying, "I am faculty here." Shocked and embarrassed, she apologized: "I am sorry, you look like a student." I never quite know what to say to this. Thanks? I am not? While I can understand how perhaps my age and height (I am five foot three) can be reasons for the confusion, these comments are nevertheless racial-gendered microaggressions and speak to the invalidation and marginalization that Chicana and Latina faculty regularly experience (Solórzano and Pérez Huber 2020). Similar to my *colega* Dr. Valadez, comments about my age, dress, and appearance have seeped into my teaching evaluations. I have had students and colleagues refer to me as "Señorita," "Miss," "Mija," and "Mamacita," or on a first-name basis. My student evaluations have included accusations of racism and sexism, as well as comments questioning my knowledge, credentials, and ability to teach effectively. In my two years as a tenure-track professor, I have already dealt with two grade appeals from students who felt that I graded them unfairly because they are white women. One of these students became so upset when the grade appeal was rejected that she filed a racial complaint with our university's Title IX office.

These racial-gendered microaggressions have affected me both professionally and personally. Professionally, all of these comments go into my Retention, Tenure, and Promotion (RTP) file for my colleagues to read, comment, and evaluate me on. Each year I find myself having to explain white fragility in the classroom and the experiences of women of color in academia to situate these comments. On a personal level, the emotional labor and exhaustion of being a Chicana feminist scholar has been daunting. What is striking to me is that I have only been in academia for four years yet have already dealt with so much racism and sexism. What keeps me grounded, focused, and motivated are other faculty and students of color who affirm me and lift my spirits up. The racial microaffirmations we engage in—the text messages "just checking in," the thank-you notes from students, the nods—are just a few examples of the subtle verbal and nonverbal strategies that people of color use to affirm each other's dignity, integrity, and shared humanity (Solórzano and Pérez Huber 2020).

Assessing the Impact of Biased Student Evaluations

Student evaluations play a critical role in the promotion and tenure process. Despite well-documented evidence of students' racial/ethnic and gender biases, these instruments continue to be used to assess whether a faculty member is a "good fit" for the department/university (Spooren, Brockx, and Mortelmans 2013; Uttl, White, and Gonzalez 2017). Faculty are expected to fit a particular gendered and racialized stereotype. Female faculty must be warm and forgiving, and must smile.

If they deviate from these gendered expectations and instill structure and rigor into their courses, they are penalized. Women of color face additional scrutiny compared to white female faculty. White female faculty are not subject to the racialized negative stereotypes that their colleagues of color face from other faculty and students.

When I (Mercedes) have shared my concerns about student evaluation bias and other related concerns, I have received mixed responses from other faculty. For instance, some junior faculty acknowledge my concerns but say that they cannot relate. At one point, I was one of four junior faculty women and the only junior woman of color in my department. When I sought advice from a tenured colleague, she not only dismissed my concerns but let me know that she would not advise me to address issues of student bias in the narrative for my retention letter. Furthermore, when I shared my experience of students questioning my qualifications, she simply stated that she does not require that her students refer to her as "Doctor." The message I received was that I was overly sensitive, that I was the problem. The widespread attitude in my department is that addressing social justice issues and racial/ethnic biases is a "fad" or "trendy." I have found that white male and female colleagues cannot relate to the issues highlighted in this essay and do not have to worry about being taken seriously in the classroom. Going to a senior colleague for guidance and advice often turns into a lecture about being careful not to "play the race card."

Recommendations and Ways to Move Forward

Our shared experiences highlight some of the most common forms of hostility and racial-gendered microaggressions experienced by women of color faculty, and in this case, Latina tenure-track faculty. Given some of the issues addressed above, we provide a few recommendations that aim to address some of the challenges we often navigate in higher education.

First, it is critical that departments and institutions reconsider the weight of student evaluations in the tenure and promotion process. Additional forms of evaluation should be given equal, if not more, weight. Furthermore, reviewers should receive implicit bias training and be familiar with the literature on bias in student evaluations of women faculty of color.

Second, institutions should be intentional in hiring more Latinx tenure-track faculty. This may include making concentrated efforts to recruit faculty from underrepresented groups, posting job advertisements in outlets that cater to a more diverse demographic, and similar tactics. Increasing representation will help normalize Latina faculty in institutions of higher education. This is particularly critical in Hispanic-serving institutions, where a large portion of the student body is Latinx. In the wake of social justice movements, institutions of higher education have proudly proclaimed that they are making efforts towards being inclusive and diverse. Yet they continue to neglect representation across tenure-track faculty, especially in the case of Latina faculty. Institutions need to make a commitment to tenure-track Latina representation and set a goal to match the student and tenure-track faculty ratio of race, ethnicity, and sex.

Too often, faculty and administrators of color become the institutional go-to people to lead discussions and training related to racism. Much of this work is done above and beyond the responsibilities of white colleagues who hold the same positions. The responsibility to disrupt racism needs to fall on institutions, not on people of color. Universities can start by not asking whether racism exists on their campus (e.g., using campus racial climate surveys) but *how* it operates through its systems, policies, and processes. Institutions should consider providing training opportunities to all faculty, students, and staff to recognize everyday racism in order to take action against it. The disruption of racial-gendered microaggressions should be a priority across all levels of the institution, particularly campus leadership. Lastly, universities generally only request consultation with a racial equity center or scholar after an incident, rather than approach racial equity as continuous long-term work. Building an antiracist campus with racially conscious leaders means that regardless of the news cycle, there should always be an ongoing effort to disrupt and challenge racism.

Works Cited

Anderson, Kristin J., and Gabriel Smith. 2005. "Students' Preconceptions of Professors: Benefits and Barriers According to Ethnicity and Gender." *Hispanic Journal of Behavioral Sciences* 27, no. 2 (May): 184–201. https://doi.org/10.1177/0739986304273707.

Chávez, Kerry, and Kristina M. W. Mitchell. 2020. "Exploring Bias in Student Evaluations: Gender, Race, and Ethnicity." *PS: Political Science & Politics* 53, no. 2 (April): 270–74. http://dx.doi.org/10.1017/S1049096519001744.

Nuñez, Anne-Marie, and Elizabeth Murakami-Ramalho. 2012. "The Demographic Dividend." *Academe* 98, no. 1 (January–February): n.p. https://www.aaup.org/article/demographic-dividend#.Yh1lb-jMI2w.

Pérez Huber, Lindsey, Ofelia Huidor, Maria C. Malagón, Gloria Sánchez, and Daniel G. Solórzano. 2006. "Falling Through the Cracks: Critical Transitions in the Latina/o Educational Pipeline." *UCLA Chicano Studies Research Center*, no. 7 (January): 1–14. https://files.eric.ed.gov/fulltext/ED493397.pdf.

Solórzano, Daniel G., and Lindsey Pérez Huber. 2020. *Racial Microaggressions: Using Critical Race Theory to Respond to Everyday Racism*. New York: Teachers College Press.

Spooren, Pieter, Bert Brockx, and Dimitri Mortelmans. 2013. "On the Validity of Student Evaluation of Teaching: The State of the Art." *Review of Educational Research* 83 (4): 598–642. https://doi.org/10.3102/0034654313496870.

Uttl, Bob, Carmela A. White, and Daniela Wong Gonzalez. 2017. "Meta-analysis of Faculty's Teaching Effectiveness: Student Evaluation of Teaching Ratings and Student Learning Are Not Related." *Studies in Educational Evaluation* 54 (September): 22–42. http://dx.doi.org/10.1016/j.stueduc.2016.08.007.

17

Who Can Be a Scholar?

Identity, Power, and Intellectual Labor in the Academy

Brandy L. Simula and Jessica Bishop-Royse

In this chapter, we draw on our combined two decades of experience as social science PhDs pursuing our research and scholarship as staff in higher education settings. Our experience comes from multiple positions across several institutions, both public and private, and we reflect on the ways that institutional structures and microlevel interactions constrain scholars working in staff positions from pursuing research as well as being taken seriously *as* scholars.

Not fully "inside" the academy as are our faculty colleagues, nor fully "outside" the academy like peers employed in government, industry, and nonprofits, PhDs employed in higher ed careers beyond the professoriate are precariously situated in relation to belonging and the academy. We explore how power, status, and belonging influence the experiences of PhD scholars. We focus on institutional betrayal and marginalization of the scholarship and intellectual labor of PhD scholars working from staff rather than faculty positions. While we focus in this chapter on our experiences as scholars in staff positions, we note that many of the structural, interactional, and status issues we identify are shared by colleagues working in teaching-oriented positions, and those working as contingent laborers in the academy, as independent scholars, and as scholars working in applied settings outside higher education.

Our reflections are grounded primarily in our lived experiences and draw from our mixed-methods study of the career experiences of

PhDs employed in higher education careers beyond the professoriate, as well as extensive conversations across our professional networks. While holding full-time staff positions, we have each continued to pursue scholarship, publishing in the areas of health inequalities (Bishop-Royse) and interactions, inequalities, and identities (Simula). We have contributed to scholarship in our fields in other capacities, including extensive work reviewing manuscripts in our fields (Bishop-Royse and Simula) and in editorial capacities (Simula).

Identities and Status

Consistently across both of our careers, our choice to continue pursuing scholarship has been called into question in both implicit and explicit ways. Our own experiences, as well as those of our research participants, have often included navigating the perception that such an endeavor interferes with our commitment to our professional careers. From questions in job interviews to conversations with colleagues and supervisors, we are often asked to justify *why* we engage in research even though we have left—or were never in—faculty positions. The assumption underlying most of these conversations is that faculty do the scholarship and staff support that scholarship.

Experiences of faculty colleagues explicitly dismissing the scholarship and scholarly identities of colleagues in full-time staff positions was a common theme that emerged in our qualitative, in-depth interview study of 50 PhDs from diverse disciplines employed in more than 30 different career paths in higher ed at 27 different colleges and universities in the United States. Although we are fortunate that some faculty colleagues recognize our research expertise, we routinely experience marginalization and microaggressions enacted by our faculty colleagues. Young, Anderson, and Stewart's (2015, 62) concept of hierarchical microaggressions—"the everyday slights found in higher education that communicate systemic valuing (or devaluing) of a person because of the institutional role held by that person"—is useful for understanding interactions between faculty and staff scholars. Frequent devaluations of our role as scholars occur through microaggressions and are normatively permissible by the devaluation of staff positions in general. For example, a new faculty member at Simula's previous institution expressed interest in chatting about a shared area of research interest and potential for collaboration. Over coffee, when Simula shared that she had just moved from a faculty appointment to a staff position but was continuing her research, the faculty member said, "Oh, well if you're not faculty, I'm not really interested in talking further," and left. Other examples include blockage or exclusion from participation in reading groups in our research area on the basis of our staff status and institutional recognition of recent scholarship failing to include our work.

What is remarkable about PhDs employed in higher education is that often, the PhD is a requirement of the position. In many of these positions, the extensive research experience of active scholars is required. For example, the knowledge and skills gained from having conducted original primary research (in the form of a dissertation or other scholarship) is essential when advising faculty on the various methodological, statistical, and logistical obstacles that arise when conducting primary research (Bishop-Royse's current position). Moreover, often PhDs in these positions are asked to provide an array of types of technical assistance, requiring currency in a variety of research methods and statistical techniques.

As sociologists who study—among other things—identity processes, we are also deeply aware of the ways in which continued challenges to one's identity can erode that identity. As individuals for whom "scholar" is an important identity central to who we are, the extra burden of having to justify our right to claim that identity is additional labor that faculty colleagues do not experience—at least, not in relation to their institutional position. As white women, our white privilege protects us from the kinds of microaggressions that scholar colleagues of color—especially Black colleagues—experience (Griffin et al. 2011). While our right to claim a scholar identity is frequently suspect, our right to be physically present in higher education spaces is never questioned in the way that it is for colleagues of color (Jones 2018; Sagar 2019).

On the other hand, our identities as women almost certainly factor in the microaggressions, erasure, and marginalization we experience as scholars. Women are routinely untitled (titles excluded or ignored when they are used for men colleagues in similar situations) and uncredentialed (credentials excluded or ignored when they are included for men colleagues in similar situations) (Devon 2019). We experience both on a routine basis. For instance, on panels when speakers are introduced, faculty colleagues are introduced as "Doctor" while we are not; we are referred to by our first names in situations where faculty colleagues are referred to as "Dr. So-and-So." Untitling and uncredentialing were also common themes among the experience of participants in our study of PhDs employed in higher ed careers beyond the professoriate. Our interview partners noted in great detail the ways they strategically signaled and reinforced their credentials, especially the doctorate. These microinvalidations (Sue et al. 2007) are the nearly constant backdrop against which we pursue our scholarship. The cumulative effects of having to continually justify engaging in research and scholarship is an ongoing harm that is perpetrated on an individual, interactional level and is embedded and reinforced in institutional structures.

Resources and Rewards

Institutional betrayals of the recognition of the expertise and accomplishments of scholars working from staff positions are facilitated by unequal power dynamics fostered in institutional status and prestige systems. These betrayals also occur when scholars in staff lines are denied access to research resources and support for scholarship that are often available only to those in faculty appointments. Staff scholars are often prevented from accessing the kinds of material support available to faculty colleagues. For instance, many funding calls for proposals require a tenured or tenure-track faculty position as part of the eligibility criteria. Similarly, research assistants—provided through departments and through undergraduate research programs—are routinely available only to scholars in faculty lines. Discretionary, individual research funds are also typically only available to scholars in faculty lines. Denial of resources to support and recognize scholarship takes place at all levels of higher education—in departments, at colleges and universities, and in academic associations.

As a result, many staff scholars are put in the position of having to self-fund their scholarship, which includes using nonwork and vacation time to conduct research. While some have access to—very limited—personal funding to support their research, many simply do not. The persistent racial and gendered wage gaps almost certainly play a role in this process. Women and scholars of color are compensated less than men and white scholars (Barbezat and Hughes 2005; Johnson and Taylor 2019; Lee and Won 2014; Toutkoushian, Bellas, and Moore 2007). The resources they could potentially have available to self-fund research are already constrained by the results of systematic disparities in compensation. Further, institutions continue to racialize academic funding, providing greater access to scholarship and research funding to white scholars than to scholars of color (Ray 2017).

When staff scholars *do* persist in conducting and publishing research, they are denied access to research support and their work often goes unacknowledged. Departments and institutions routinely fail to include the academic publications of staff scholars in announcements of new scholarship. The research of staff scholars is also often undercited. As with many other experiences in higher ed, this process is exacerbated for women and scholars of color, whose work is routinely undercited compared to that of white and men colleagues (Chakravartty et al. 2018; Delgado 1984; Dion, Lawrence Sumner, and McLaughlin Mitchell 2018; Dworkin et al. 2020). Efforts to address racist and sexist citational practices have appeared on social media in recent years, for example through the hashtags #womenalsoknowstuff, #citeblackwomen, #citeasista, #POCalsoknowstuff, #womenalsoknowhistory, and other campaigns to recognize and redress the routine exclusion of scholars of color and women scholars. It's beyond time to recognize that #staffscholarsalsoknowstuff.

Additionally, recognition of outstanding research in the form of awards often overlooks staff scholars. Indeed, research awards and recognition in many cases explicitly define eligibility criteria in ways that limit consideration to scholars in faculty lines. Although institutional structures are flexible enough to include staff scholars, institutions disallow opportunities to support and recognize scholars working in staff positions (Bickford and Mitchell Whisnant 2013).

Conclusion

While the betrayals we identify in this chapter are long entrenched in institutional structures and in the status and prestige hierarchies of academia, we contend that the marginalization and devaluation of staff scholars can be reduced by directly addressing the issues we have identified. To that end, we conclude by providing specific recommendations for affirming and supporting the work of staff scholars.

Recommendations for Staff Scholars

The onus for changing conditions that marginalize and betray the intellectual contributions of staff scholars is an obligation of institutions rather than individuals. Yet we also recognize that staff scholars have considerable agency in pursuing strategies that improve their own scholarly engagement.

First, we affirm and encourage staff scholar colleagues to claim and enact identities as scholars, recognizing that one's identity as a scholar is based on their scholarship, not their appointment type. Second, we suggest that connecting with—and creating—communities of scholar colleagues working from similar positions can provide affirmation and support of both one's scholarship and one's scholarly identity. In our own experiences, support and accountability groups, as well as conversations with staff scholar colleagues facing similar challenges, has been important for our ability to persist in scholarly pursuits despite myriad institutional roadblocks. Third, we encourage staff scholars to take active roles in advocating for policy changes in their institutions and professional organizations.

Recommendations for Faculty Colleagues

Faculty are important as allies and advocates—particularly those who enjoy the privilege and security of tenure. Faculty allies can advocate for more inclusive institutional policies and practices. They can also be mindful of their citation practices, ensuring that they are citing relevant scholarship regardless of the appointment type of the people producing that scholarship. Faculty colleagues can also be intentional in including staff scholars in events, collaboration opportunities, professional networks, etc. At the most basic level, faculty can critically examine the ways their practices may—often unintentionally—marginalize scholar colleagues working in staff positions. We both have had positive experiences co-creating intellectual communities and pursuing collaborative scholarship with faculty colleagues. We know how productive these communities can be when we are intentional in creating them.

Recommendations for Institutions

Higher education institutions, academic associations, and funding agencies serve as gatekeepers for material and social resources, contributing to the devaluing of staff scholars and their work. Policy changes at the institutional level have the potential to affect the experiences of staff scholars.

First, departments, institutions, and academic associations should make research funding and access to research assistants available to scholars based on the strength of their scholarship, regardless of appointment type. Departments and institutions should also develop "mini sabbaticals" for staff scholars—four-to-six-week sabbaticals that assist staff scholars in executing their research. These shorter sabbaticals would be less disruptive to units employing such scholars than the traditional semester- or yearlong sabbatical model, while still providing an extended, uninterrupted period for staff scholars to focus on research. Many of these scholars' day-to-day work is driven by student and faculty needs; during the times when requests for support are low, employers can allow these scholars to direct their own time for research.

In addition to expanding access to material resources and support, colleges and universities must also include the publications, grants, and research-related awards of staff scholars in publicity about the institution's scholarship. Academic and professional organizations (such as disciplinary associations) should similarly actively seek to include and make visible the research of staff scholars.

Departments should also make an "Affiliated Scholar" title available to staff scholars working in their disciplinary tradition. Such a title would not need to carry a salary or direct funding, but it would help illuminate staff scholarship through departmental websites and social media platforms. Additionally, these scholars should be included on departmental mailing lists and invited to colloquia, talks, and social events to ensure their inclusion in relevant intellectual communities.

Across institutional levels from departments to academic associations, institutions should take an active role in supporting staff scholars by offering programming and professional development that support the work of staff scholars. Professional and academic associations must recognize that many staff scholars are self-funded and there should be a membership category for these scholars. Moreover, the associations should consider directing travel funds to support participation by staff scholars.

The Social and Intellectual Cost of Preserving the Status Quo
Finally, while we have focused on how the marginalization of staff scholars causes harm to those working in those positions, we also recognize the immense cost to knowledge production that results from pushing out scholars working from these contexts. Preserving the current system harms not only individual staff scholars but negatively impacts the state of knowledge in the fields in which those scholars work. The primary focus of doctoral training is to produce research experts who are highly skilled in substantive areas as well as in research design and analytical techniques. Institutions betray the PhDs they produce by preventing us from using the research expertise in which we have been trained. Institutions also risk betraying the broader communities they purportedly serve by preventing the development of research and knowledge that could contribute to addressing pressing challenges and questions in those communities. Institutional courage (Freyd and Smidt 2019) in this context requires higher education institutions to take immediate, concrete steps to reduce the harms caused in the betrayal of staff scholars by enacting policies and procedures that provide equitable access to resources and recognition.

Works Cited

Barbezat, Debra A., and James W. Hughes. 2005. "Salary Structure Effects and the Gender Pay Gap in Academia." *Research in Higher Education* 46, no. 6 (September): 621–40. https://doi.org/10.1007/s11162-004-4137-1.
Bickford, Donna M., and Anne Mitchell Whisnant. 2013. "A Move to Bring Staff Scholars Out of the Shadows." *Chronicle of Higher Education*, November

25, 2013. https://www.chronicle.com/article/a-move-to-bring-staff-scholars-out-of-the-shadows/.

Chakravartty, Paula, Rachel Kuo, Victoria Grubbs, and Charlton McIlwain. 2018. "#CommunicationSoWhite." *Journal of Communication* 68, no. 2 (April): 254–66. https://doi.org/10.1093/joc/jqy003.

Delgado, Richard. 1984. "The Imperial Scholar: Reflections on a Review of Civil Rights Literature." *University of Pennsylvania Law Review* 132, no. 3 (March): 561–78. https://doi.org/10.2307/3311882.

Devon, Karen Michelle. 2019. "Call Me by My Name: Doctor." *Annals of Surgery* 270, no. 1 (August): 29–30. http://dx.doi.org/10.1097/SLA.0000000000003327.

Dion, Michelle L., Jane Lawrence Sumner, and Sara McLaughlin Mitchell. 2018. "Gendered Citation Patterns Across Political Science and Social Science Methodology Fields." *Political Analysis* 26, no. 3 (July): 312–27. https://doi.org/10.1017/pan.2018.12.

Dworkin, Jordan D., Kristin A. Linn, Erin G. Teich, Perry Zurn, Russell T. Shinohara, and Danielle S. Bassett. 2020. "The Extent and Drivers of Gender Imbalance in Neuroscience Reference Lists." *Nature Neuroscience* 23, no. 8 (August): 918–26. https://doi.org/10.1038/s41593-020-0658-y.

Freyd, Jennifer J., and Alec M. Smidt. 2019. "So You Want to Address Sexual Harassment and Assault in Your Organization? *Training* Is Not Enough; *Education* is Necessary." *Journal of Trauma & Dissociation* 20 (5): 489–94. https://doi.org/10.1080/15299732.2019.1663475.

Griffin, Kimberly A., Meghan J. Pifer, Jordan R. Humphrey, and Ashley M. Hazelwood. 2011. "(Re)Defining Departure: Exploring Black Professors' Experiences with and Responses to Racism and Racial Climate." *American Journal of Education* 117, no. 4 (August): 495–526. http://dx.doi.org/10.1086/660756.

Johnson, Jessica A., and Barrett J. Taylor. 2019. "Academic Capitalism and the Faculty Salary Gap." *Innovative Higher Education* 44, no. (February): 21–35. https://link.springer.com/article/10.1007/s10755-018-9445-z.

Jones, Stacy Holman. 2018. "Making Our Stories Count: Racial, Gendered, and Sexualized Antagonisms in the Academy." *Departures in Critical Qualitative Research* 7 (2): 1–7. https://doi.org/10.1525/DCQR.2018.7.2.1.

Lee, Young-joo, and Doyeon Won. 2014. "Trailblazing Women in Academia: Representation of Women in Senior faculty and the Gender Gap in Junior Faculty's Salaries in Higher Educational Institutions." *Social Science Journal* 51, no. 3 (September): 331–40. https://doi.org/10.1016/j.soscij.2014.05.002.

Ray, Victor. 2017. "The Racialization of Academic Funding." *Inside Higher Ed*, February 9, 2017. https://www.insidehighered.com/advice/2017/02/10/how-academic-funding-racialized-essay.

Sagar, Aparajita. 2019. "Institutional Climates and Women Faculty of Color: Overcoming Aversive Racism and Microaggressions in the Academy." *Susan Bulkeley Butler Center for Leadership and Excellence and ADVANCE Working Paper Series* 2 (2): 4–15. https://www.purdue.edu/butler/documents/5-WPS_Fall-2019-Sagar_Institutional-Climates-and-Women-Faculty-of-Color_Final.pdf.

Skallerup Bessette, Lee. 2020. "Staff Get Little to No Say in Campus Governance. That Must Change." *Chronicle of Higher Education*, September 22, 2020. https://www.chronicle.com/article/staff-get-little-to-no-say-in-campus-governance-that-must-change.

Sue, Derald Wing, Christina M. Capodilupo, Gina C. Torino, Jennifer M. Bucceri, Aisha M. B. Holder, Kevin L. Nadal, and Marta Esquilin. 2007. "Racial Microaggressions in Everyday Life: Implications for Clinical Practice." *American Psychologist* 62, no. 4 (May–June): 128–42. https://doi.org/10.1037/0003-066x.62.4.271.

Toutkoushian, Robert K., Marcia L. Bellas, and John V. Moore. 2007. "The Interaction Effects of Gender, Race, and Marital Status on Faculty Salaries." *Journal of Higher Education* 78 (5): 572–601. https://doi.org/10.1080/00221546.2007.11772330.

Young, Kathryn, Myron Anderson, and Saran Stewart. 2015. "Hierarchical Microaggressions in Higher Education." *Journal of Diversity in Higher Education* 8 (1): 61–71. http://dx.doi.org/10.1037/a0038464.

Mapping Place and Constructing Space

How Black Students Respond to Nonbelonging at a Predominantly White Institution

Jasmine L. Harris

Tensions between Black and white students on college campuses continue to rise around racism, perpetuating difficulties "fitting in" for Black students at predominantly white institutions (PWIs) despite institutional attempts to improve inclusivity. Though it's clear that Black students' experiences at PWIs are tenuous, what is less clear is how campus culture and campus space work together to impact how students feel about their integration in the campus community. Analysis of interview, focus group, and spatial mapping data from students at a PWI suggests that belonging is constructed via trust on campus. Black and white students distrust one another. For Black students, that lack of trust translates to feeling unsafe and disconnected in most common spaces on campus, like dorms, dining halls, and classrooms, and requires a reenvisioning of the campus map to maintain individual and group perceptions of safety. The inability of Black students to establish trust across racial and ethnic community groups on campus, and the subsequent necessity to rely on each other to ensure their safety, represents an institutional betrayal—a failure of the institution to live up to its claims of inclusivity to the detriment of Black students explicitly.

•

Higher education in the United States starts with the founding of Harvard in 1636, and then a ripple of institutions founded over the next 250 years. They trained all-white male students in professions like law, medicine, and ministry (Eckel and King 2004). This history created a cultural expectation of whiteness in higher education (Harris 2020). The broader institution is structured around white men. Their needs are prioritized in the organization and in the creation of college norms, values, language, and expectations (Ray 2019; Pauker, Apfelbaum, and Spitzer 2015; Gulati-Partee and Potapchuk 2014; Calmor 1995), despite the increasing introduction of "diversity initiatives" in these predominately white spaces.

In the 1960s, colleges and universities transitioned from all white, by law, to *predominantly* white institutions (PWIs); laws mandated the admission of minorities by race, sexuality, and religion (Clotfelter 2004; Brown v. Board of Education II 1955). In response, schools revamped institutional responses to growing tensions between white and nonwhite campus populations (Tatum 1997; Wilkerson 1992). However, even as institutions have become hyperaware of the potential for racist violence on campus, steps taken to change institutional practices over the last 60 years have not worked. In fact, there was a 77% year-to-year increase in incidents of white supremacist propaganda on college campuses during the 2017–18 academic year (Bauman 2018), a statistic that highlights the continued institutional betrayal of Black students attending PWIs. This paper seeks to understand how Black students construct belonging in a setting where they *should* belong, but don't. It asks where Black students perceive belonging at PWIs.

The Problem

There is something specific about the relationship between Black students and higher education that is not found among Asian and Latinx students and therefore demands study. Black students have lower graduation and retention rates (*JBHE* 2006; Nichols and Evans-Bell 2017), there are few Black faculty available for support on campus (McFarland et al. 2018; Li and Koebel 2017), and there are disproportionately few resources for programs targeting Black students (Ray 2017). Establishing belonging in this context must be difficult for Black students.

Individual belonging is part of one's conceptualization of identity (Butler 1990; Hall 2000; Lähdesmäki et al. 2016). Identity impacts belonging and vice versa (Derlan and Umaña-Taylor 2015). On college campuses, where unwelcome identities are predetermined (Juvonen 2006; Read, Archer, and Leathwood 2003) so, too, is accessible belonging. At PWIs, the "student" identity is immediately and perpetually fractured for Black students (Du Bois 1935; Tatum 1997; Ray 2017). Conversely, white college students are assured of at least basic belonging (Goldin and Katz 1999) because institutions are structured to meet their needs (Deil-Amen 2011).

Here, belonging is grounded in definitions of safety, as a condition of physical and psychological protection on campus and of having connections to other students, faculty, and staff on campus. This conceptualization captures the complicated relationship between students' desire for integration into the campus community and the need for safe havens to experience success on campus. Belonging is a contextually dependent (Benson 2014; Cuervo and Wyn 2014), public-versus-private concept (Poe et al. 2014; Fenster 2005). College campuses are uniquely both residential spaces, meant to feel like "home" (Winkle-Wagner 2009; Turner 1994), and public spaces where entrance is conditional (Antonsich 2010). For Black students, these simultaneously public and private contexts have acute impacts on their sense of belonging on campus (Harris 2020; Harper and Quaye 2007).

Perceived belonging, both geographic and social, is based on the development of boundaries and the potential penalties for crossing boundaries (Bennett 2014; Huot, Dodson, and Rudman 2014; Marcu 2014). Existing research on race and belonging agrees that for Black people in predominately white spaces, regular interactions with other Black peers is important to a prolonged sense of belonging (Derlan and Umaña-Taylor 2015; Solórzano, Ceja, and Yosso 2000). The availability of such interactions is determined by boundaries, real or imagined, in the space.

Campus spaces, the primary purposes of which are decided by the institution, become marked by the shared identities of those students who most frequent the spaces (Turner 1994). For Black students then, classrooms, residence and dining halls, gyms, and outdoor spaces dominated by the predominately white student body cannot also be spaces of contextual "affirmation-belonging" (Derlan and Umaña-Taylor 2015) because regular interactions with other Black students can't be guaranteed. Belonging on campus is multidimensional, based on fixed and fluid identities of race, ethnicity, and gender (Solórzano, Ceja, and Yosso 2000) but also on perceptions of fit, inclusion, and physical access (Bennett 2014; Marcu 2014). When colleges and universities pledge to provide equal educational experiences across racial lines but fail to provide these kinds of safe spaces, it constitutes a betrayal of both students and the institutional mission. This paper explores how Black students at a PWI responded to such failures.

Methods

The site of research is approximately 1,400 students, predominantly white (73%) and female (53%), with about 17% students of color. Data was collected October 2017–May 2018. An online survey was emailed to all students three times between October and December 2017. The demographic breakdown across the student body is 73% white, 8% Latinx, 7% Black, 5% Asian, 3% multiracial, and 4% "other." All students had an equal likelihood of participation regardless of racial and ethnic identity. At the end of the survey, students interested in interview participation were prompted to provide contact information and were contacted by student research assistants for scheduling. The same process was undertaken among interview participants to solicit focus group participants. Overall, 363 students completed the survey, 34 students participated in interviews, and 26 in focus groups. Ten-dollar Amazon gift cards were distributed as compensation for survey participation, and an additional $10 card was provided if students participated in interview or focus group data collection. The project was funded via grant support from the Pennsylvania Consortium for the Liberal Arts Colleges and the Arthur Vining Davis Foundations.

Principal data collectors were a mix of six Black students and three non-Black students on campus. Survey, interview, and focus group participation was predominately white, about 72% white students to 10% Black students, and the remaining were other students of color, representative of the overall student population. Student researchers also participated in group coding sessions with faculty principal investigators to analyze data. Buildings, paths, and public areas on campus mentioned in data collection as important to perceptions of belonging were mapped using ArcGIS software to create spatial understandings of belonging in the site.

Findings

Data was collected from all willing participants, regardless of racial or ethnic identities, and analyzed as a whole. Patterns of belonging development were identified within and across groups. In this section, Black student participants responses' are aggregated to highlight patterns specific to them and to avoid the trap of comparing their experiences to a white baseline. Instead, Black students' experiences on campus should be understood relative to the published institutional values in the site of research, which include establishing a welcoming, equitable, and inclusive environment for a diverse community of students, faculty, and staff. The findings detail, often using students' own words, interventions they've undertaken to overcome this institution's inability to match values and action.

Overall, Black students felt less safe and less connected on campus than their white peers, and therefore were more concerned with space and spatial boundaries in their movements across campus. Black students reported hyperawareness of their spatial location and other people present because they perceive their race as perpetually influencing their experiences. Most importantly, they don't perceive the institution or its representatives as being invested in improving their experiences, intensifying perceptions of nonbelonging among Black students in the site.

What Is Safety on Campus?

Black students at this PWI made direct connections between the consistency of their perceived nonbelonging and their sense of safety on campus. In spaces dominated by students, like dorms, dining halls, and party spaces, their sense of safety is low, especially compared to academic buildings. For white students, however, there's little difference in perceived safety building-to-building. Instead, their sense of safety is steeped in fear of the other, only focused on times (nighttime is seen as inherently unsafe among these students) when the belonging of strangers is harder to "identify" and is perceived as endangering students.

The social and psychological costs of feeling unsafe on campus mean Black students have entirely different experiences than white students. Their racial identity is as important to what happens to them on campus as any other characteristic. Toni, a junior Black woman, and Nicole, a senior Black woman, put it best in their focus group session:

TONI: I can't change the color of my skin, so [feeling unsafe] is [my] reality.

NICOLE: I don't think someone like me can feel safe on this campus. . . . I feel like we constantly have to walk on eggshells around this campus because we're Black.

Black students defined safety on campus as feeling "comfortable, relaxed, and at ease," and "like [I'm] not in any danger," where there are "no apparent threats," but few identified public spaces where that sense of safety was present. White students only noted feeling unsafe in areas where "it's so dark at night," or when "locals show up at parties," where and when the barriers between the private campus and the surrounding communities become unclear for them. Black student participants, by contrast, identified their dorm room as the only place available to feel safe, and even there, describe fellow white students as unpredictable, making all their moves across campus precarious ones.

Sophomore Lisa discusses her inability to feel safe and comfortable even in her dorm.

LISA: There's been a lot of racial . . . not discrimination, but there are just things that people who live [in my dorm] say and do that make me uncomfortable. Especially my roommates.

INTERVIEWER: Have you addressed these issues with your roommates?

LISA: Yes.

INTERVIEWER: Has anything changed since then?

LISA: No.

Sam, a senior Black man, synthesizes the relationship between race, space, and belonging on campus. His certainty in the shared experiences of other Black students leads him to believe the institution is responsible for problems he perceives as "known." Sam tells us, "For

Black students there's never really a safe space . . . I think it's [the institution's] job to really support us." Toni adds the qualifier, "[where] you get to be yourself," to the first part of Sam's statement. For her, and many Black participants, lack of safety also means limited self-expression and an expectation of nonbelonging on campus. Both Sam and Toni are expressing feelings of betrayal, where the school administrators promised safety and equity, but Black students feel neither. The inability to feel safe anywhere reveals the tenuousness of Black students' situations. Small numbers prevent the development of appropriate spaces on campus and leave Black students without the social and psychological protections offered by deep intragroup connections.

Connections

Part of what makes students, regardless of identity, feel like they belong on campus is the availability of support systems catering to their needs and interests. Student perceptions of campus belonging are influenced by the amount of integration and regulation across identity groups. Groups provide a sense of safety and connection, especially among minorities in marginalized spaces. For Black students with very few means of institutional support, it's hard to perceive belonging at all. To attain some marginal membership within the college community, Black students compartmentalize their cultural membership in exchange for their college student identity. They aren't afforded the opportunity to exist as whole people; instead they must develop a "double-consciousness, this sense of always looking at one's self through the eyes of others'" (Du Bois [1903] 2012, 8). Without the support of deep, interconnected networks, Black students instead develop bonds based on survival rather than commonalities, weakening their resolve to withstand racism in the site and leaving them feeling lonely in comparison to their white peers.

Here again, Nicole details the burdensome minutiae of being Black at a PWI. She finds the weight of representation perpetual, explaining, "My biggest adjustment was the race difference. I grew up in a Black city and here I am the only Black person in the classroom. . . . I have to defend everything Black." Nicole's statement means her learning is affected by her race, adding an extra layer of stress in the classroom. At PWIs, a lack of support systems for Black students negatively impacts their daily lives.

This stress and anxiety manifests physically. Toni reveals, "I have panic attacks constantly because [I'm] so stressed and anxious." As a junior, she's already spent almost three years in a perpetual state of psychological distress.

Sam reveals that the perpetual experiences of stress and anxiety described by Toni drove him to stop actively engaging with other members of the campus community. He adds, "I isolated myself here and I just don't want to interact with people [anymore]." This isolation stunts Black students' development of belonging on campus. For them, it is important to identify a few private spaces where smaller, and, therefore, safer networks are developed. Thus, a sense of safety is increased and at least a little belonging is perceived. This approach allows Black students to make connections with like-minded students without threats to personal safety.

Black students' belonging directly impacts their mental health even if that isn't the language they use. Black students who perceive low perceptions of belonging have greater fear and anxiety. They feel threatened and are in constant fear of being accosted, specifically because of their racial identity. If conflict occurs, they feel as though authorities will quickly believe white students because of their identity. Ultimately, this causes Black students to feel helpless, creating a greater strain on them as they try to complete undergraduate degrees. To be Black students at a PWI means never truly belonging, so their safety is always in jeopardy.

Mapping Campus

Black students' perceived disconnections from the campus community are evidence of poor integration and limited development of support networks. Black student participants were explicit in descriptions of campus engagement vis-à-vis complex space-making. Not only do they make note of racist experiences on campus, but they're also sharing those anecdotes across a network of Black students. These anecdotes are translated into warnings of where to go, and more importantly, where not to go—in the spirit of *The Negro Motorist Green-Book* (Green 1936–1951), a written record of safe spaces for Black folks traveling across the United States under the tyranny of Jim Crow. In this section, interview and focus group data is overlayed on to a physical map of the campus to create visual representation of these welcome versus unwelcome spaces building-to-building and place-to-place.

Black students develop and reference revised versions of the campus map, built on their verbal warnings, to construct safety, support, and connection in tangible form. For example, almost every Black student participant identified Party Hall, a dorm on campus well known as a space where large parties are regularly held (often hosted by student athletes), as an unsafe space, one they actively and purposefully avoid. There is no written record of this among them, but Black students still asserted their expectations of poor treatment should they enter this space and their continued willingness to opt out of attendance at events there as a mode of protection.

Junior student Carmen understands the importance of space on campus to exist without constant reminders of her race. She explained: "I had such horrible experiences dealing with white [people], and I think [on campus] they see me more as a Brown student, so I never feel they [think] 'you matter.'" To "matter" here is to be fully integrated and as accepted on campus as their white peers. Space is an important piece of belonging. Black students admitted those spaces where white students feel comfortable often feel "off limits" to them. Lin, a senior, describes his inability to "fit in": "[I feel safe] nowhere . . . because there's always a white person who probably doesn't want me there."

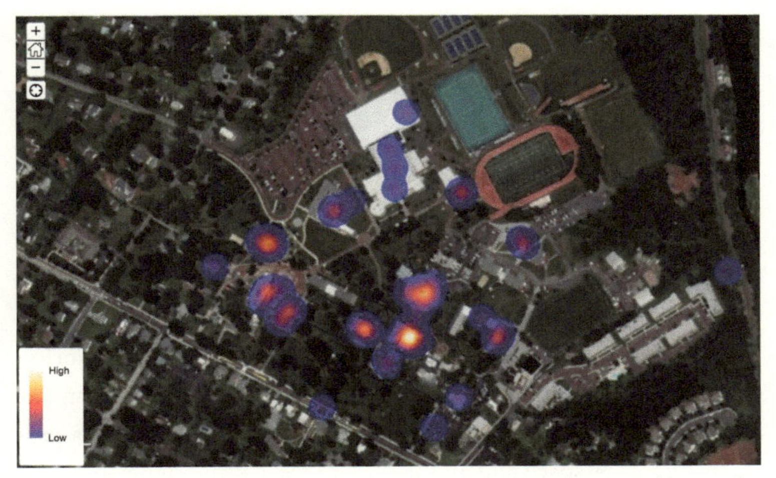

Heat Map of Perceived Safety & Connection on Campus (Low–High). Map by author.

The map above takes the verbal description of safe and unsafe spaces from interview and focus group data to create a physical representation of where students feel safe and connected on campus. Heat mapping is a method of visualizing social phenomenon via geographic clustering. Aggregating this data into map form using GIS software creates an index of student belonging across the site. The mostly purple areas are spaces where Black students perceive greater belonging because their sense of safety, and perceived connection to their peers, is more likely. By contrast, red and orange areas denote spaces with the number of Black students who reported incidents of racism are higher, increasing their need for hypervigilance on campus. For Black students, a sense of safety and connection is only high where they are assured about the absence of white students. Because the vast majority of the campus is comprised of white student spaces, Black students make more effort in planning their movements across campus than do white students.

Belonging among all students, regardless of racial or ethnic identity, is lower in public campus spaces like the dining hall, gym, field house, and administrative buildings like the president's home and the deans' offices. But Black students were more likely to report feeling unsafe in these settings, and were also more likely to report feeling unsafe and disconnected in private spaces like dorms, bathrooms, and entire academic buildings.

Students across campus develop affinities for particular spaces and reconstruct the purpose and primacy of said spaces using a majority-rules policy, where those students with the largest numbers impact who else can or will enter. Black students, therefore, describe a proverbial fight for space and an inability to feel a sense of belonging in spaces where they are always outnumbered. Instead, Black students map their movements across campus in a deliberate fashion, particularly to maintain a sense of safety.

Black and white students distrust one another, and for Black students, that lack of trust translates to feeling unsafe and disconnected in most common spaces on campus. This distrust manifests as a general sense of nonbelonging that is not perceived by white students. Weak feelings of belonging lead to more negative experiences because they create anxiety and a commitment in students to splitting their social identities.

Conclusions

The construction of belonging is predicated on a unique mix of perceptions of safety, purposeful integration, and access to campus spaces where belonging is guaranteed. For Black students, trusting the predominately white students, faculty, and administrators around them is important to a positive construction of belonging and perceived safety and connection on campus. Overall, there is a disconnection between Black students' perceptions of belonging, their perceptions of the institution's allotments of space, and success in their continued efforts to improve inclusion on campus.

Though administrators in the site of research cannot control Black students' feelings, participants describe an environment where trust and support are low. Because administrators, faculty, and students are mostly white, policies developed to improve student experiences are innately beneficial to white students, despite institutional pledges to improve inclusivity, leaving Black students feeling, at best, unsupported, and, at worst, wholly unwelcome. They are unable to become seamlessly integrated members of the campus community, as white administrators want them to be, because their orientation to and relationship with the college campus is racialized in ways it isn't for white students. They cannot focus exclusively on schoolwork or socializing because of this extra level of effort required to protect their safety and find community in inherently unwelcoming environments. This puts Black students at a disadvantage academically, socially, and psychologically, compared to their white peers. As PWIs seek to improve inclusion policies and programs, leaders need to develop a better understanding of how minorities construct and perceive belonging, in order to ensure those policies' effectiveness for Black students.

Works Cited

Antonsich, Marco. 2010. "Searching for Belonging—An Analytical Framework." *Geography Compass* 4 (6): 644–59. https://doi.org/10.1111/j.1749-8198.2009.00317.x.

Bauman, Dan. 2018. "Hate Crimes on Campuses Are Rising, New FBI Data Show." *Chronicle of Higher Education*, November 14, 2018. https://www.chronicle.com/article/Hate-Crimes-on-Campuses-Are/245093.

Bennett, Julia. 2014. "Gifted Places: The Inalienable Nature of Belonging in Place." *Environment and Planning D: Society and Space* 32 (4): 658–71. https://doi.org/10.1068/d4913p.

Benson, Michaela. 2014. "Trajectories of Middle-Class Belonging: The Dynamics of Place Attachment and Classed Identities." *Urban Studies*, 51 (14): 3097–112. http://dx.doi.org/10.1177/0042098013516522.

Brown v. Board of Education II. 1955. 349 U.S. 294.

Butler, Judith. 1990. *Gender Trouble: Feminism and the Subversion of Identity*. London: Taylor & Francis.

Calmore, John O. 1995. "Racialized Space and the Culture of Segregation: Hewing a Stone of Hope from a Mountain of Despair." *University of Pennsylvania Law Review* 143, no. 5 (May): 1233–73. https://doi.org/10.2307/3312475.

Clotfelter, Charles T. 2004. "Private Schools, Segregation, and the Southern States." Paper presented at the Conference on the Resegregation of Southern Schools. Chapel Hill, NC, August 29–30, 2002.

Cuervo, Hernan, and Johanna Wyn. 2014. "Reflections on the Use of Spatial and Relational Metaphors in Youth Studies." *Journal of Youth Studies* 17 (7): 901–15. http://dx.doi.org/10.1080/13676261.2013.878796.

Deil-Amen, Regina. 2011. "Socio-Academic Integrative Moments: Rethinking Academic and Social Integration Among Two-Year College Students in Career-Related Programs." *Journal of Higher Education* 82 (1): 54–91. https://doi.org/10.1080/00221546.2011.11779085.

Derlan, Chelsea L., and Adriana J. Umaña-Taylor. "Brief Report: Contextual Predictors of African American Adolescents' Ethnic-Racial Identity Affirmation-Belonging and Resistance to Peer Pressure." *Journal of Adolescence* 41 (1): 1–6. https://doi.org/10.1016/j.adolescence.2015.02.002.

Du Bois, W. E. B. (1903) 2012. *The Souls of Black Folk*. Edited and with an introduction by Brent Hayes Edwards. Reprint, Oxford: Oxford University Press.

Du Bois, W. E. B. 1935. "Does the Negro Need Separate Schools?" *Journal of Negro Education* 4, no. 3 (July): 328–35. https://doi.org/10.2307/2291871.

Eckel, Peter D., and Jacqueline E. King. 2004. *An Overview of Higher Education in the United States: Diversity, Access, and the Role of the Marketplace*. Washington, D.C.: American Council on Education. https://www.acenet.edu/news-room/Documents/Overview-of-Higher-Education-in-the-United-States-Diversity-Access-and-the-Role-of-the-Marketplace-2004.pdfn.

Fenster, Tovi. 2005. "The Right to the Gendered City: Different Formations of Belonging in Everyday Life." *Journal of Gender Studies* 14 (3): 217–31. https://doi.org/10.1080/09589230500264109.

Goldin, Claudia, and Lawrence F. Katz. 1999. "Human Capital and Social Capital: The Rise of Secondary Schooling In America, 1910–1940." *Journal of*

Interdisciplinary History 29, no. 4 (Winter): 683–723. http://www.jstor.org/stable/206979.

Green, Victor H. 1936–1951. *The Negro Motorist Green-Book*. New York: V. H. Green. Available at New York Public Library Digital Collections, http://digitalcollections.nypl.org/collections/9ea5d5b0-1117-0132-7932-58d385a7b928.

Gulati-Partee, Gita, and Maggie Potapchuk. 2014. "Paying Attention to White Culture and Privilege: A Missing Link to Advancing Racial Equity." *Foundation Review* 6, no. 1 (April): 25–38. http://dx.doi.org/10.9707/1944-5660.1189.

Hall, Stuart. 2000. "Who Needs 'Identity'?" In *Identity: A Reader*, edited by Paul du Gay, Jessica Evans, and Peter Redman, 15–30. London: Sage.

Harper, Shaun R., and Stephen John Quaye. 2007. "Student Organizations as Venues for Black Identity Expression and Development Among African American Male Student Leaders." *Journal of College Student Development* 48 (2): 127–44. https://psycnet.apa.org/doi/10.1353/csd.2007.0012.

Harris, Jasmine L. 2020. "Inheriting Educational Capital: Black College Students, Nonbelonging, and Ignored Legacies at Predominantly White Institutions." *WSQ: Women's Studies Quarterly* 48, no. 1–2 (Summer): 84–102. https://www.jstor.org/stable/26979203.

Huot, Suzanne, Belinda Dodson, and Deborah Laliberte Rudman. 2014. "Negotiating Belonging Following Migration: Exploring the Relationship Between Place and Identity in Francophone Minority Communities." *Canadian Geographer* 58, no. 3 (February): 329–40. http://dx.doi.org/10.1111/cag.12067.

JBHE (*Journal of Blacks in Higher Education*). 2006. "Black Student College Graduation Rates Remain Low, But Modest Progress Begins to Show." http://www.jbhe.com/features/50_blackstudent_gradrates.html.

Juvonen, Joana. 2006. "Sense of Belonging, Social Bonds, and School Functioning." In *Handbook of Educational Psychology*, edited by Patricia A. Alexander and Philip H. Winne, 655–74. Lawrence, KS: Erlbaum Associates Publishers.

Lähdesmäki, Tuuli, Tuija Saresma, Kaisa Hiltunen, Saar Jäntti, Nina Sääskilahti, Antti Vallius, and Kaisa Ahvenjärvi. 2016. "Fluidity and Flexibility of 'Belonging': Uses of the Concept in Contemporary Research." *Acta Sociologica* 59 (3): 233–47. https://doi.org/10.1177/0001699316633099.

Li, Diyi, and Cody Koedel. 2017. "Representation and Salary Gaps by Race-Ethnicity and Gender at Selective Public Universities." *Educational Researcher* 46 (7): 343–54. https://doi.org/10.3102/0013189X17726535.

Pauker, Kristin, Evan P. Apfelbaum, and Brian Spitzer. 2015. "When Societal Norms and Social Identity Collide: The Race Talk Dilemma for Racial Minority Children." *Social Psychological and Personality Science* 6, no. 8 (November): 887–95. https://doi.org/10.1177/1948550615598379.

Marcu, Silvia. 2014. "Geography of Belonging: Nostalgic Attachment, Transnational Home, and Global Mobility among Romanian Immigrants in Spain." *Journal of Cultural Geography* 31 (3): 326–45. https://doi.org/10.1080/08873631.2014.945719.

McFarland, Joel, Bill Hussar, Xiaolei Wang, Jijun Zhang, Ke Wang, Amy Rathbun, Amy Barmer, Emily Forrest Cataldi, and Farrah Bullock Mann. 2018. *The Condition of Education 2018* (NCES 2018-144). U.S. Department of Education. Washington, D.C. *https://files.eric.ed.gov/fulltext/ED583502.pdf.*

Nichols, Andrew H., and Denzel Evans-Bell. 2017. *A Look at Black Student Success: Identifying Top- and Bottom-Performing Institutions.* Washington, D.C.: Education Trust. https://edtrust.org/wp-content/uploads/2014/09/A-Look-at-Black-Student-Success.pdf.

Poe, Melissa R., Joyce LeCompte, Rebecca McLain, and Patrick Hurley. 2014. "Urban Foraging and the Relational Ecologies of Belonging." *Social & Cultural Geography* 15 (8): 901–19. http://dx.doi.org/10.1080/14649365.2014.908232.

Ray, Victor. 2017. "The Racialization of Academic Funding." *Inside Higher Ed*, February 9, 2017. https://www.insidehighered.com/advice/2017/02/10/how-academic-funding-racialized-essay.

Ray, Victor. 2019. "A Theory of Racialized Organizations." *American Sociological Review* 84 (1): 26–53. https://doi.org/10.1177/0003122418822335.

Read, Barbara, Louise Archer, and Carole Leathwood. 2003. "Challenging Cultures? Student Conceptions of 'Belonging' and 'Isolation' at a Post-1992 University." *Studies in Higher Education* 28 (3): 261–77. https://doi.org/10.1080/03075070309290.

Solórzano, Daniel, Miguel Ceja, and Tara J. Yosso. 2000. "Critical Race Theory, Racial Microaggressions, and Campus Racial Climate: The Experiences of African American College Students." *Journal of Negro Education* 69, no. 1 (Winter–Spring): 60–73. https://www.jstor.org/stable/i326903.

Turner, Caroline Sotello Viernes. 1994. "Guests in Someone Else's House: Students of Color." *Review of Higher Education* 17 (4): 355–70. https://doi.org/10.1353/rhe.1994.0008.

Tatum, Beverly D. 1997. *"Why Are All the Black Kids Sitting Together in the Cafeteria?" and Other Conversations About Race.* New York: Basic Books.

Wilkerson, Isabel. 1992. "Racial Tension Erupts, Tearing a College Apart." *New York Times*, April 13, 1992. https://www.nytimes.com/1992/04/13/us/racial-tension-erupts-tearing-a-college-apart.html.

Winkle-Wagner, Rachelle. 2009. "The Perpetual Homelessness of College Experiences: Tensions Between Home and Campus for African American Women." *Review of Higher Education* 33 (1): 1–36. http://dx.doi.org/10.1353/rhe.0.0116.

Part IV

Disability, Health, and (Non)Normative Bodies

Disability (In)Justice

Disabled Scholars in an Ableist World

Rachael McCollum and Krista L. Benson

One of the experiences of disability that disabled people share with each other, but rarely with abled people, is that few people can imagine disabled potential or creativity. Too often, disabled people are targets of pity or anxiety from abled people. This limitation in the understanding and imaginations of abled people produces circumstances that make it difficult for disabled people to thrive. We crafted this essay to share our experience of proposing a disability studies research project that was stopped by ableism before it could begin.

We are, respectively, a recently graduated student and an assistant professor at Grand Valley State University. In 2019 and 2020, we submitted a project proposal to a program for undergraduate student research or creative projects mentored by a faculty member at our institution. This program is designed to give undergraduate researchers the opportunity to engage in research design and implementation with a faculty mentor, one of the undergraduate high-impact activities that can encourage retention and graduation. Rachael outlines the experience of submitting to—and subsequently being denied by—this program. Although the rejections started as a form of tacit ableism—the committee neither understanding disability studies as a field nor the field's conversations around language—the second rejection moved into explicit ableism. Because of the way the committee read a disability studies project framed by a disabled undergraduate scholar, the project was never given a chance.

We explore this experience as a form of institutional failure, one in which the everyday norms of disability injustice become apparent. We frame disability injustice as the opposite of disability justice. Disability justice is a framework that was created by people who were often invisibilized by disability rights activists and movements. These populations include those people with disabilities (or disabled people; see "person-first" discussion below) who are BIPOC, queer, transgender, unhoused, immigrants, and other communities caught up in the intertwinings of ableism, racism, settler colonialism, heterosexism, and other systems of domination. From this vantage point, "Disability Justice holds a vision born out of collective struggle, drawing upon the legacies of cultural and spiritual resistance within a thousand underground paths, igniting small persistent fires of rebellion in everyday life" (Berne 2017, 150). We write this piece as two disabled people in academia, one who is queer and disabled and trying to figure out if we have a place here. We see this essay as an opportunity to highlight a case of institutional failure and systemic ableism and to explore the larger stakes of ableism as embedded in higher education in the United States. We ask: Is there a way to find disability justice in higher education? We worry the answer is no.

Disability Injustice: A Research Project Stopped in Its Tracks (Rachael's Story)

I have always been a curious person. I like to learn new things, and I fill my time absorbing information about things that catch my interest. This is one of my favorite things about being autistic. When I like something, I love it. When I'm learning new information, I dive in headfirst. When I'm interested in something, I want to drown myself in it, to let the information and the experience fill my mind until there is nothing else there and I am happy.

This desire to learn has driven me forward in my educational experience and has allowed me to find great joy and fulfillment in my studies. I enjoy being in college more than I enjoyed high school, for a number of reasons but primarily because college allows me much greater choice in the subjects I learn about.

I was a double major in women, gender, and sexuality studies, and film and video production. I love both of these majors, but I especially love the places where they overlap. I have taken as many classes as I can on subjects related to marginalized groups in film, representation in the media, and how society and media are influenced by each other. But this wasn't enough. I still wanted to learn more.

As a disabled person, I was particularly interested in learning about disabled individuals on and behind the screen, but there were no classes on the subject at my university. I decided that I wanted to commit to learning more and sought out the Office of Undergraduate Research and Scholarship to explore my options.

The first year that I submitted a research application, I was denied. I was told that my plans for the project had not been sufficiently clear; I received a handful of other comments providing secondary reasons for my rejection. I was disappointed, but I accepted it. I could understand their point about clarity, and I resolved that I would do better on those matters on a future application. But I also sent an email to the office immediately after reading the letter to inform them of an issue I saw with one of the secondary comments.

The comment suggested that I should have utilized "person-first language" in my application, using terms like "person with a disability" rather than "disabled person." I took issue with this attempt to correct my language, as I knew that the discussion around person-first or identity-first language was far more complicated than they were suggesting. In particular, within the autistic community, the common consensus (though not universally agreed upon) is identity first: "autistic person" rather than "person with autism." It's also the language I use to describe myself, and I bristled at the reviewer's attempt to police the language I use for myself.

Despite this disheartening first attempt, I submitted a second application the following year, knowing it would be my last chance to do so. I knew that my writing ability and grades had improved since the first application, and I ensured that the proposal took into account the advice from the previous year and explained a bit more about the field of study, so that the faculty review committee could better understand both the project goals and the choice to use identity-first language. I disclosed my disability in this application, as it was important to mention that I was a disabled person writing within disability studies. I also wanted to clarify that my GPA was not an accurate measure of my abilities, as my GPA was higher after diagnosis, and to show that I was capable of the work without needing the extra support my GPA might suggest. I felt very good about my application, and I believed my chances of approval were high, so I was crushed when a second rejection letter arrived.

In the committee's feedback, I was told that a "lack of clear project description and student motivation and preparation statement" were the reasons for this rejection. I was told that the goals and significance of the project were unfocused, despite the time taken to explain the relevance of my project to the field of disability studies. The committee didn't seem to understand what the goals were of research in the humanities. I had been told previously that the projects handled through the office were generally more focused on the sciences, and disability studies is a little-known field even within some humanities. They didn't understand the point of my research from the start.

Despite being the primary author of the proposal, I was told that it was unclear if "the student" understood the project. The strengths of the proposal were attributed to Professor Benson rather than myself, though I was the one who took the lead on the proposal, with support from Professor Benson.

Most upsetting of all, it was explicitly stated that my preparation and commitment to the project were in doubt because of my prior academic performance and "self-identified disability." Rather than understanding that this disclosure was to inform the committee of my *strengths* on this project, they seemed to view it as a statement that I would need more support than average. I was devastated and angry. I had been turned down *because* I am disabled. No matter what other flaws my proposal had, my disability had been assumed to be one of them. The committee didn't seem to realize that it was discriminatory. My ability status should not have been mentioned as a problem in the review, let alone in the letter.

Yet it was. And in that light, the rest of the letter took on a different meaning. It was assumed that my professor took the lead on the proposal, which now seemed to be a damning slight against my abilities. The strengths of the proposal were attributed to the person the committee presumed was abled, rather than the one they knew to be disabled. Because they knew of my disabilities, there was an assumption that I couldn't create knowledge from my own experience that was also informed by the academic literature. This was a failure of the institution to provide disability justice—a kind of betrayal.

In effect, my chances were slim from the beginning. The decision was grounded in ableism on two fronts. First, the committee didn't understand the importance of disability studies as a field and assumed that my project was meaningless because it would have provided an interpretive analysis rather than a specific set of numbers or facts. Second, I was assumed to be less capable of research because of my disability, even though I had shown myself to be far more adept at schoolwork since I had been diagnosed and began to receive treatment.

I am an optimist at heart, and I had trusted that disclosure of my disability would be understood as relevant only to my prediagnosis performance rather than to my overall ability. The betrayal I felt upon learning it had not been understood this way was made worse by my inexperience with discrimination of this kind. I have experienced ableism my entire life, but most of it has not been directly attributed to my disability. As someone with an undiagnosed but lifelong disability, much of the ableism I have encountered was unknowing. I was judged for my autistic *traits*, not my autism, because no one had known that I was autistic at the time.

I try to give people the benefit of the doubt, and though previous ableism in my life was still discriminatory, I had convinced myself that at least people hadn't realized what they were doing. If they had known about my disability, they might have been kinder. But now I had no such excuses for their unfairness. They knew that I was disabled, and this was the exact reason they rejected me. It was a stark reminder that my ability status is tied to assumptions about my capability and intelligence.

The reason that I contacted the Office of Undergraduate Research and Scholarship after the first rejection was not to appeal my case and be allowed to ask for reconsideration. I was willing to accept their reasons that I had not been chosen, without questioning whether I had ever had a fair chance to begin with. On that occasion, all I wanted to do was educate them about the language issue that they had clearly misunderstood. My concern was that other disabled students would run into the same issue when they applied or that those committee members would take their ignorance into the rest of their academic lives, feeling content to correct disabled students, colleagues, and people outside academia on the language they use. The second rejection suggested I was right to be concerned.

Broader Impacts of Ableism in Higher Education

Any story of institutional failure is a story of loss—of opportunity, connection, the promise of education. In the case of ableism in higher education, individual stories of institutional failure also connect to concerning patterns of exclusion of disabled people. The U.S. Congress passed laws to require and structure inclusion of disabled people in K–12 and higher education. These include Section 504 of the Rehabilitation Act (1973), the Individuals with Disabilities Education Act (IDEA) (1990), and the Americans with Disabilities Act (ADA) (1990). However, despite these laws and the structures they embed in education to provide accessible education to disabled people, we still see disabled people disproportionately underserved in higher education. One of the reasons we wanted to write this article is because we are worried about disabled students who will apply for intensive research grants or other high-impact learning opportunities who may run into the same barriers we experienced. Our experience highlights why accommodations are useful but not in themselves sufficient if we seek to include and value disabled people in and across higher education.

These structures of exclusion extend into the workplace as well, and educational exclusion of disabled people is connected to professional exclusion. According to a report from the U.S. Bureau of Labor Statistics (2020), in 2019 only 28.2% of disabled college graduates were employed, compared to 75.5% of nondisabled college grads. According to this same source, only 15.5% of disabled high school graduates were employed. For disabled people who are employed, they earn just $0.61 for every dollar a nondisabled person earns, with disabled people of color earning even less (Yin, Shaewita, and Megra 2014).

Universities have not succeeded in being places where justice for disabled people is likely or even possible. Aimee Morrison points to a tension in disability accommodations in universities for students, staff, and faculty when she notes that these processes attempt "to contain and control difference in such a way as to leave intact the fundamentally ableist set of values, practices, and built environments that constitute the institution known as 'the university'" (2019, 694). This does not call into question the ways that disability accommodation structures provide avenues for more equitable access to education—

they absolutely do that work. However, as Morrison points out, the bureaucratic processes of accommodation and the medical legitimacy of diagnosis do not address the structures of ableism that are embedded in higher education.

Can There Be Disability Justice in Higher Education?

In the end, we each attempted to use the systems available to us at our institution to try to address these issues of institutional failure and betrayal. We met with one of the associate vice presidents of diversity and inclusion at the institution to discuss our concerns of disability discrimination. She spoke with the director of the Office of Undergraduate Research and Scholarship, and there were some assurances of changes at the committee level, specifically that members would be more aware of structural and interpersonal ableism. Yet no real change has happened at the time of our writing.

The question remains for us, but also more broadly in higher education, Where is the space not only for disability inclusion but disability justice? This essay highlights a set of circumstances that affected the two of us, though obviously, circumstances that most directly negatively impacted Rachael, as the author with less institutional power. Of course, we are not the only disabled people trying to carve out spaces in higher education that allow us to thrive. In reflecting on this experience, Rachael considers: "These events hurt me personally, but they also make me worry for the disabled students to come along behind me. These individuals on committees are making decisions that will have a great impact on many students' lives, and they think that these are acceptable reasons to hold disabled students back. This is about more than just me and my desire to do a research project. This is a symptom of a problem that affects disabled students across academia." The myth that we are individuals whose experiences only impact us is an ableist (and colonial and racist) fiction. Disabled people function in communities whenever possible because we must. It's impossible to see this experience as only reflecting our experiences—instead, it tells us exactly how little higher education institutions value *all* disabled people.

Acknowledgments

We would like to thank Dr. Jae Basiliere for their feedback on an earlier draft of this essay, and we offer many thanks to the editors of this volume for their helpful edits, questions, and thoughts that helped improve the quality of the final essay. Rachael would also like to thank her family and friends for encouraging her to stand up to this and all other instances of ableism, without which encouragement she would likely not have written this.

Works Cited

Berne, Patty. 2017. "Skin, Tooth, and Bone—the Basis of Our Movement Is People: A Disability Justice Primer." *Reproductive Health Matters* 25 (50): 149–50. https://doi.org/10.1080/09688080.2017.1335999.

U.S. Bureau of Labor Statistics. 2020. "Persons with a Disability: Labor Force Characteristics News Release." https://www.bls.gov/news.release/archives/disabl_02262020.htm.

Morrison, Aimee. 2019. "(Un)Reasonable, (Un)Necessary, and (In)Appropriate: Biographic Mediation of Neurodivergence in Academic Accommodations." *biography* 42 (3): 693–719. https://www.jstor.org/stable/26849029.

Yin, Michelle, Dahlia Shaewitz, and Mahlet Megra. 2014. *An Uneven Playing Field: The Lack of Equal Pay for People with Disabilities*. Washington, D.C.: American Institutes of Research, December 2014. https://www.air.org/sites/default/files/Lack%20of%20Equal%20Pay%20for%20People%20with%20Disabilities_Dec%2014.pdf.

20

Audre Lorde's Army of One-Breasted Women

Sara A. Mata

Exploring the experiences of women faculty diagnosed with breast cancer, the women's voices provided visibility to their circumstances, including maneuvering gendered institutional structures of higher education. Historical context and other factors influence and contribute to gender inequities in faculty experiences, particularly for those with cancer, suggesting they do not belong. Bringing awareness to circumstances of experiencing breast cancer while in a tenure-track role is meant to enlighten and advocate for equity in academia for those dealing with a life-threatening disease. This study was based on five women representing various institutions across the United States, all of whom agreed to share their stories. I use quotes from Audre Lorde's *The Cancer Journals* (1997) as captions for each painting included herein, speaking to themes describing the many ways women with cancer felt they did not belong in academia. The paintings are my own.

Agency and support are critical to enduring inequitable organizational cultures and power dynamics. For the women in this study, finding agency and supportive spaces required intentional and strategic efforts on their part. Rather than feeling an innate sense of belonging and support, the women had to manage, adjust, and respond to circumstances of dealing with cancer, at both personal and professional levels. These efforts were personally taxing and professionally critical, as being a faculty member was an important piece of their identity, especially when so much of the academy was unforgiving

I could die of difference, or live—myriad selves.

and left women feeling detached and invisible. Balancing treatments versus teaching, time off versus tenure, the myriad of their selves often became an indefinite spectrum of identities that each woman had to balance while managing their professional contributions and personal well-being.

A sense of belonging and connectedness should not be underestimated, especially for individuals who identify as being part of one or more socially minoritized identities. The stories shared by the women highlighted how valuable and important a sense of connection was to their self-preservation. Actions such as negotiation, comfort, and reassessing responsibilities demonstrate how the women survived an

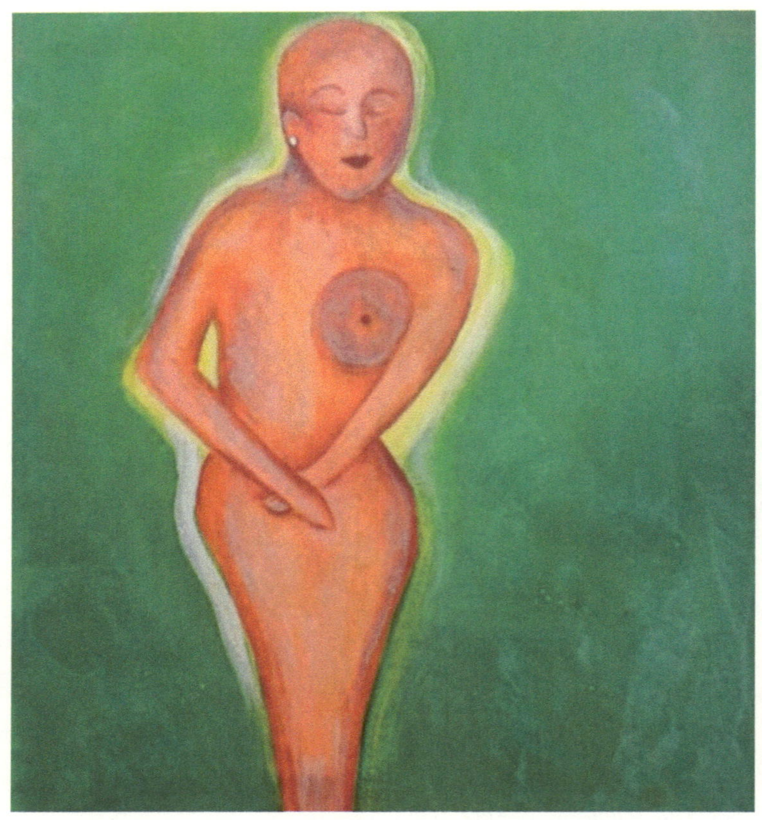

I say the love of women healed me.

organizational structure that did not demonstrate an ethic of care or support. It was the relationships the women built and sustained, particularly when they felt higher education had betrayed them, that provided personal support and encouragement as their personal and professional lives intersected in ways that created a divergence of identities and expectations. The women's experiences highlighted the importance of personal circles of support to sustain them during their journey.

The women felt pressured to conform to socialized expectations and power dynamics of patriarchy. The women negotiated wearing

Being one-breasted does not mean being unfashionable.

head wraps, scarves, and even wigs at times as they navigated the social narrative of femininity and their efforts to conceal their personal fights and experiences with cancer. Further demonstrating feelings of invisibility, vulnerability, and institutional betrayal, the women's stories showcase concerns and uncertainties about the academy's expectations of what a woman professor should look like.

Dynamics of cancer caused women to feel both visible and invisible. These feelings came to light as the women described the pressures of physical representation associated with being a woman fac-

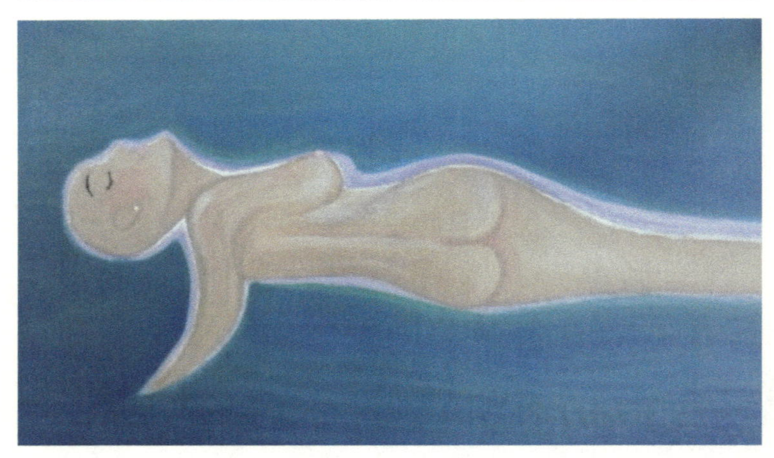

And that visibility which makes us most vulnerable is that which also is the source of our greatest strength.

ulty member. Further, the women highlighted acts of institutional betrayal—feeling shunned and discarded by the institution because of the impacts of their cancer and disconnects with their experiences and needs as faculty members. Women had to gauge who was trustworthy and potentially supportive; the presence and value of trust was incredibly significant to counter the vulnerability of visibility and unfortunate circumstances of having cancer.

A recent article from the *Philadelphia Inquirer* (Reyes 2021) describes how Temple University's sick-leave policy caused library worker Latanya Jenkins to go to work sick and in pain, and "ran her into the ground." Latanya died of metastatic breast cancer, and co-workers say the school's policy made her choose between her health and her job. Despite all her efforts of balancing the aftereffects of her treatment, she worried about disciplinary actions for taking time off. Through ten years of service, Latanya maintained a dedication to her career, applying for permanence and attempting to appease her institution. Yet her situation, and many others similar to Latanya's, demonstrates the lack of humanity and the betrayal by institutions of higher education.

My hope is that bringing visibility to the women who shared their experiences brings an awareness of how institutions do little to accommodate those who do not fit the norm. A lesson the past years have taught us all is that no position should ever be worth the sacrifice of a life. And yet we must continue to challenge policies, procedures, and the lack of support in institutions that fail to provide an inclusive environment for all to belong.

Works Cited

Lorde, Audre. 1997. *The Cancer Journals*. San Francisco: Aunt Lute Books.

Reyes, Juliana Feliciano. 2021. "After a Temple Librarian Died, Coworkers Said the Sick-Leave Policy 'Ran Her into the Ground.'" *Philadelphia Inquirer*, August 4, 2021. https://www.inquirer.com/news/temple-university-librarian-sick-leave-policy-cancer-20210804.html.

21

Un/Due Hardship and Class(Room) Struggles

Pedagogies and Procedures of Accommodation

C. Goldberg

After COVID-19 protocols shifted my 2020–21 teaching assistant (TA) job online, I found myself working almost exclusively from my laptop. As a graduate student with a chronic collagen condition, I was not surprised when a flare-up of musculoskeletal pain hit me hard during the first weeks of the fall semester. The stress of an increased workload combined with unprecedented screen time were bound to take a toll on me. I was scared of the damage that I might inflict on my body while trying to stay on top of my tasks in a virtual workspace designed without accessibility in mind. So, when a senior administrator attending a TA meeting recommended that I consult my university's Office of Employee Well-Being if I had disability-related concerns, I did.

My research focuses on how people navigate access needs when dealing with nonobvious and episodic impairments, so I was cautiously optimistic that my "disability support specialist" could help me find ways to thrive in (or at least survive) the pandemic teaching environment. Maybe she could even advise me on how to better support my students with their own access needs. I willingly jumped through the bureaucratic hoops set out for me. I provided medical documentation. I explained the kinds of difficulties I was experiencing. I even proposed possible solutions that required few resources and would cost little more than others' understanding, buy-in, and willingness to accommodate.* For example, static versions of the PowerPoint slides shown in video lectures could be provided in screen-reader-friendly pdf or PowerPoint format, couldn't they?

Having answered all the disability support specialist's follow-up questions, I awaited her assessment. In the coming days, I looked forward to her creative suggestions about how I could make use of any available access-oriented resources and work with my course instructor and department to navigate the academic year with more ease. Unfortunately, things did not go quite the way I had imagined.

Less than a month after my initial "employee well-being" consultation, my TA contract was cut short, midsemester. Despite my strongly stated preference to keep teaching, my termination was rubber-stamped, a fait accompli before I had a chance to question it, let alone consent to it. How was the unilateral decision to sever my yearlong contract made? What "hardships" had the alternate proposals discussed with my disability support specialist presented (and why would any such hardships be considered "undue")?† And how had initiating the very process intended to help reduce employment barriers resulted in my being dismissed from my duties altogether—all in the name of "accommodation"?

This piece draws from snippets of emails I received the week I learned I'd been removed from my 2020–21 teaching appointment. Between its irreverent lines lies a basic plea: that people in charge of facilitating accommodations processes and communicating their outcomes respect the humanity and dignity of those participating in them.

---

* See Bonaccio et al., whose overview of concerns expressed by managers about workers with disabilities notes that "accommodations are typically not expensive; however, they must be implemented appropriately and be tailored to the person" (2020, 148).

† "Organizations covered by the [Ontario Human Rights] Code have a duty to accommodate to the point of undue hardship. Some degree of hardship may be expected—it is only if the hardship is 'undue' that the accommodation will not need to be provided" (Ontario Human Rights Commission 2016).

By no means do I wish to vilify diligent individuals charged with implementing accessibility mandates, who are working hard to do their jobs, often with insufficient resources. Even under "normal" circumstances, but especially lately, we all have a lot on our plates. Constraints—financial, time, legal, and otherwise—abound, and imperfect outcomes are unavoidable.

Yet ableism often comes down to the sometimes subtle distinction between making decisions *for* people with disabilities—whether they are seeking formal accommodations in institutional settings or informal consideration in more casual situations—and collaborating *with* them. Additionally, addressing discrimination goes beyond critiquing individuals' attitudes and choices. We need also to examine how day-to-day practices reflect (or don't reflect) larger-scale policies, regardless of the intentions behind them.

For "accommodations" to be adequate, those on whose behalf they exist must deem them so. Only then can those charged with the "duty to accommodate" claim to have fulfilled it. Yet, apparently, much work remains to be done before we collectively shift from procedures that perpetuate systemic injustices to those that combat them—in the classroom and beyond.

A: Good Afternoon

3:14 p.m. November 11, 2020.

"Good afternoon," the Equity Studies administrative coordinator's email begins cheerily.

She has learned from my own department's administrator that I am "an individual still looking for a TAship."

Still looking for a TAship, eh? As of yesterday, I had a TAship. According to my contract, I should still have one!

(Incidentally, I am not having a particularly good afternoon.)

1: Beyond Normal

Those of us who can learn to be or seem "normal" do so, and those of us who cannot meet the standards of normality usually achieve the closest approximation we can manage.

—Susan Wendell, *The Rejected Body*

I don't look physically disabled—not unless you know what to look for.* In many situations, depending on the moment and setting, I am (or pass as) "normal" (or normal enough).† This privilege is a mixed blessing.

That my "quirks" seldom register to others as limitations helps me to avoid the stigma and discrimination faced by folks whose differences are more legible as incapacities. "Crip pride" aside, our world is not overly kind or welcoming to people with obvious disabilities. So, flying under the radar has its perks. Then again, access goes beyond anticipating wheelchairs by building ramps and so on.

Still, I mostly make out fine without attracting undue attention.

You might not even notice the little ways my behaviors fail to align with unspoken expectations. For example: I make anachronistic, old-fashioned phone calls, voice to voice, instead of texting back. I recline or sit cross-legged or askew, while others plant both feet on the ground or cross one leg uniformly over the other. When out for a stroll, I often step, semi-surreptitiously, from the sidewalk onto that patch of grass alongside it—and I did so before "physical distancing" was a global phenomenon. I have long eschewed traditional hand-

---

* This piece picks up from (and moves beyond) my writing in "Getting To(o) Normal" (Goldberg 2020).

† See Samuels for a discussion of "the shifting and contested meanings of disability; the uneasy, often self-destroying tension between appearance and identity; the social scrutiny that refuses to accept statements of identity without 'proof'; and, finally, the discursive and practical connections between coming out—in all the meanings of the term—as queer and as disabled" (2003, 233).

shakes; even before the current pandemic, I would offer up a menu of alternative greetings instead.

Or maybe you'll jump to conclusions. You might assume, for example, that I respond curtly by text because I'm uninterested, angry, or impolite (not because the physical act of typing—or even "swyping"—can be painful). My "informal" posture indicates disrespect or an overly casual vibe (not physical bracing). I stroll slightly off the path because I'm a weirdo (not because soil is infinitely more cushioning than concrete). My hand's failure to meet your perfunctory grip represents my rejection of your friendly or professional overtures;* alternately, my proposed hugs or cheek kisses symbolize unabashed sexual interest (rather than safer options for my joints and ligaments).

Don't get me wrong: I'm not claiming *not* to be a weirdo (or to never be inappropriate, rude, unpolished, dismissive, flirtatious, etc.). But unless I bring them up, do the less obvious possibilities occur to you?

B: No-Show

4:30 p.m. November 11, 2020.

An hour after the Equity Studies administrative coordinator's good-afternoon-wishing email arrives in my inbox, "my" students start showing up for "our" Zoom tutorial. I am not there.

Not because I can't be there. *(No, I haven't caught the plague or had a flare-up.)*

Not because I don't want to be there. *(Quite the contrary.)*

Never before have I "no-showed" at a scheduled tutorial. *(I hadn't planned to start now.)*

---

* Pre-pandemic, at least. COVID-19 has opened up spaces to negotiate greetings from a place where fewer "touch" (or accompanying "squeeze") norms are assumed to be universally good or comfortable. Whether the default distancing and more nuanced negotiation practices I witnessed proliferating in 2020–21 persist into the now-only-hypothesized "new normal" post-pandemic era remains to be seen.

So, if I am both willing and able to attend "my" pandemic-proof Wednesday tutorial, which I was contracted in the summer to lead from September through April, why am I absent today?

Because, apparently—according to the associate dean (AD), per my department—I have received an "accommodation."†

2: Different Spokes

You will take the heavy stuff / And you will drive the car / And I'll look out the window and make jokes / About the way things are.

—Ani DiFranco, "You Had Time"

I regularly surprise folks by pointing out—or simply defying—assumptions. How much do *you* consider the technical and practical "rules" at play in how bodies (your own and others') and other "things" (e.g., machines, policies, social norms, etc.) function? In my experience, few (especially able bodied and otherwise privileged) people give these matters much thought. Not until something goes wrong.‡ Or clashes with their expectations.

For example, folks with no reason to consider the impact of every step they take often equate failing (or refusing) to walk as much as dis/humanly§ possible with "bad" things: laziness, unhealthiness, self-indulgence . . . Shame on you for stopping work before the job is done! Did you order in or eat out instead of grocery shopping and cooking? Shame. Do you have others do more than their "fair share"

† Per the *Cambridge English Dictionary*, "accommodation" (noun uk /əˌkɒm.əˈdeɪ.ʃən/ us /əˌkɑː.məˈdeɪ.ʃən/) means: 1. "a place to live, work, stay, etc." *(but I have been asked to leave)*; 2. "an agreement between two groups who have different opinions on a subject, or the process of reaching an agreement" *(but no agreement has been reached).*

‡ The term "temporarily able-bodied" (or TAB, for short) and related phrases (e.g., "aging is disabling") are used by disability activists and theorists to highlight that the state of being "able bodied" is impermanent and everyone will experience disability in their lifetime if they live long enough.

§ See Liddiard 2018 for an elaboration of different engagements with the terms "dis/human" (176, 179) and, alternately, "DisHuman" (13, 161–63, 168, 174–79).

of the lifting, carrying, commuting, chopping, window closing, jar opening, etc.? Shame!

Despite knowing of the individual and community-level injuries our globalized neoliberal economic system inflicts, I certainly haven't purged all of the (ableist, racist, sexist, transphobic, homophobic, etc.) judgments I internalized growing up. Not to mention other seemingly benign notions, such as "mind over matter," reciprocity as "tit for tat," and—this one particularly insidious in my adult-child-of-a-workaholic-Holocaust-survivor psyche—the misguided intergenerational promise that self-sacrificing work will somehow set you free . . .

But, that brisk "healthy" stroll you've suggested?

Well, it could put me out of commission for a week . . .

Oh, it didn't occur to you?

Wait, wait, no, don't get me wrong. I'm not turning you down. Actually, I'd love to come along! I like fresh air as much as the next guy, and I like spending time with you. So, would you mind if I ride along beside you?

(See, as long as my hands/wrists/shoulders are holding out, rolling is smoother than plodding . . .)

Oh, you prefer that your walking companions *walk*?

(I can try to keep apace on foot. I'll just probably pay for it later.)

No worries, I understand. Really.

(As honed as my bike-balancing skills are, sometimes I attract scowls and jeers from passersby who claim the path as theirs alone. That can be awkward. Speaking of which, cycling on pedestrian walkways with me-sized wheels is illegal. Regardless of how agonizingly slowly and carefully I ride, I risk getting a ticket every time I bike on the sidewalk. No local law or custom recognizes the bicycle, traditional purview of the able bodied—innocent children and athletic adults alike—as a mobility device.)*

* See Fritsch 2013 for another discussion of the challenges associated with using a bicycle (or, in Fritsch's case, a tandem bike) as an unrecognized mobility device.

One sec, just let me put on my mask and shoes!

C: Sunny Days

11:36 a.m. November 6, 2020.

Two business days after what I soon learn *was* my final Wednesday Zoom tutorial of the year, I get an email from my home department's administrative coordinator.

It begins optimistically: "Hoping you are enjoying the unseasonably warm and sunny weather . . ."

(That's nice.)

I read on, scanning the second sentence: "I'm writing to let you know . . . [we] heard from [the] AD . . . of your accommodation earlier this week . . ."

(Good news—I am being accommodated!)

As I continue reading, my belly sinks.

"As instructed, I have adjusted your [teaching] assignment to a half TA for the Fall term only—paid through December. Your accommodation (removed from the course but paid) begins on November 11 through December 31. For the Winter term, I have been asked to keep an eye out for TA opportunities for you . . . I don't anticipate any in our unit . . ."

Instead of reasonable accommodations† that would allow me to keep doing my current job through April, per my contract and disability rights protected by relevant labor laws, I seem to be getting some

† "Accommodation" (noun ac·com·mo·da·tion | \ ə-ˌkä-mə-ˈdā-shən), per the *Merriam-Webster Dictionary*: 1. "something supplied for convenience or to satisfy a need" *(but whose convenience or need-satisfying is being considered?)*; 2. "the act of accommodating someone or something : the state of being accommodated" *(where, in theory, the accommodation is serving the person supposedly being accommodated, not just conveniencing those doing the unilateral accommodating; here, the timing, tone, and substance of the process, minus adequate consultation, undermined the spirit of an "act" that might otherwise have represented a collaborative and mutually satisfactory resolution).*

severance to tide me over for a month or two (in lieu of being paid overtime for extra hours worked prior to being summarily dismissed).

This is not the "workplace accommodation plan" that I was expecting. In my understanding, meaningful consultation with the person being accommodated is a critical component of reasonable accommodations. Arguably, decision-making on behalf of people with disabilities that does not account for their perspectives is itself one of the most prevalent and insidious manifestations of ableism. However, neither the AD nor the disability support specialist from the Office of Employee Well-Being (whom the AD explicitly instructed me to consult to resolve my access concerns) checked in prior to implementing their so-called accommodation plan. In fact, nobody even told me that a verdict on my case had been reached, let alone offered viable alternatives, before my replacement was hired.

To me, it sounds a whole lot like I'm being fired.

(Incidentally, I am a bit too distracted by my sudden loss of employment to really enjoy the warm, sunny weather.)

3: Self-Accommodation

"You must have wished a million times to be normal. . . . No?"
"I've wished I had two heads. Or that I was invisible. I've wished for a fish's tail instead of legs. I've wished to be more special."
"Not normal?"
"Never."

—Katherine Dunn (*Geek Love*, 1989)

I seldom notice that my "normal" way of doing things isn't like everyone else's—until *they* point it out.* Even then, my irregularities usually feel fairly benign.

Like, who cares that I usually work lying down? Throughout childhood and adolescence, I read on my bed . . . never studied at the desk in my room . . . dragged the circular cushion from our communal un-

* As discussed previously in Goldberg 2020.

dergrad student living room bucket chair into our "fifth bedroom"—a coffin-shaped three-foot-tall, three-foot-wide, six-foot-deep storage closet—to cram for exams . . . surrounded every hard surface in my home with a plethora of pillows . . .

This embodied need—to rest horizontally (or at least partly reclining), propped up on squishy surfaces atop a solid base, to concentrate—never made me question my able-bodied identity. Only recently did I start reconsidering my need for soft but supportive full-body workspaces (and my failure to find generically "ergonomic" desk setups suitable) in accessibility terms. That, and the myriad other ways I do things: sliding to the ground when uncomfortable chairs are the only other option; pushing elevator buttons with my cell phone instead of my fingers; opening jars with a baby boa constrictor wrench; overusing the Ctrl+C and Ctrl+V functions to copy-paste quotes from digital texts into essays instead of typing them out.

In disability parlance, I've been "self-accommodating" all along.

Strictly speaking, "self-accommodation" is at least partly a misnomer. We all rely on one another's support—acknowledged and unacknowledged—even in accommodating our*selves*.

That baby boa constrictor wrench? A thoughtful gift from a friend to whom I recounted the sad tale of a particularly hungry night when the spaghetti was cooked but I couldn't get the lid off the sauce. Those digital texts? Furnished by Claudio at Library Accessibility Services. Sitting on the ground during events? Infinitely less lonely when I'm not the only one.

In my experience, in atmospheres of communal care and respectful collegiality, my physical particularities and "accommodation needs" (as well as those of my students with disabilities) can generally be accommodated through a combination of creativity, communication, and collaboration. Universal design (UD) principles suggest making common accessibility features (e.g., subtitles and screen-reader-friendly PowerPoint slides) available by default in pedagogical settings to reduce our collective reliance on one-on-one negotiations. While even the most rigorous and consistent application of UD principles does not eliminate the possibility that additional accommodations may be required, the attitude underlying UD shifts us away from seeing accessibility as "special" treatment for some and toward creating spaces where all of us are welcome.

At the other end of the spectrum, sometimes a course instructor pits their intellectual property rights against the university's duty to accommodate, thus undermining the disability human rights protected in educational and workplace settings. Could this be why, when I advocated for the provision of accessible copies of slides to TAs (as well as to students whose letters of accommodation specifically requested them), I was flat-out refused—and, soon thereafter, terminated?

D: Terminal Accommodation

10:45 a.m. November 11, 2020.

Unbeknown to me or "my" students at the time, the tutorial I led last week was my last of the year (and with them).

Yesterday I received a message saying "it should be fine . . . to say goodbye to the students tomorrow."

I'm relieved at this consolation—to at least get some closure and do justice by the students with whom I still need to meet about outstanding grades and other pending issues.

Now, the final blow: "It has come to my attention that your access to the course comes to an end formally with the end of your contract, the outcome being that you won't be able to attend a portion of the tutorial today after all. . . . Nevertheless, thanks very much for your initial offer."

I am silently ushered away from my virtual desk.

4: Contracted Contract

Like ten thousand spoons when all you need is a knife.

—Alanis Morissette, "Ironic"

At the time of this writing (over a month after my contract was abruptly ended) . . .

My disability support specialist has not produced a workplace accommodation plan that might justify calling my 2020 dismissal an "accommodation"—such as its leading to barrier-free employment in 2021.

Neither the AD nor any other involved party has offered any explanation as to why accommodating me within my 2020–21 contract would have caused the university or department "undue hardship."

I still have no contract for the upcoming winter semester (although I have considered some offers).

E: Rights in the Workplace

3:14 p.m. November 11, 2020.

The Equity Studies administrative coordinator's email continues: "I have winter assignments in the following courses available. Please let me know if any . . . may be of interest to you."

The first TAship on the list? "Rights in the Workplace."

(Ironic . . . Don't you think?)

I'm finding it unduly hard to accommodate* that I need to start a new job in the middle of the school year because the university failed

* "Accommodate" (transitive verb ac·com·mo·date | \ ə-ˈkä-mə-ˌdāt), per the *Merriam-Webster Dictionary*: 1. "to provide with something desired, needed, or suited"; 2a. "to make room for"; 2b. "to hold without crowding or inconvenience"; 3. "to bring into agreement or concord : reconcile"; 4. "to give consideration to : to allow for"; 5. "to make fit, suitable, or congruous."

to protect my rights as a worker, and now they want me to teach students about workers' rights.

(A little too ironic? Yeah, I really do think.)

Works Cited

Bonaccio, Silvia, Catherin E. Connelly, Ian R. Gellatly, Arif Jetha, and Kathleen A. Martin Ginis. K.A. 2020. "The Participation of People with Disabilities in the Workplace Across the Employment Cycle: Employer Concerns and Research Evidence." *Journal of Business and Psychology* 35:135–58. https://doi.org/10.1007/s10869-018-9602-5.

Fritsch, Kelly. 2013. "The Neoliberal Circulation of Affects: Happiness, Accessibility and the Capacitation of Disability as Wheelchair." *Health, Culture and Society* 5 (1): 135–49. https://doi.org/10.5195/hcs.2013.136.

Goldberg, C. E. 2020. "Getting To(o) Normal: Critical Reflections on Being 'Fitted' by an Occupational Therapist and Related Artefacts." *Disability Studies Quarterly* 40 (2): 1–11. https://doi.org/10.18061/dsq.v40i2.6752.

Liddiard, Kirsty. 2018. *The Intimate Lives of Disabled People*. London: Routledge.

Ontario Human Rights Commission. 2016. *Policy on Ableism and Discrimination Based on Disability*. https://www.ohrc.on.ca/en/policy-ableism-and-discrimination-based-disability.

Samuels, Ellen Jean. 2003. "My Body, My Closet: Invisible Disability and the Limits of Coming-Out Discourse." *GLQ: A Journal of Lesbian and Gay Studies* 9 (1–2): 233–55. http://doi.org/10.1215/10642684-9-1-2-233.

22

Is It Just Me?

Mental Health and Institutional Perspectives from a Graduate Writing Consultant

Doreen Hsu

Researchers widely acknowledge that graduate students in the United States commonly experience widespread and severe mental health issues. For example, a 2014 study showed 43–46% of doctoral students were clinically depressed (Evans et al. 2018, 282). Across disciplines at private and public universities, 12% of surveyed students had contemplated suicide in the past year (Bolotnyy, Basilico, and Barreira 2018, 11). Furthermore, 41% of graduate students report "moderate to severe anxiety," about six times more prevalent than the general population (Evans et al. 2018, 282). In everyday life, 17.5% of students even stated that they "often lack companionship" and "feel isolated" from other people (Bolotnyy, Basilico, and Barreira 2018, 18). These existing statistics suggest a range of mental health concerns that may impede students' abilities to learn, express emotions, form relationships, and cope with challenges. In this essay, I focus on these signs of distress "far above and beyond healthy levels of stress or anxiety" that would usually help us pursue goals, recognize challenges, and persist against setbacks (Bolotnyy, Basilico, and Barreira 2018, 9). Such mental health concerns may be expressed visibly as signs of nervousness or explicit statements of distress. While I do not intend to diagnose people, I explain my analysis based on signs of distress that I have observed as a graduate writing consultant who works with graduate students across disciplines. Using my experiences, I show how the university creates stresses for graduate students through a deficit model that focuses solely on weaknesses without acknowledging students' diverse needs and strengths.

In adhering to a deficit model, the university frames student stresses as individual failures, especially for women and students of color, who are historically less represented on campus. The university thus absolves itself of further responsibility to address these concerns as institutional issues that require large-scale solutions. I base this deficit model upon existing scholarship that defines "deficit thinking" as a values framework that explains students' weaknesses as "self-imposed" and inevitable products of "culturally disadvantaged" backgrounds (Valencia 2019, 10–11). The deficit model shapes graduate student education, and it is this model that connects to graduate student stresses in university. In action, university departments that follow a deficit model assume students "should know what to do" in their graduate programs. However, students do not know how to succeed because they are not receiving training from the university that holistically acknowledges their diverse perspectives, needs, and strengths. The university thus betrays its students by contributing to stresses through a deficit model. These stresses are not new and will continue if we do not critically examine these institutional conditions. We must address this model in higher education by immediately enacting short-term and long-term solutions.

Graduate students' symptoms of distress have real consequences in academic performance. Studies show that nearly 45% of graduate students have experienced stresses that "significantly affected their wellbeing and academic performance" (Gray 2018, 226). A specific example is the lack of participation in seminars, as most grads feel uncomfortable interacting with faculty and peers in such academic settings. Only 29% of students believe they are "moderately or very comfortable speaking up in seminars," and only 19% of women feel comfortable participating, compared to 35% of men (Bolotnyy, Basilico, and Barreira 2018, 18). Women and international students also report fewer interactions with faculty overall (Bolotnyy, Basilico, and Barreira 2018, 19). Many grad students may feel anxious about the quality of their ideas and feel hesitant to speak their thoughts in front of their peers and instructors. Students may also believe that they are alone in their academic challenges, and wonder, "Is it just me?" This self-consciousness can prevent students from participating in discussions. If students feel this way about participating in seminars and have fewer faculty interactions, they could feel increasingly anxious about their work and receive less guidance.

Another potential consequence of mental health stresses is the low completion rate in PhD programs. The average completion rate across disciplines in the United States is 50%, which has stayed consistent in the past decade (Wollast et al. 2018, 143; Sowell et al. 2008, 48). Furthermore, students who identify as women, Asian American, Hispanic American, and African American finish their programs more slowly and have lower completion rates. On average, white doctoral students finish their programs at a 55% rate, while Hispanic Americans complete at 51%, Asian Americans at 50%, and African Americans at 47% (Sowell et al. 2008, 48). These rates differ across disciplines. For example, within social sciences, white students complete at 57% by year ten, compared to 55% of Hispanic American students, 47% of African Americans, and 44% of Asian Americans (Sowell et al. 2008, 77). For men and women of all racial groups, 58% of men complete their PhD programs compared to 55% of women, but these rates vary greatly among disciplines that have historically maintained a gender imbalance (Sowell et al. 2008, 48). Latest statistics show that these differences remain in schools such as University of California, San Diego (UCSD), in which 75% of UCSD "domestic non-underrepresented minority" doctoral students starting in 2007–9 completed within ten years, compared to 63% of "underrepresented minority" students (Division of Graduate Education and Postdoctoral Affairs, n.d.). Evidently, grad students experience stresses in widespread and severe ways that perpetuate historical patterns of exclusion and inequity. It is not enough for us to consider such stresses as individual, microlevel challenges. Rather, we must focus critically on the institution that grad students depend on.

Psychologist Jennifer Freyd defines institutional betrayal as "wrongdoings perpetrated by an institution upon individuals dependent upon that institution" (Freyd 2020; see also Smith and Freyd 2014, 575). As graduate students, we are completely dependent upon the institution in which we study. Almost all grad students are employed by the university to conduct research, publish, teach, mentor students, and apply for grants that fund university research projects. Across disciplines, grad students receive financial support, education, and credentials from the university, all of which support and legitimize our intellectual inquiries, even long after our graduation. In turn, the institution depends on grad students to conduct scholarly activities that support faculty and undergraduate students, who build the institution's reputation and fund the university. Grad students were even treated as essential employees under strict COVID-19 lockdown restrictions and were required to conduct in-person, on-site research activities that the university deemed necessary. Despite serving essential functions, graduate students are betrayed by their institution in ways that severely impact mental health and academic performance. Institutional betrayal can manifest in different ways and through different avenues, but the graduate student stresses I explain here as a writing consultant can be traced to consequences of a deficit model.

The deficit model is a framework of values that shapes graduate education in various ways, including pedagogical approaches and understandings of grad student problems. Within graduate programs, students are often educated through courses and academic interactions; these focus exclusively on picking out weaknesses without assessing individual needs or strengths. Consequently, graduate students' diverse backgrounds, needs, and skills are often overlooked by university departments. In adhering to a strict deficit model, departments assume that graduate students know how to succeed on their own, and when students do encounter challenges, these struggles are then interpreted as individual problems. To explain how such institutional betrayal occurs and contributes to mental health stresses, I discuss my experiences as a graduate student writing consultant employed by a university writing center. As a writing consultant, one of my tasks is meeting grad students in one-on-one tutoring sessions to understand the student's needs and provide professional feedback based on the student's perspectives. I pose questions, comments, and recommendations from a position of peer empathy, and I work with students across disciplines on various projects, including dissertations and academic manuscripts. Graduate writing consultants recognize that writing occurs throughout the research process, and I work with students to plan, brainstorm, draft, and revise texts. Furthermore, as a Taiwanese American woman with a multilingual and multicultural background, I serve as an ally and role model for students who are also underrepresented in academic spaces. Overall, our writing center is founded on the principle of providing a unique intersectional space for academic tutoring, professional development, and "social/emotional well-being" (UCSD Writing Hub, n.d.). As a grad writing consultant, I am one of the only academic service staff members specifically trained to support grad students holistically across these dimensions of academic, professional, and emotional success.

The university's adherence to a deficit model translates into a near-complete lack of helpful support in graduate student research and writing projects. University departments assume that students are doing well because they "should know what to do" as mature grad students, hence only needing feedback on deficits or "things to fix" in their projects. For example, graduate students schedule consultations because they are unsure how to start complex projects like a dissertation proposal, qualifying field exam paper, or seminar essay. Students often ask me to help them understand "what to do" in their projects. Although students come to me for writing support, graduate students' "problems with writing" often include challenges with understanding expectations in their programs and learning the conventions of writing in their disciplines. When grad students are not specifically taught the academic expectations, they feel "stressed out" in trying to figure everything out on their own, especially when students feel like they "should know what to do, but [they] don't." Grad students are betrayed by a university that does not explicitly teach them what they need to learn as advanced scholars within their disciplines.

In the absence of departmental and faculty leadership in clarifying expectations, assignment objectives, and providing helpful feedback, peer support becomes the default course of action that students rely on for academic guidance. However, peer support among graduate students is made even more precarious by departments that create competitive environments. For example, institutions may provide very limited funding support for grad students. By withholding material resources, the university may force many of its students to constantly compete against each other for fellowships that reward academic excellence. Grad students have shared with me that they sometimes feel "uncomfortable asking other grad students for their grant or fellowship application essays" to use as sample texts. This reluctance to ask for help in the form of a peer writing sample is based on a real fear of disclosing vulnerabilities and risking negative judgments from peers who would view them as "competition." Thus, when grad students do interact with each other, they are often socializing in hostile environments that do not promote collaboration and empathetic feedback as fundamental pillars of higher education.

It is no surprise that many grad students struggle with developing and completing writing projects throughout their career. When students do receive adviser feedback as part of their academic training, the comments often focus on deficits in the product and do not provide further explanation on how to "fix the writing." A student once mentioned that they were stressed about a faculty member's feedback: "My adviser says this part is confusing because I should clarify the analytical modeling. But I don't know what that is and how I can explain that." Students such as this individual may feel distressed because departments often do not train faculty on effective strategies to teach writing at the graduate level. Teaching advanced writing requires "a profound sensitivity" to the highly specific academic conventions of one's discipline and "the best ways of introducing newcomers to those peculiarities" (Paré 2011, 60). Graduate students need to learn the writing conventions of their disciplines, and students learn best when they are taught in ways that account for their backgrounds and needs. Although faculty can expertly recognize issues in student writing, advisers often "struggle to find the words that would help the student" learn how to write like an advanced scholar in the discipline (Paré 2011, 72). Without a common vocabulary to discuss writing projects, some faculty use disciplinary-specific, expert jargon to teach grad students, many of whom are novice learners. Subsequently, faculty may offer writing advice "without full explanation" (Paré 2011, 65). Thus, within graduate programs that follow a deficit model, students often struggle to start their writing projects because they receive little guidance from within their departments. When students do complete their projects, they face challenges in revising and improving their writing, since students are often working from comments that only focus on deficits. As such, the institution contributes to significant obstacles for grad students at every stage of their academic process.

With all these challenges, students can feel stressed, insecure, and confused about who they are as graduate students. Grad students need to be explicitly taught and trained in the expectations of their disciplines, which includes academic writing as a necessary skill. However, university departments assume that all grad students enter their programs with the same level of knowledge and skills, without ensuring that students have equal access to academic resources. Students have mentioned to me that they "feel like there is nowhere to go within the department to look for feedback or guidance," even for milestone projects like qualifying field exam papers, which have highly specific expectations that only a faculty adviser or disciplinary peer would be familiar with. Thus, the institution operates on a deficit model that does not engage with students in an individualized, holistic, and continuous fashion. Engaging with grad students to understand their needs at various stages of their programs is a pedagogical practice that requires time, energy, and skillful mentorship that many institutions do not invest in. Subsequently, when grad students encounter obstacles at every stage of their programs, it is debilitating to work through the challenges alone.

This deficit model in graduate student education is corroborated in existing research. Scholars emphasize how universities have "normalized disciplinary conventions of knowledge production" to the point that departments view these traditions as "universal" (Starke-Meyerring 2011, 77). As universities normalize these traditions, departments may assume that all grads know these conventions and do not need guidance for academic projects. When students do need explicit guidance on their work, their needs are often unrecognized or dismissed by their departments. Students' academic struggles are interpreted as individual weaknesses or problems that students should address on their own. Graduate students often feel like they are the only ones "not managing time well," or that they are not succeeding because they are "not smart," hence needing more time to finish research and writing. Furthermore, when peer interactions are hostile or infrequent, grad students are even more likely to internalize stresses as individual inadequacy rather than symptoms of institutional failure to provide guided support at every stage of the academic career. Students wonder repeatedly, "Is it just me?" This institutional betrayal contributes to severe stress among grad students who feel like they "should know what to do" but are extremely insecure about their writing and research progress because they are not receiving training from their departments. Thus, grad students are betrayed by their institution, which does not teach them what they need to learn to succeed within their programs. Students need individual and sustained engagement at every stage of their career to learn disciplinary expectations and develop their own strengths. Without institutional structures that ensure grads have equal access to the academic training they need, students feel increasingly stressed and anxious about whether they even belong in their graduate programs.

The institution contributes to especially complex stresses for certain students. Almost all of my student clients are women, students of color, and students for whom English is not their primary language. The gendered use of academic support is documented in research, which shows that women are "significantly more likely" than men to use university writing centers (Salem 2016, 154). Women may be more likely to seek help, or they may be told more often to seek help. From my experiences, it is primarily the latter. For example, a woman grad student once mentioned that whenever she talked with her adviser about a project, she felt "really emotional because [the adviser] always says to revise." It is critical for graduate students to learn how to write through "gradually increasing and mentored participation in the [normalized] discursive practices" of their disciplines (Starke-Meyerring 2011, 81). Revising texts is a necessary part of learning how to write, but it is the lack of guidance that makes revision especially stressful. It seems that women grad students are frequently asked by advisers to revise, often without specific feedback that can promote learning in the discipline. The lack of guidance may be a result of women grad students' interactions with faculty advisers, as existing scholarship already demonstrates that women interact less with faculty (Bolotnyy, Basilico, and Barreira 2018, 19). Some faculty may doubt women's capability to write accurately about complex ideas. This potential gender bias is supported by audit research that show women academics are critiqued significantly harsher by "objective" peer reviewers and grant committees, even when application content is identical (Kaatz, Gutierrez, and Carnes 2014, 1). Thus, some women grad students may feel as if their work is "never good enough," because their writing is constantly critiqued with limited feedback. Students may feel as if they should always present polished writing to prove that they belong in the institution.

Such women grad students schedule writing consultations to "get help," often because they are trying to develop projects and revise with limited guidance. Students may also seek to preemptively avoid their advisers' requests for revision by presenting "more polished" drafts to their advisers. Subsequently, some women grad students ask writing consultants to review their work first, before sending their writing to faculty advisers. In doing so, many women grad students often apologize for showing me "messy writing" that they want to "fix" for their advisers' approval. These students may feel as if they must apologize for causing confusion or inconvenience, even though writing consultants are dedicated to supporting students' writing in a positive, empathetic manner. Combined with the isolation and anxiety that grads face, some women students may feel especially anxious and self-conscious about their academic work. These negative feelings about academic progress can feed into students' perspectives about their own identities and capabilities as graduate students. Overall, the institution has established a deficit model in which students are constantly asked to fix a perceived, individual weakness that shows in their writing. These perceived inadequacies may be related to existing societal biases based on race, class, and gender. The deficit model is not neutral—it is tied to existing inequalities that benefit privileged white men at the cost of everyone else.

We must consider the institution as an active agent that creates specific conditions for students' lives. The university betrays its grad students by contributing to significant stresses and then framing such struggles as individual weaknesses that do not require institutional intervention, hence absolving the university of further responsibility. Through this deficit model, the institution focuses only on critiquing students' weaknesses without developing students' strengths. Subsequently, to address grad student mental health concerns, we must confront the university's use of the deficit model, through short-term and long-term solutions that reduce isolation, raise consciousness, and develop student services like the writing center. For example, our university writing center is dedicated to helping students succeed academically, professionally, and emotionally throughout their programs (UCSD Writing Hub, n.d.). We must continue developing services that hold similar motivations. Although additional funding would help, it is imperative to raise consciousness about the value and benefits of this student-centered approach that continuously engages with individual students at every stage of their postgraduate career. Once we assess students' needs, then we can provide effective training and empathetic mentorship that directly accounts for students' diverse strengths and perspectives.

Students must have equal access to academic services and resources that can develop their individual skills and strengths within the institution. My recommendation would be to establish a required writing course for all beginning graduate students and incorporate contacts with academic services as required peer feedback in course syllabi. As a writing consultant who collaborates with various departments and campus units, I have seen significant success in seminars that have required students to make a certain number of contacts with grad writing consultants as a form of peer feedback. Specifically, students find it freeing to discuss their ideas and writing with a peer outside of the course. Writing consultations can help students consolidate their understanding of course content without feeling like they are competing with classmates or disclosing weaknesses to faculty instructors. Once graduate students make an initial contact with a writing consultant, many students return to the writing center for another consultation or explore other resources to further develop their learning as an advanced scholar.

As for a required writing course as part of a graduate curriculum, our writing center already provides workshops that can serve as the foundation for a low-stakes graduate writing course across disciplines. In fact, I have facilitated these writing workshops myself as part of a required summer program for certain incoming grad students. Such writing workshops provide necessary opportunities for grad students to develop their academic projects, practice professionalization skills, and build supportive peer networks across disciplines. We should be expanding and incorporating such services into graduate curricula to ensure that all students have equal access to academic training and support. Graduate students arrive in their programs with diverse needs that are not acknowledged by the deficit model, which only focuses on weaknesses without developing holistic strengths and skills. Overall, we must recognize that one outcome of the deficit model is that it selectively retains students who "know what to do" and can produce with the least amount of support. Subsequently, this model saves the neoliberal capitalist university from further expenditures, maximizing returns while minimizing investment in supporting all students.

The institution is part of the problem of graduate student stresses. As such, the institution must also be part of the solution. These acts of institutional betrayal occur through a deficit model that connects to stresses on mental health and academic performance. Thus, a long-term solution to these acts of betrayal is to dismantle the deficit model, reframe graduate education, and rebuild the university foundationally. Historically, institutional remediation has been ineffective because our society is structured along lines of race, class, and gender that benefit some at the cost of others. Current university agents of power have survived and benefited from such oppressive models. To dismantle the deficit model, we need to shift the university away from its neoliberal capitalist foundation. We must raise consciousness about the institution's responsibility for acknowledging students' diverse needs and developing their strengths based on their perspectives. In doing so, we can build a student-centered institution that structures its programs to assess students' perspectives at every stage of their learning process. Graduate students must learn clear expectations and receive training based on their specific needs at various stages of learning, such that students can succeed academically, professionally, and emotionally within and beyond their graduate programs. Departments must formally acknowledge students' diverse backgrounds as strengths through curriculum changes and pedagogical practices that incorporate sustained mentorship and individualized guidance from faculty and staff.

This institutional reformation requires a complete "revolution of values," like the one Dr. Martin Luther King Jr. argued for in 1964 at the University of Oslo. Dr. King warned us: "There is no deficit in human resources; the deficit is in human will" (1967, 187). The deficit model in our institutions is a deficit in human will to prioritize student perspectives. Our institutions and societies do not lack technological and material resources, only the motivation to affect short-term and long-term change. This lack of human will is a profound "poverty of the spirit" that will lead to our "violent coannihilation" (King 1967, 181, 202). The "spirit" of the university must not be drained by the status quo of neoliberal capitalist values that contribute to student stresses. Even as we return to "more normal" in-person learning settings under the COVID-19 pandemic, we must continue to evaluate and reawaken the university "spirit." We must restore universities as educational institutions that fully acknowledge students' identities by assessing students' diverse needs, perspectives, and strengths. In doing so, we can truly ensure that students understand they belong in the university. We need to stop students from wondering, "Is it just me?" These institutional acts of betrayal will worsen if we do not confront our human will. We must immediately use our resources to reorder priorities and revolutionize our human spirit.

Works Cited

Bolotnyy, Valentin, Matthew Basilico, and Paul Barreira. 2018. "Graduate Student Mental Health: Lessons from American Economics Departments." *Journal of Economic Literature* 60 (4): 1188–1222. https://doi.org/10.1257/jel.20201555.

Division of Graduate Education and Postdoctoral Affairs. n.d. "Completion Rates." Accessed August 15, 2024. https://grad.ucsd.edu/about/grad-data/completion-rates.html.

Evans, Teresa M., Lindsay Bira, Jazmin Beltran Gastelum, L. Todd Weiss, and Nathan L. Vanderford. 2018. "Evidence for a Mental Health Crisis in Graduate Education." *Nature Biotechnology* 36 (3): 282–84. https://doi.org/10.1038/nbt.4089.

Freyd, Jennifer J. 2020. "Addressing Sexual Violence Through Institutional Courage (Fall 2018–Winter 2020)." Project on Institutional Courage. https://www.jjfreyd.com/project-on-institutional-courage.

Gray, Marilyn. 2018. "More Than Dissertation Support: Aligning Our Programs with Doctoral Students' Well-Being and Professional Development Needs." In *Re/Writing the Center: Approaches to Supporting Graduate Students in the Writing Center*, edited by Susan Lawrence and Terry Myers Zawacki, 223–39. Logan: Utah State University Press.

Kaatz, Anna, Belinda Gutierrez, and Molly Carnes. 2014. "Threats to Objectivity in Peer Review: The Case of Gender." *Trends in Pharmacological Sciences* 35 (8): 371–73. https://doi.org/10.1016/j.tips.2014.06.005.

King, Martin Luther, Jr. 1967. "The World House." In *Where Do We Go From Here: Chaos or Community?* 167–91. Boston: Beacon Press.

Paré, Anthony. 2011. "Speaking of Writing: Supervisory Feedback and the Dissertation." In *Doctoral Education: Research-Based Strategies for Doctoral Stu-*

dents, Supervisors and Administrators, edited by Lynn McAlpine and Cheryl Amundsen, 59–74. New York: Springer.

Salem, Lori. 2016. "Decisions . . . Decisions: Who Chooses to Use the Writing Center?" *Writing Center Journal* 35 (2): 147–71. https://www.jstor.org/stable/43824060?seq=1.

Smith, Carly P., and Jennifer J. Freyd. 2014. "Institutional Betrayal." *American Psychologist* 69 (6): 575–87. https://doi.org/10.1037/a0037564.

Sowell, Robert, Ting Zhang, Nathan Bell, and Kenneth Redd. 2008. *Ph.D. Completion and Attrition: Analysis of Baseline Demographic Data from the Ph.D. Completion Project*. Washington, D.C.: Council of Graduate Schools.

Starke-Meyerring, Doreen. 2011. "The Paradox of Writing in Doctoral Education: Student Experiences." In *Doctoral Education: Research-Based Strategies for Doctoral Students, Supervisors, and Administrators*, edited by Lynn McAlpine and Cheryl Amundsen, 75–95. New York: Springer.

UCSD (University of California, San Diego) Writing Hub. n.d. "Graduate Student Services." Accessed August 15, 2024. https://writinghub.ucsd.edu/what-we-do/graduate-services.html.

Valencia, Richard R. 2019. "The Construct of Deficit Thinking." In *International Deficit Thinking: Educational Thought and Practice*, 1–29. New York: Routledge.

Wollast, Robin, Gentiane Boudrenghien, Nicolas Van Der Linden, Benoît Galand, Nathalie Roland, Christelle Devos, Mikaël De Clercq, Olivier Klein, Assaad Azzi, and Mariane Frenay. 2018. "Who Are the Doctoral Students Who Drop Out? Factors Associated with the Rate of Doctoral Degree Completion in Universities." *International Journal of Higher Education* 7 (4): 143–56. https://doi.org/10.5430/ijhe.v7n4p143.

Part V

Resistance and Resilience

I Am Not Just a Body but Also a Soul

The Power of Erasure amid Hypervisibility on a Faculty Search Committee

Jennifer M. Gómez

And that visibility which makes us most vulnerable is that which also is the source of our greatest strength.

—Audre Lorde, "The Transformation of Silence into Action"

Prologue

Lying naked from the waist down with a sheet to cover me, I am violated by the gynecologist. Dr. White Woman inserts the speculum without warning, removes the IUD without telling me, inserts the new IUD with no notice, and then digitally penetrates me without my permission. I know that she knows I'm here. But my presence doesn't matter. To her, I am just a body but not a soul.

Background

Though not unique (Washington 2006), the abuse at the doctor's office, which happened outside of academia, is a physical parallel of what it is like for me as a Black woman assistant professor on a search committee for a tenure-track faculty position in my department. Both occurred within the same fall semester of the same 2020 year, in which the devaluing of Black people in the United States could not be more apparent. The difference in academia is they *say* they want us there. But do they really?

The university I am affiliated with at the time of this search* has some understanding of the value of diverse representation in searches. So much so, they require a certain level of racial diversity on all search committees. But that performative diversity (Ahmed 2012) is where the understanding ends. Our search committee has two Black faculty on it, of which I am one. I know that they know we're here. But our presence doesn't matter. To them, we're bodies but not souls.

Since this is academia, our soulless bodies are also presumed to have no knowledge worth respecting. With the institutional betrayals (Smith and Freyd 2014) being numerous, I cannot help but speak up. After all, my experience on the job market was also full of discrimination (Gómez 2018, 2020). Through sheer serendipity, I got my job at this institution—a job that confounds me by simultaneously including (1) remarkable, unwavering exaltation, support, and tangible power and influence on one end; (2) on the other, the predictable, almost-boring-if-it-weren't-so-harmful, direct and indirect discrimination. *But at this job and on this search committee, I can finally make a difference!* Or so I thought.

Institutional Betrayal Within Search Committee Meetings: An Excerpted Play

Me: *In this Excel sheet of applicants, I see columns to check if the applicant would bring diversity to the department by race, gender, or other. This is nominal diversity* (AACU 2002). *What is the priority for underrepresented expertise, such as commitment and experience to studying*

* Though this piece was originally written in fall 2020, I have chosen to retain present-tense verbiage for these past events (known as *translation temporum*), as I wish to stay true to the dire immediacy of the events I describe . . . events that so many others continue to experience in academia.

Black and Brown populations in their research, marginalized theoretical perspectives, ability to teach and mentor underrepresented minority students, those kinds of things that would bring diversity?

Them: *We are looking for the best candidate. Any diversity is . . . a bonus, I would say. We want the best person.*

Me: *I compiled a list of phone and video interview questions from myself and colleagues on the job market from the past several years. I can share it with the committee as a starting point for creating standardized questions for all interviews. This way, we home in on what we are looking for with the questions, and each candidate gets the same opportunity. That'll make it easier for us to compare across interviews as well. I'd also suggest that we share this list of questions with all candidates before the interview. That way, we create an even playing field, instead of privileging those candidates who are more prepared for such interviews, since their parents are professors, for example, while disadvantaging first-generation applicants. That taps into what we're wanting to measure too. Not people who are more in-grouped or people who are slick at the mouth, but those who are actually the most qualified. This way, everyone has the opportunity to prepare and to shine. I can send the list of questions to the committee after this meeting.*

No response. In vivo or to the email.

Next meeting:

Me: *Oh, we're talking about phone interviews again. [Reiterates the importance of standardized questions.]*

Them: *But I may have a specific question I want to ask a candidate based on their application. To get clarity.*

Me: *We could do a combination, right? Same base-level questions for everyone. Then one or two questions for each that are unique to their application.*

Silence.

I know that they know I'm here . . . but I'm just a body.

Me: *Speaking of these initial, preliminary interviews being on a virtual conference platform, there's one equity concern. Since we're all working from home now [in the COVID-19 pandemic], not everyone lives in a presentable, professional, quiet place to conduct the interview. Kids running around, dogs barking, et cetera. So I've been reading about how phone interviews might be preferable and not cause this undue burden—stress—for some people. They can take the phone call in their car, for instance. And this then reduces the potential for bias on our end.*

Them: *We've been seeing cats and kids and people in their homes on videoconferencing for months. People in their basement. Not a big deal . . . I guess if someone doesn't want to do a video call, they can say no. We won't make them. But it'll make it easier for the applicants too—they can see us, know when someone wants to talk. That sort of thing. Less awkward than a phone call.*

Now it's my turn for silence: that means that certain candidates will have the advantage of the video call and others won't. That difference will be systematic, based on class and other factors. But I don't say it. Cos now I remember: I'm just a body.

But wait, I tell myself. It's not over. I can't give up. This is high stakes. A tenure-track faculty position (big deal), equity in hiring (big deal), and potential to increase the pipeline for underrepresented minority students by having a professor who, instead of conducting research, teaching, and service with white supremacist ideals, actually works from brilliance that is so often marginalized (huge deal!). My gosh! And then maybe our faculty discussions wouldn't be so painful because it wouldn't just be me, the Black Martian, talking about equity and equality! And then our department culture and climate could be better! And we could change the world institutionally: one university, one department, multiple faculty, and many students at a time!

So I keep trying . . .

Me: *I want to bring up X candidate. They have fewer publications, but one in [very high-impact journal], which I know was mentioned as important last time. They're junior, that's true. But their work is groundbreaking. In psychology, using critical race theory [Bell 1995] to research these concepts is revolutionary. We were just talking about how a theoretical perspective is important. They have it. And experimental methodology, which has been mentioned over and again as so central to this position.*

The other Black faculty member on the search committee provides additional points of this candidate's stellar, innovative work.

Them: *But . . . and maybe this is a bias. My general rule is that people who are ABD aren't ready for a faculty position. It's too much. They need a postdoc, some other experience. Cos with being faculty comes a lot of more stuff. And graduate students just aren't ready.*

Me: *Oh, well, I'm looking here. They have teaching experience as a graduate student. Instructor of record for multiple classes. Very high teacher evaluation ratings and comments from students. So they're already balancing some of this stuff at this level—research, teaching. Have been funded. Also, for scholars so junior, my frame is that I look for potential. What potential are they showing for future scholarship? They're showing quite a bit here to me.*

Silence.

Them: *Well, I like to look at the evidence. Maybe they'll go on to do great things, but without the evidence right now, you know, I can't know that.*

Many voices screaming in my head: The evidence was just presented!!! Groundbreaking research, published in a high-impact journal, and has gotten funding, all while balancing teaching as well! Already! At this early stage in their career! But I feel pretty confident that you are not qualified to assess this candidate given you probably haven't even heard of critical race theory. Maybe you've caught a whiff of it in discussions regarding the recent Executive Order on Combating Race and Sex Stereotyping (2020), though you probably weren't able to grasp that either. Fortunately, you have two Black faculty on this search committee who do recognize this scholarship, as well as this candidate's brilliance. Both have spoken enthusiastically and concretely about this candidate. This is why diverse representation is so important! Until I remember: We're just a collection of bodies . . .

. . . moving on.

Preliminary virtual-conference interviews have happened, with two faculty members on each and the student member additionally attending some. For one of my interviews, I augment the senior faculty's written summary that will be shared with the full committee: *Seemed to be not fully developed in terms of incorporating various components of diversity, equity, and inequality into his research (see above) or teaching (see here). Unclear of potential for growth in these domains. [Fleshed out teaching example from the interview.]*

The senior faculty removes my words from the summary, including the example I gave. Instead, she writes a diluted interpretation of my words, ending with the following: *Reading Jennifer's comments, [another committee member's name in the third person] isn't sure it was a contradiction—we moved on to another topic after that without following up*. Of course, there is not a way for the remaining members of the search committee to know what apparent "contradiction" she is referring to—or that a follow-up was unnecessary—given she removed my words of explanation.

This was perhaps the most unequivocal, and painful, silencing. Even I cannot second-guess my perception of what happened. It is impossible to misunderstand an interview summary for my colleagues in which Senior White Woman removes my words and publicly disagrees with my erased appraisal.

The Power of White Mediocrity

It is too early to know how this search will end. I do feel confident that, regardless of outcome, this search is neither fair nor equitable, as three themes are self-evident: (1) "just a body"—erased and rendered invisible throughout the process; (2) highest-status members of the search committee are not serious about diversity, equity, and inclusion in this hire or in the hiring process; and (3) coded racism—multiple excuses to uplift inferior white candidates and eliminate superior candidates of color, are employed, with ignorance, arrogance, and power. As such, this committee is an example of the ways in which faculty search committees reproduce whiteness (Ray 2019; Sensoy and DiAngelo 2017), including using the excuse of "fit" (White-Lewis 2020). Never in my presence has white mediocrity (Mitchell 2018) been so heavily concentrated while wielding so much power. The powers that be in this search committee cannot manage to be consistent in delineating what they are actually looking for in a hire, much less provide an equitable appraisal of applicants within a fair decision-making process. As sung by Selena Quintanilla Pérez in "God's Child (Baila Conmigo)" (Quintanilla Pérez and Byrne 1995), a mirror of academia: "¡Es nuestro reino, pero vean lo que hemos hecho!"

What of Resistance?

For myself, I continue to resist by not giving up: not resigning from the search committee, not disengaging from the process, and not being silent. I continue to try. And yet, try as I might on an individual level, nothing felt quite as soothing as a message I got from my friend and colleague, who is also the other Black faculty member on this search committee. After one particularly grueling meeting, he sent me a text that said, "Thank you for always being unapologetically you." The simple comment brings tears to my eyes now just as it did then. That solitary statement touched me deeply, showing me that I am not in fact invisible in this space. We went on to briefly commiserate on the reality of what was happening in these search committee meetings, while sharing joy, respect, and understanding with each other. It is in instances like these where I remember that this fight is not mine alone.

I Am Not Just a Body but Also a Soul

Though no one has given me negative feedback about my behavior, the highest-status faculty members on this search committee have consistently shown me what they think of me: *Just a body. Just a quota. Just an irritation. Just a squeaky wheel. Just a junior faculty member who doesn't know her Black woman place. Just a bitch nigger.*

To them.

But not to me.

To me, I have a soul so beautiful that I transcend all the discrimination, oppression, anti-Blackness, and sheer stupidity that I remain constantly surrounded by. From the doctor's office to the university. And I hold that truth so close and so dear. As a deliberate act of self-preservation and political warfare (Lorde 2017), I launch the fight for equality within myself.

With that, my internal whisper becomes a rallying cry: *I am not just a body but also a soul!*

Works Cited

AACU (Association of American Colleges and Universities). 2002. *Greater Expectations: A New Vision of Learning as a Nation Goes to College*. Washington, D.C.: AACU.

Ahmed, Sara. 2012. *On Being Included: Racism and Diversity in Institutional Life*. Durham, NC: Duke University Press.

Bell, Derrick A. 1995. "Who's Afraid of Critical Race Theory?" *University of Illinois Law Review* 4:893–910.

Executive Order on Combating Race and Sex Stereotyping. 2020. Executive Order 13950, 85 FR 60683. September 22, 2020. https://www.federalregister.gov/documents/2020/09/28/2020-21534/combating-race-and-sex-stereotyping

Gómez, Jennifer M. 2018. "A Time for Arrogance: A Minority Scholar Describes the Challenges She Experienced on the Academic Job Market." *Inside Higher Ed*, February 16, 2018. https://www.insidehighered.com/advice/2018/02/16/minority-scholar-describes-challenges-she-experienced-academic-job-market-opinion.

Gómez, Jennifer M. 2020. "Exposure to Discrimination, Cultural Betrayal, and Intoxication as a Black Female Graduate Student Applying for Tenure-Track Faculty Positions." In *Presumed Incompetent II: Race, Class, Power, and Resistance of Women in Academia*, edited by Yolanda Flores Niemann, Gabriella Gutierrez y Muhs, and Carmen G. Gonzalez, 204–14. Logan: Utah State University Press.

Lorde, Audre. 2017. *A Burst of Light and Other Essays*. Mineola, NY: Courier Dover Publications.

Mitchell, Koritha. 2018. "Identifying White Mediocrity and Know-Your-Place Aggression: A Form of Self-Care." *African American Review* 51, no. 4 (Winter): 253–62. https://doi.org/10.1353/afa.2018.0045.

Quintanilla Pérez, Selena, and David Byrne. 1995. "God's Child (Baila Conmigo)." Track 4 on *Dreaming of You*. London: EMI Records.

Ray, Victor. 2019. "A Theory of Racialized Organizations." *American Sociological Review* 84 (1): 26–53. https://doi.org/10.1177/0003122418822335.

Sensoy, Özlem, and DiAngelo, Robin. 2017. "'We Are All for Diversity, but . . .': How Faculty Hiring Committees Reproduce Whiteness and Practical Suggestions for How They Can Change." *Harvard Educational Review* 87, no. 4 (Winter): 557–80. https://doi.org/10.17763/1943-5045-87.4.557.

Smith, Carly P., and Jennifer J. Freyd. 2014. "Institutional Betrayal." *American Psychologist* 69 (6): 575–87. https://doi.org/10.1037/a0037564.

Washington, Harriet A. 2006. *Medical Apartheid: The Dark History of Medical Experimentation on Black Americans from Colonial Times to the Present*. New York: Doubleday.

White-Lewis, Damani K. 2020. "The Facade of Fit in Faculty Search Processes." *Journal of Higher Education* 91 (6): 833–57. https://doi.org/10.1080/00221546.2020.1775058.

24

Institutional Compassion

Counterstories to Betrayal in Sociology

Jennifer Lai and Angélica Ruvalcaba

Developing superpowers seems preordained for women of color in the academy. Every day, we must stay vigilant to the unmaking of our instincts, cultures, values, and upbringing, even as we inevitably succumb to it. When we enter academic spaces, we are immediately forced to examine, cast doubt upon, and ultimately contort our names, language, behavior, bodies, even our modes of thinking, or we are ignored or excluded. We stretch and strain ourselves to meet these expectations, presaging the consequences of what might happen if we do not submit to the comfort of those with privilege. Hence, superpowers.

Ironically, as sociologists, our intellectual mandate is to study structures, systems, and processes that produce and enable these harms; our discipline claims unique insight into a comprehensive picture of social injustice. And yet, race, gender, sexuality, disability, and other intersecting identities are still treated by many scholars as abstract concepts rather than lived experiences. A sort of hopeless hypocrisy is revealed when our assertions of "But this is *us*!" are met with backlash and contempt.

So what do you do when the scientific "experts" in your field struggle to acknowledge your everyday experiences with unjust processes that contribute to the very inequities they supposedly study? One option is to forge another narrative—although this is a skill that takes time to develop. It takes time because our everyday encounters with overt and covert discriminations leave Black, Indigenous, and people of color (BIPOC) scholars swaddled in doubt about our own ambitions and abilities. In our case, over the course of a year, we deliberately set aside small chunks of time to learn about each other's experiences, which unexpectedly contributed to a sense of catharsis and healing. Although the people, professional norms, and operating procedures of our predominantly white institution continue to make us feel like we do not belong, we have drawn upon our strength and mettle as critical BIPOC sociologists to center our own experiences as an inextricable part of the higher education narrative. As such, the aim of this essay is to demonstrate this skill of telling each other's stories. We also discuss the generative work that has followed.

Angélica's Story, as Told by Jennifer

In Angélica's story, multiple processes constitute the institutional betrayal she has faced. At the forefront of these processes are consistent patterns of negligence, racial stereotyping, and a practice of reducing students to their failures—patterns that, due to their subtlety, are among the most destructive forms of racism. Angélica entered our doctoral program in the fall of 2017 as the only student of color in a cohort of three. She was immediately subjected to a different experience than the other two students. For example, it took several weeks for our department to provide her with a desk, even though an individual workspace was supposed to be guaranteed by our graduate student employees' contract. I do not know where she worked in the interim, but the fact remains that a first-generation student of color was made to feel like she did not belong—unlike her peers, Angélica did not have access to a secure location on campus where she could do her work.

As sociologists, we are trained to identify individual actors and/or sequences of events that may have contributed to this result; certainly, some would describe Angélica's experience as mundane, incidental, or the result of an unlucky set of circumstances that made her desk assignment "slip through the cracks." But this narrative is precisely what we want to push back against. Patterns of negligence are not shaped by random mistakes. Angélica's status as a stakeholder in our department was swiftly communicated to her when the department failed to provide the most basic resource to facilitate her work as a scholar in training. Although she was intensely recruited, as soon as Angélica arrived on campus, the performative aspect of her recruitment made itself known. After being denied a space to work, Angélica could no longer take seriously the function of the department as an academic unit that would ensure the professional training of its students. Angélica was then forced to question if there would have been such a delay in accessing a desk if she did not occupy the positionality she does.

Ultimately, the emotional toll that accompanied her unmet expectations made it difficult for Angélica to actively engage with the department in all forms—not just the people and procedures but also its physical spaces. Physical spaces reproduce meanings and ideologies that are shaped by existing power relations (Neely and Samura 2011). When her other cohort members received desks and she did not, Angélica had no choice but to interpret her experience as colonial and racist ideologies made material. The absence of a space to do her work reinforced the idea that individuals like her did not belong in academic spaces like these. Such tangible imbalances of power are a key feature of ongoing legacies of exclusion and marginalization that BIPOC scholars consistently encounter within institutions of higher education (Barajas and Ronnkvist 2007; Anderson 2015).

The department's failure to provide a desk for Angélica set the tone for other incidents of institutional betrayal. Angélica was forced to find another community of peers, advisers, and mentors for emotional support and professional development. The fact that institutions must rely on the survival tactics of their most marginalized students to prevent attrition is further evidence that they are not the safe spaces they claim to be. Upon realizing that she had found her own community, the department wasted no time pigeonholing Angélica as a student of her found community as opposed to a scholar of sociology. Her found community happened to be in the Chicano/Latino Studies Program, meaning that when our department described Angélica as a "student of Chicano/Latino studies," they revealed that Angélica's racial identity would always feature foremost, rather than her interdisciplinary scholarship. This conflation of racial identity with professional expertise is commonly encountered in institutions of higher education; that is, our credibility as critical scholars is based on the fact that we are not white, rather than on the ideas we produce. As such, BIPOC scholars have a complicated relationship with our own scholarship: Revealing our positionalities and personal experiences as motivations for our research feels like sharing too much of ourselves to an undeserving audience. Yet these topics are precisely what our white colleagues express the most interest in "learning" from us.

Racial stereotyping that is upheld and, indeed, rewarded by institution-level metrics is another form of institutional betrayal. Angélica joined the Chicano/Latino Studies Program as a dual-major student; she did so not only because of her Latina identity but because she was able to easily access appropriate forms of support for her professional development. Consequently, being a dual-major student produced challenges that affected Angélica's "good standing" in our department. Even with the informal understanding that dual-major students must fulfill additional academic requirements, the bureaucratic procedures that classify students as "good" or "bad" based on their progress—a status that affects eligibility for funding, research, and teaching opportunities—do not account for these additional requirements. Rather than celebrate Angélica's commitment to two programs, as well as her scholarly engagement with two disciplines, the sociology department instead judged Angélica as a student who was "not meeting expectations" regarding the timely completion of departmental milestones. This stripping away of a student's story and context is another instance of institutional betrayal that disproportionately affects students who are driven by a sense of service and community building—here, a woman student of color.

Angélica's experiences, accumulated over four short years, show that institutional betrayal, rather than institutional support, was the primary feature of her sociology doctoral program at a predominantly white institution. Such incidents of institutional betrayal are symptomatic of an overarching structure of people and processes incentivized to reduce Angélica's talents, ambitions, and accomplishments into a metric, or to a matter of race, or to their perception of her failures. It is no wonder that when BIPOC students talk about their experiences in higher education, they describe them as matters of survival.

Jennifer's Story, as Told by Angélica

Institutional betrayal takes many forms. Yet when I reflect on Jennifer's journey through the sociology doctoral program, I can see the betrayal most clearly in the lack of representation, the double standards that professors have placed on her, and the lack of support she has received from our department. These are only a few out of many betrayals that Jennifer has endured and has had to overcome, not to prove that she is strong or capable enough but because there is no other way to thrive in the academy as a woman of color.

In 2014, Jennifer entered an institution and program that was predominantly white—which is common, as most institutions of higher education have historically been white, elitist, and exclusionary to BIPOC, and have upheld colonial values and systems of oppression (McCabe 2009; Shotton et al. 2018; Ayala and Ramirez 2019). Although the department's demographics have changed over time to be more inclusive of BIPOC scholars, true representation is lacking. There remains a lack of Asian American, and more specifically Chinese American, students in the department, with Jennifer currently being the only one. Some might defend the demographic makeup of departments or entire institutions with the tired excuse that it is "just a result of recruiting based on expertise." But as women of color, we know this is not the case. We know that, when compared to the rate of hiring white candidates, institutions fail to hire and retain BIPOC and individuals of other marginalized identities (Bensimon 2005; Zambrana et al. 2015). So when I state that the department has failed Jennifer in providing representation, this is not just a coincidence. It is part of a wholesale rejection of BIPOC scholars as experts and a devaluing of their unique experiences and positionalities.

Concrete representation provides a window for students to see what the academy values. When students are not represented, the message is clear: they do not belong in the academy. This has serious consequences; scholars have found that a lack of demographic representation often leads BIPOC students to feel out of place and more likely to question the legitimacy of their merits (González 2002; Yosso and Benavides Lopez 2010). Even as departments and institutions publicly declare their commitment to diversity, equity, and inclusion (DEI), we often see that it does not take the form of representation. They are yet again betraying their students by proclaiming something they do not materialize in practice.

Jennifer also encountered institutional betrayal in how she was steered away from and eventually deprived of her abilities to creatively present research findings and collaborate with her peers. Coming from an engineering background, Jennifer was used to working in teams to accomplish project objectives. She also enjoyed the challenge of finding creative ways to present scientific information to diverse audiences; her personal style involved using colorful graphics to emphasize major takeaways from her research. Yet when she tried to draw on these strengths, she was told by faculty advisers that these approaches were not professional or appropriate for academic work. Likewise, when Jennifer pursued professional opportunities or engaged in community activities, she was scolded for spending her time on work that was not "relevant" to her scholarly training. What made these remarks worse was the fact that these same faculty advisers celebrated and praised Jennifer's white colleagues when they used colorful graphics or pursued similar opportunities outside of our department. This betrayal was specifically targeted to Jennifer; the lack of support she received felt calculated, like she had become a container for her faculty advisers to pour their own frustrations and trauma into. Her faculty advisers enacted this treatment under the guise of "academic advising," the net effect being that Jennifer was made to feel like nothing she did would be good enough for the academy.

This potent mix of emotional exploitation prompted Jennifer to change the composition of her committee four times over the past six years. Over and over again, Jennifer's faculty advisers projected their insecurities and mentoring deficiencies onto her. Despite this, Jennifer found ways to thrive. Eventually, she revived her instincts of engaging in creative and collaborative work and has since led multiple sociological projects that combine critical ideas from our field with a diverse assortment of research methods. Jennifer has accomplished this despite being thoroughly detached from most forms of departmental support. The department celebrates some student accomplishments, but they have never reconciled their inaction and, at times, their complicity in working against students like Jennifer. They take their students' accomplishments as their own but do not view the student's experiences with racism and other injustices as equally their own; they leave these for the students to bear alone. This betrayal is well known among BIPOC; we are tokenized and celebrated when convenient, but we are rarely given the same attention when we need it the most.

It is important to understand that the institutional betrayals Jennifer has faced did not just suddenly emerge. Rather, they are engaged with by perpetrators who serve as catalysts for experiences of harm to BIPOC students. As we share these stories, we want to emphasize that intent and impact matter. Such institutional betrayals are not unique to Jennifer, our department, our institution, or our discipline. I see our histories reflected in one another; I see her experiences with institutional betrayal in my own experiences. But it should not be up to Jennifer, other BIPOC scholars, or me to address alone. Eliminating institutional betrayal requires an institutional dismantling.

Discussion

Across time, space, and cohorts, we expected our institution to provide us with the tools we needed to thrive. Instead, it has cut us down and held us back. It has engendered a continuous and endless cycle of betrayal. Despite this, we are resilient. Our ability to thrive in our department was not a result of the institution itself. The term "institutional courage" has been used to describe actions that seek and promote "the truth" despite high inertia within institutional settings (Center for Institutional Courage, n.d.). It then follows that courageous institutions are those that do all they can to protect and care for the people who depend on them. But even if being courageous was enough to transform institutions into "more accountable, equitable, effective places for everyone" (Center for Institutional Courage, n.d.), it would not be enough to redress the totality of BIPOC experiences within these institutions. Addressing the injustices and inequities that we have experienced would mean dismantling the very foundations of these institutions, since they are rooted in nothing less than scientific racism (Simpson 2017; Smith 1999). Doing so would not only be unpleasant; it would result in extreme pushback from the white majority. It would require long-term commitments, not short-term inconveniences. There is little to suggest that institutions of higher education are ready for such commitments. But we, as BIPOC, cannot idly wait as institutions pursue DEI projects that serve as Band-Aid solutions.

By learning how to tell each other's stories, we have come to realize that *institutional compassion* has been the driving force behind our ability to thrive in our departments. Institutional compassion does not rely on the rigmarole of the institution itself but on the defiant and often quiet labor of those within it. In a sea of betrayal, competition, and gatekeeping, we have learned how to recognize those who reject such an unsustainable version of the academy. Rather than reproduce harm, individuals who exercise institutional compassion use the infrastructure of the academy to establish accessible communities, initiate and maintain meaningful forms of mentorship and collaboration, and create spaces for rest and recuperation for students, staff, and faculty on the margins.

For graduate students like us, hitching our everyday work to the idea of institutional compassion is both motivational and generative. We found that we could listen to only so many stories of betrayal before we realized we were waiting for something that was not coming. Ultimately, our institutions betray us because they reveal themselves to be hollow in their promise of being a safe learning environment, a reliable provider of professional development, and a beacon for equality and justice. They do not know how to do the work of protecting students and ensuring opportunities for self-actualization and learning. But we do—and we have been doing the work! By learning and validating each other's stories, and by practicing compassionate collaboration, we leverage the knowledge of each other's experiences of injustice to propel our present actions—a necessary precursor to leaving a place better than we found it.

The term *institution* suggests a center of operations that relies on a consolidation of power and top-down practices. But institutional compassion as a mechanism for meaningful and reliable support is disperse and yet focused on centering marginalized scholars, specifically BIPOC, so it cannot be something that is forced by the institution itself. Institutional compassion cannot arise out of a workshop or be checked off a to-do list; in practice, it arises out of mundane acts of care and consideration. To make room for this essential work, we recommend that institutions recognize students, specifically BIPOC and other marginalized students, as significant stakeholders within their communities. We recommend that institutions trust BIPOC and marginalized students as they explore their ways of knowing and cultivate their expertise. In doing this, they are directly challenging the oppressive norms instilled within institutions of higher education. It is thus the duty of institutions that wish to practice compassion to stand by those students.

Works Cited

Anderson, Elijah. 2015. "The White Space." *Sociology of Race and Ethnicity* 1 (1): 10–21. https://doi.org/10.1177/2332649214561306.

Ayala, Maria Isabel, and Christian Ramirez. 2019. "Coloniality and Latinx College Students' Experiences." *Equity & Excellence in Education* 52 (1): 129–44. https://doi.org/10.1080/10665684.2019.1635542.

Barajas, Heidi and Amy Ronnkvist. 2007. "Racialized Space: Framing Latino and Latina Experience in Public Schools." *Teachers College Record* 109 (6): 1517–38. https://doi.org/10.1177/016146810710900605.

Bensimon, Estela M. 2005. "Closing the Achievement Gap in Higher Education: An Organizational Learning Perspective." *New Directions for Higher Education*, no. 131, 99–111. https://doi.org/10.1002/he.190.

Center for Institutional Courage. n.d. "Institutional Courage." Accessed December 10, 2020. https://www.institutionalcourage.org.

González, Kenneth P. 2002. "Campus Culture and the Experience of Chicano Students in Predominantly White University." *Urban Education* 37 (2): 193–218. https://psycnet.apa.org/doi/10.1177/0042085902372003.

Liboiron, Max, Justine Ammendolia, Katharine Winsor, Alex Zahara, Hillary Bradshaw, Jessica Melvin, Charles Mather, Natalya Dawe, Emily Wells, France Liboiron, Bojan Fürst, Coco Coyle, Jacquelyn Saturno, Melissa Novacefski, Sam Westcott, Grandmother Liboiron. 2016. "Equity in the Author Order: A Feminist Laboratory's Approach." *Catalyst: Feminism, Theory, Technoscience* 3 (2): 1–17. https://doi.org/10.28968/cftt.v3i2.28850.

McCabe, Janice. 2009. "Racial and Gender Microaggressions on a Predominantly-White Campus: Experiences of Black, Latina/o and White Undergraduates." *Race, Gender & Class* 16 (1–2): 133–51. http://www.jstor.org/stable/41658864.

Neely, Brooke, and Michelle Samura. 2011. "Social Geographies of Race: Connecting race and space." *Ethnic and Racial Studies* 34 (11): 1933–52. https://doi.org/10.1080/01419870.2011.559262.

Shotton, Heather J., Amanda R. Tachine, Christine A. Nelson, Robin Zape-tah-hol-ah Minthorn, and Stephanie J. Waterman. 2018. "Living Our Research Through Indigenous Scholar Sisterhood Practices." *Qualitative Inquiry* 24 (9): 638–45. https://doi.org/10.1177/1077800417744578.

Simpson, Leanne Betasamosake. 2017. *As We Have Always Done: Indigenous Freedom Through Radical Resistance*. Minneapolis: University of Minnesota Press.

Smith, Linda Tuhiwai. 1999. *Decolonizing Methodologies: Research and Indigenous Peoples*. London: Zed Books.

Yosso, Tara, and Corina Benavides Lopez. 2010. "Counterspaces in a Hostile Place." In *Culture Centers in Higher Education: Perspectives on Identity, Theory, and Practice*, edited by Lori D. Patton, 83–104. Sterling, VA: Stylus.

Zambrana, Ruth E., Rashawn Ray, Michelle M. Espino, Corinne Castro, Beth Douthirt Cohen, and Jennifer Eliason. 2015. "Don't Leave Us Behind: The Importance of Mentoring for Underrepresented Minority Faculty." *American Educational Research Journal* 52 (1): 40–72. https://doi.org/10.3102/0002831214563063.

25

Out of the Shadows

Kathy Diehl

Terminal contract
Budget cuts
Program dissolution
I sit in shock, feeling paralyzed
Taking in the cold stares
Of those who control the strings
Terminators

How did I become this silent body?
A feeling of gray descends and settles
I sink into my new reality
A reality that is now a void where the dream of tenure used to be
A vast space of uncertainty
I try to fill it with anger and resentment
But remain powerless
Invisible/Erased

Retreating into the heartbreak
Of this unexpected, unknown path
Existing in a state of suspended disbelief
So much dedication, time, investment . . .
No rationale, No explanations

Questions without answers
Including questioning myself . . . gaslighting?

Confronted with limitations of
Hiring freezes
Program closures
Devaluing of the arts
Devaluing female artists over forty
Fear and Intimidation
COVID
How will I recover? Survive?
How does a fifty-year-old dance educator start over?

I remind myself of what I know
about
Embodied Resiliency

Slowing down
Acknowledging
Reconnecting to my Body's wisdom
With a rush of gratitude
I find my feet again
Grounded
Forging a new path

Shifting toward a new
Perspective
I *choose* to embrace the Spiraling Journey
Dancing my way out of the Lies
Inhumanity
Hostility and Toxicity

While the future remains unclear
I have to try
I begin to find more clarity
I reclaim what I know
Move beyond the secrets and degradation
Out of the shadows of questioning my worth
Into an open space of
Creative Possibilities
Reinvention

Freedom.

26

La Llorona of the Academy

Shantel Martinez

The purpose of this poem is to reclaim the monster of la llorona into a figure of power, freedom, and beauty. By weaving together elements of her myth with my lived experience, this poem illuminates the ways in which I have been positioned and become the wailing woman of the academy through the haunting presence of colonization, intergenerational trauma, racism, sexism, and betrayal. Through owning my monstrosity, I create a new path of being and belonging.

I am the wailing woman.
Drowning what I birthed into the world
The bringer of death
The wailing woman
La traidora
The goddess of monstrous woman
How could it come to this?
With no regrets
And no remorse
I reclaimed what belonged to me
    My life
    My body
    My tongue
    myself

Letting the dark water wash over my sins
Hands fighting the turbulent currents
  I chose to let go
  To free myself from what tethered me to that   life
The silver full moon,
My sole witness
Guiding and illuminating my path
of no return.

I am the wailing woman.
Whose cries
fill the colonial and colonized halls
                    of the ivory tower
My virginal white robes
Cloak the eternal suffering of ancestors.
Bound.
Chained.
Gagged.
Silenced.
  For daring to speak back. Speak their truth.
  Bruised and battered,
  Their words mix in my blood, fueling life through death
  Haunting the present.
    Trauma can be a bitch.
The academy said I was too much
  Too loud, proud, Brown, and mad.
   Uncivil.
   Fiery.
   Unfit.
   Impostor.
  But they never admitted
   That they too were responsible for my monstrosity.

I am the wailing woman.
My story is infamous. A myth in the making. A ghost story.
With words whispering in the wind, I warn you.
To stop the cycle of trauma.
The story of the young woman
who fell in love
    with knowledge and education
Thinking that it would be my one true love
Bringing me happiness for a new future.
And so I left my family, my community, my place of safety
To be with my lover, *my education*
Not for the degree or credentials
But for freedom to create
    To be curious
    To speak my story into existence
        Thinking this would be the ultimate gift,
                Not knowing this would be the
                ultimate sacrifice.
And through time, I birthed you children:
    New knowledge
        Papers
            Articles
                Dissertation.
I birthed these things
thinking that you would love me more.
That your love would be faithful
but the closer I thought I would get to you
the more you pushed me away.
Telling me I was unfaithful
That I was no longer a blind believer.

I am the wailing woman.
Yelling that
The power of pipelines
is actually the power of
pipe/lies.
Where mentors become sister wives
intertwined for the same love
and competition
is spirited against both women
tearing their loyalties apart.
And so,
I became *la llorona.*
Drowning my training
drowning your lessons
Drowning what I have birthed
in order to be the fierce and feared
Latina that you could not kill.
That you could not silence.

I wail
to warn those,
not of my presence
but of yours.

27

Becoming a Problem

James M. Thomas (JT)

I remember what compelled me to become a problem. It was that image of those migrant children. Seventeen of them, standing single file between makeshift tent barracks within a newly constructed detention camp in Tornillo, Texas. At the end of that single-file line, a child stands several feet apart from the rest, hanging their head.

When I was eleven years old, my grandmother took me to Washington, D.C., to see the Holocaust Memorial Museum, which had opened that year. Growing up, I often attended synagogue with my grandmother. Among her temple friends was a Polish woman named Tola. When Tola was a child, the Nazis put her family into a camp. Tola was the sole survivor. Even at a young age, I was made to understand the significance of what the Nazis had done to Tola, her family, and six million others. Because Tola was my grandmother's friend, and a Holocaust survivor.

And yet it was not until I visited that memorial museum in 1993 that the Holocaust became visceral for me. Two memories from that visit remain etched into my person, indelible marks just below the surface. The first was the memorial museum's entranceway. As a child, I recall thinking while passing through it that I was entering into a camp like other children before me. Perhaps like Tola. Yet I was just visiting, while those children never left.

My second memory is of the room filled with shoes. There were some four thousand of them, in a large pile. The smell of rot and decay hung in the air. The longer you stood in the room, the stronger the smell became. Even if you turned your eyes from that pile of shoes, there was no way to escape that smell. You simply had to bear it. But in bearing that smell, you bore witness to both the sheer terror and utter mundanity of the Holocaust. There, in that room, was just a pile of shoes. Shoes not unlike those on my feet, on the feet of other passersby. And yet, of those men and women and children who had hopes, dreams, love, and laughter, all that remained were their shoes. Only their shoes, and that lingering smell of rot and decay.

If I close my eyes, I can still see those baby shoes. In my mind, they are still white, like new. They sit atop the remaining pile, a backdrop of faded shades of brown and gray. And if I close my eyes, I can still smell what my eleven-year-old self thought was the smell of death. When I saw that picture of those migrant children in Tornillo, Texas, and when I look upon that picture today, I see those shoes in that room. And I smell death.

In early October of 2018, the Trump presidency was only half-complete. By then, the racial dog whistles of my youth had already become full-blown foghorns. The Senate had just voted to confirm Brett Kavanaugh to the U.S. Supreme Court despite Christine Blasey Ford's testimony alleging he sexually assaulted her when they were teenagers. Meanwhile, MSNBC's Joe Scarborough was condemning protestors for interrupting the meals of U.S. senators, rather than condemning those senators for having put migrant children in detention camps and appointing an alleged rapist to the Supreme Court.

But it was the image of those migrant children that compelled me to become a problem. "Don't just interrupt a senator's meal, y'all," I posted to Twitter on October 6, 2018. "Put your whole damn fingers in their salads. Take their apps and distribute them to the other diners. Bring boxes and take their food home with you on the way out.

They don't deserve your civility." In hindsight, I should have more forcefully condemned those senators who enabled the internment of migrant children. In hindsight, I should have known that my comments, guised as humor and as milquetoast as they were, would make me into a problem.

•

Within a few short weeks, my tweet had become the focus of a right-wing harassment campaign. The chancellor of my university had condemned my remarks on his university-managed Facebook account. That condemnation was subsequently reported on first by *Campus Reform*, then *Fox News*, and, later, *Breitbart*. The chancellor had given the mob carte blanche. And now, to many, I was a problem that needed to go away.

The first wave of hate mail hit my university inbox beginning in mid-October.

> Stop talking, walk in some upscale restaurant full of Oxford Conservatives and Provoke the Man. Stick those spindly Quadroon fingers of yours in their Cob Salad—and get your mostly White Ass kicked. (October 17, 2018)

> I hope someone tortures you to death. (October 17, 2018)

> You are disgusting and this won't end well for you. It will suck to be you very shortly. (October 17, 2018)

> Incivility is nasty business, it cuts both ways. We may be slow to violence, but we're much better at it. (October 18, 2018)

> Hey Scumbag. I don't want you dead, I just want to see you bleeding out on the floor from the holes in your head, and then watch you

> go to the hospital to recover, only to get beat on again. (October 18, 2018)

From mid-October through early November, I received some three hundred emails, voice mails, and letters, many similar to those above. Burial insurance brochures arrived in my campus mailbox. One person posted my home address to Twitter, encouraging others to pay me a late-night visit while my children are sleeping.

Along with threats of violence, university administrators and staff fielded hundreds of other phone calls and emails calling for my firing. A Mississippi state senator referred to my actions as disgusting and demanded the chancellor take immediate action. The state senator made no mention of those migrant children, standing in a single-file line under that Texas sun. In 2022, this same state senator sponsored a bill to end tenure in Mississippi public colleges and universities. The bill, Senate Resolution 2692, died in committee (2022).

The governor of Mississippi responded to my remarks on his own Twitter account: "This is troubling and disappointing to see from one of our university professors. There is no place in a civilized society, and particularly on a college campus, for urging individuals to harass anyone." The governor offered no opinion on whether the forced internment of migrant children has any place in a civilized society. The governor was a person of interest in a federal investigation for his role in the misspending of $77 million in federal Temporary Assistance for Needy Families funds while he was in office (Ganucheau 2022).

What I recall most clearly about these threats of violence and calls for my termination was how unbothered I was by it all, and how off-putting that appeared to others. Many of my colleagues in my department were especially concerned for their own safety, presumably because anyone wanting to do me harm might also harm them. In response to their concerns, the dean of my college, working with my department chair and university police, placed a security detail on the floor of the academic building in which our department is housed. Outside the building, a university police officer regularly patrolled the surrounding parking lots.

The dean and chair also encouraged me to pass along to the university police any messages I deemed threatening, so that they could investigate. I complied, in large part because of their concerns, not my own.

There are some who believe my lack of concern over these threats was a kind of masculine posturing or a defense mechanism. I find that idea reductive. I grew up and attended school in Kansas City, Missouri, at the height of its crime wave. I was robbed more than once, including at gunpoint. To enter into my middle and high schools I had to walk through metal detectors. Once, in the sixth grade while waiting in line with the other children to enter my school building in the early morning, I watched a friend pull a kitchen knife from his winter jacket and attempt to stab a seventh grader who had been bullying him.

It's not that I didn't take these threats seriously. I know there are any number of people in this world willing to go to great lengths to hurt others. The difference between my colleagues and me is that because I know this, I also know those people who would hurt me would do so no matter how I choose to move in this world. So, I choose to be unbothered. But by being unbothered, I became a problem.

•

A few days after my social media post, I and three other colleagues made public our research report on racial microaggressions at the University of Mississippi (Johnson et al. 2018). The report was the culmination of three years of work. The research was solid, and the report was thorough. The report was also not flattering to the university.

Our report documented over 1,300 incidents of microaggressions, from more than 600 students on our campus (Johnson et al. 2018). Our study was approved by our university's institutional review board, which allowed us to collect sensitive data on the condition that we not publicize identifying information.

While our report was shared with the public in early October, it was not news to the university's leadership. We had been in conversation with the Office of the Provost and the Office of the Chancellor for months prior to the release of the report. We even worked closely with the provost and the Office of Diversity and Community Engagement to plan a public presentation of our findings to the campus public later that spring semester.

Despite our good faith efforts to work with campus leadership, the same chancellor who had condemned my social media post also penned a letter to the campus newspaper in which he questioned the accuracy of our claims (Vitter 2018). "I must take exception," he wrote, "with the assertion in the report that the University of Mississippi 'has made halting but tangible progress toward creating an inclusive campus environment.'" The chancellor then cited the share of Black student enrollment since our integration in 1962 as evidence of "sustained, substantial, and measurable progress." But, of course, our own report did not question enrollment numbers. Rather, we drew attention to the experiences of those students once they arrived on our campus.

The chancellor also questioned our research integrity. "I must add," he continued, "that I am disappointed by the fact that the report is silent on whether the research group helped the students who self-reported these incidents by referring them to local authorities or encouraging them to take advantage of resources available on our campus." Here, the implication was clear. While the incidents we documented were difficult to read, they were not the real problem. Rather, the real problem was our own supposed neglect of those students in the aftermath of their racist encounters. Never did the chancellor consider that an institution that so effortlessly enables a climate where racist encounters are commonplace is also likely ill equipped to provide the resources required to navigate that climate.

•

The chair of my department called a departmental meeting in mid-October to address the fallout from my social media post and the publication of the microaggressions report. One of my colleagues encouraged me to use that meeting as an opportunity to tell my side of things, reasoning that if people understood what I was trying to convey in my tweet, they might be more supportive. At the time, it seemed like well-intended advice. Yet at the meeting, I chose instead to simply listen. I do not regret that decision. I wanted to know what my colleagues thought of what was happening to me. I learned in that meeting that many of them felt something was happening to them. That they were being made into a problem of which they wanted no part.

At the meeting, our chair described the past weeks' events as "two bombs going off." One bomb was the chancellor's undermining of faculty research. The other was the public reaction to my tweet. He encouraged us to hold together as a department. Some colleagues suggested that we draft a departmental letter defending our research report. There was less enthusiasm for a letter defending my remarks. These were two separate bombs, they argued, and a defense of my tweet required a different strategy. Yet no real strategy was offered in that meeting, though several suggested that we should all refrain from posting on social media.

Complicating matters was the fact that there were four of us going up for tenure and promotion that fall. Several colleagues expressed concern at this meeting that if the department appeared to rebuke the chancellor, it might jeopardize our chances of success. Better to say nothing, they argued, and let this blow over. Ultimately, my department offered no defense at all, of our research report or my remarks.

Looking back, it seems as though the invocation of strategy was one way for my department, and my university, to avoid dealing with a problem. Our research report was a clear exercise of academic freedom. My speech was a clear exercise of my First Amendment rights. Neither require complex strategy to defend. But they do require institutional will. And there was little, if any, of that.

•

In *Living a Feminist Life*, the philosopher Sara Ahmed writes of institutional spaces, "When you expose a problem you pose a problem. It might then be assumed that the problem would go away if you would just stop talking about it or if you went away" (2017, 37). I became a problem in 2018 because my colleagues and I dared to document the scale and scope of racist experiences on our campus. I became a problem in 2018 because I could not stomach the image of migrant children interned in detention camps. I became a problem in 2018 because I refused to apologize, publicly or privately, for suggesting that the politicians who enabled the internment of those migrant children did not deserve a moment of peace. I remain a problem to this day because I refuse to stop talking or to go away.

Institutions are organized around ignoring, minimizing, and avoiding problems like me. Institutions work to render problems like me invisible or irrelevant. I am an expert on diversity, equity, and inclusion (DEI) efforts, and I am rarely asked to participate on university committees organized around DEI. I have a national reputation as a leading scholar on race and racism, and I have never taught my department's graduate seminar on race.

I have been described by my colleagues as "combative," "stubborn," and "difficult." I am none of those things, of course. I am a dedicated scholar, teacher, and mentor. I am collaborative, kind, and generous. But I am also a problem, because I dare to expose other problems.

Becoming a problem is my choice. I could choose silence. I could choose to "play possum," as it was once advised to me while I was receiving death threats. I have a choice. I choose to become a problem. I choose to become a problem that will not go away and that cannot be ignored.

Works Cited

Ahmed, Sara. 2017. *Living a Feminist Life*. Durham, NC: Duke University Press.

Delgado, Edwin. 2018. "Texas Detention Camp Swells Fivefold with Migrant Children." *The Guardian*, October 3, 2018. https://www.theguardian.com/us-news/2018/oct/02/texas-detention-camp-swells-fivefold-with-migrant-children.

Ganucheau, Adam. 2022. "Congressman Asks Feds to Investigate Former Gov. Phil Bryant's Welfare Spending Influence." *Mississippi Today*, July 15, 2022. https://mississippitoday.org/2022/07/15/phil-bryant-federal-investigation-welfare-scandal/.

Johnson, Kirk, Willa Johnson, John J. Green, and James M. Thomas. 2018. *Microaggressions at the University of Mississippi: A Report from the UM Race Diary Project*. Oxford: University of Mississippi.

Senate Resolution 2692. 2022. Mississippi Legislature, Regular Session 2022. https://billstatus.ls.state.ms.us/documents/2022/pdf/SB/2600-2699/SB2692IN.pdf.

Vitter, Jeffrey. 2018. "Guest Column: Ole Miss Chancellor Jeffrey Vitter." *Daily Mississippian*, October 11, 2018. https://thedmonline.com/editorial-from-chancellor-vitter/.

Afterword

Institutional Violence, Complaints, and Betrayals

Behind Closed Doors

Reshmi Dutt-Ballerstadt

The site of violence is the site of protesting that violence, saying no to that violence. That complaints are made is how we come to know something happened there: no as a tale, as trail.

—Sara Ahmed, *Complaint!*

The Complaint

During spring break in March 2022, I received an email from my university's HR director about an investigation that was being launched against me about my social media activities. The email noted that there would be an external investigation. This email marked the end of my spring break.

Who complained? What was the complaint about? What was I being accused of? I had answers to none of these questions. I was both curious and angry at the lack of institutional transparency and the school's avoidance of using any internal investigative process. That evening, I made a bold decision. I decided to go public on social media (Twitter) about the letter I had just received from HR targeting me due to my social media activities. I was acutely aware that as a result of my public stance I could receive further retaliations, or even be fired.

But I did not want this complaint to remain a "secret" or become a "behind closed doors" affair. After all, complaints are made when a complainer locates a problem. Yet when the complainer or the complainant is a BIPOC or an LGBTQIA+ person or a woman of color in a predominantly white institution, they are often marked as a problem. To address this, I wanted a hearing—because I did not want my institution to *secretly* monitor my social media activities, like authoritarian regimes do, and then weaponize the rhetoric of civility to discipline me and others who want to speak up. Dana Cloud has called such methods of surveillance "soft repressions" (2021, 17).

Instead of receiving a hearing, I learned a few things about the complaint process that need redressing. In fact, the complaint process itself when used to harass or intimidate scholars (rather than to protect them) is a form of institutional betrayal. Anyone who has ever had the courage to file a complaint or stand up against a false complaint knows about power, abuse of power, and tacit and active retaliations. Then, there are the various gag orders given by "human resources" to all those involved (the complainant, the accused, the witnesses), under the cloak of "confidentiality," prohibiting parties from getting any information about what exactly happens "behind closed doors." The expression "behind closed doors," as Ahmed says, "can refer to the actual doors that might need to be closed before someone can share information in confidence. It can also be used to signal how information is kept secret from a public" (2017, 179).

While complaints serve as an institutional inventory of wrongdoings, they also capture how institutions discourage complaints (particularly complaints of racism, sexual assault, sexism, and pay gaps). Such discouragements, or blockages, thereby lead to suppression of otherwise legitimate complaints, and the reproduction of institutional violence, silencing, and harm exposes deeply asymmetrical power distributions.

We have repeatedly seen the repercussion of complaints (that were either suppressed, not fully investigated, or made not in good faith) in recent times in cases involving sexual harassment (Hartocollis 2022), racism (AAUP 2023), and pay gap discriminations (Spiggle 2022). What becomes apparent is that the complaint process in most academic institutions serves to protect the institutions rather than the well-being of the complainants. The entire process operates in deep secrecy, lacks transparency, and its outcomes are often micromanaged by the institution's legal counsel. Taken together, the complaint process and its outcomes (often not in the favor of women and faculty of color when issues of racism and differential treatments are raised) not only harms the complainants but also obstructs the realization of a "just" university.

In the era of constitutionally protected free speech, protected activities, and "extramural speech" (Whittington 2019), I wanted my accuser(s) to witness how such a complaint filed (as a result of surveillance of my social media activities on my personal accounts) registered with the public. This is also a kind of a hearing. Rather than closing the door, I wanted to open the door wide so that my institution and others who prefer such one-sided investigations could witness the nature of their transgressions. I was also clear that if a complaint was indeed filed against me, the accuser should be allowed their right to due process and the complaint should be fully investigated. My only request was that I be made aware of the accusations, so that I could prepare a proper defense and avoid a Kafkaesque scenario.

The Next Morning and Thereafter

By the next morning, my tweet had gone viral. The following day, FIRE (Foundation for Individual Rights and Expression),* published

* FIRE stood for the Foundation for Individual Rights in Education at the time the letter was written.

an open letter demanding an explanation from the university (Conza 2022). Within a few days, outraged colleagues around the country circulated a national petition. This was followed by an article in *Inside Higher Ed* by Colleen Flaherty, reporting on the alleged intimidation by my university against me for my extramural speech.

In the meantime, I waited for the investigator to contact me. There was radio silence. While I was grateful to have support from colleagues across the country, and my two attorneys who stood by me, my body was experiencing acute stress and trauma. I was literally bleeding. A nurse confirmed that the bleeding was induced by acute stress.

Then, after twenty-eight days of waiting, I received an email from HR titled "Status of Investigation." *After twenty-eight days*. This letter thanked me "for [my] patience" and said, "We investigated the complaints filed against you of creating a hostile work environment." This was followed by a brief paragraph that read, "We have a system in place to evaluate complaints fairly and thoroughly. An outside investigator investigated these complaints and found an interview with you will not be necessary. No further action is required by you or the university and there were no findings."

I noticed how the language of the alleged investigation had shifted. There was no longer any mention of a "social media"-related investigation or, as the original HR letter had stated, that my actions "were unprofessional to colleagues in the building." The investigation, as it stood, was about me "creating a hostile work environment."

The day after I was exonerated, my bleeding stopped. While my stress level decreased, I was still angry for being treated with such hostility and carelessness. There was no apology for putting me through this horrific ordeal for three weeks and harming my well-being or my professional reputation. FIRE deemed the entire complaint to be "bogus" (Conza 2022), simply an effort to intimidate me for being a vocal critic of our administration.

The Cost of Institutional Violence

Sara Ahmed has written, "To be a complaint activist is not necessarily to enter a process believing it can deliver an end such as justice. Complaint activism does not come from an optimism in the law or in complaints procedures; if anything, complaint activism comes out of the knowledge of institutional violence that comes from making complaints" (2021, 258).

This is a narrative about institutional violence, institutional failures, institutional harassments, institutional betrayals—narratives of institutional disease and disorders. This is a narrative not just about my institution but about how institutions behave, or rather misbehave, when their subjects, particularly women, BIPOC, and gender-nonconforming subjects, demand equity and justice. It is ultimately a reportage about how institutions want to expel bodies, bodies that aim to disallow institutions from keeping their secrets from the public—secrets that expose their Title IX and diversity, equity, and inclusion failures. Finally, this is a piece about how institutions weaponize HR departments to deploy a complaint process to routinely discipline, punish, silence, and gaslight those who show institutional courage. In fact, "all too often, institutions fail the very people they should protect" (Center for Institutional Courage, n.d.).

According to the Center for Institutional Courage, "institutional courage" is defined as "an institution's commitment to seek the truth and engage in moral action, despite unpleasantness, risk, and short-term cost. It is a pledge to protect and care for those who depend on the institution. It is a compass oriented to the common good of individuals, institutions, and the world. It is a force that transforms institutions into more accountable, equitable, effective places for everyone" (n.d.).

Yet the reality is quite different. To those who are employed by the institutions (even when one is tenured and has the protection of academic freedom), showing institutional courage is costly, both emotionally and financially.

Oftentimes, those who show institutional courage to expose the wrongdoings of their institutions are disruptors and are punished for their disruptions. They are portrayed as "bad citizens," charged with trying to harm the institution. And such charges of harm can also come from one's colleagues who benefit from the institution. Even though the complainant is the one who has been betrayed by the institution, in order to protect itself, the institution often portrays the betrayed as the betrayers.

Oftentimes, it is women and BIPOC faculty and staff who challenge the status quo and refuse to protect the "secrecy" of complaints of harassment, racism and microaggressions, sexism, sexual misconducts, and differential treatments. Yet when they stand up against their aggressors (who are often colleagues or administrators) and file complaints to their HR departments, they are often charged with "unprofessionalism" or violating the "codes of civility" or "mutual respect." They experience both structural and lateral violence, as Cathy Park Hong (2020) articulates in her book *Minor Feelings*, which documents the racism that poet Prageeta Sharma experienced at the University of Montana.

Oftentimes, the complainant experiences isolation, bullying, silent treatments, humiliations, loss of institutional resources, gaslighting, and various tacit ways to discredit and harm their reputation.

Oftentimes, the internal investigations that are micromanaged by the institution's legal counsel are meant to protect the institution and not the complainant. In fact, internal investigations have the potential to create an even more hostile environment (post the complaint) than prior to the complaint.

Oftentimes, the complainants have to seek the help of outside attorneys to file their complaints, in some cases turning to federal agencies such as the Equal Employment Opportunity Commission or the Department of Labor. Not only do such complaints against their institutions delay the process, adding to more stress, but these outside institutions are often overworked, leading to investigations that are incomplete and conclusions that signal a miscarriage of justice and a broken system.

Oftentimes, the "ungrateful citizens" who are also marked as "troublemakers" make the power structures anxious. If these power structures are predominantly white, any complaints about racism increase both the white fragility and racial anxiety of these institutions. Yet the bad actors who cause tremendous harm to the complainants remain protected by confidentiality and continue the cycle of maintaining a toxic environment.

The Negligence

It is not just the language of the complaint that struck me as being negligent. After all, the language of "unprofessionalism," as the nationally led petition pointed out, is coded in racist and sexist rhetoric—it is wielded to discipline and punish the accused. What struck me as most negligent is that the email noted, "There were no findings." So I kept wondering what had happened "behind these closed doors" that rendered "no findings."

Did I violate any institutional policy or not? I asked myself.

If I violated any institutional policies, then that is a finding.

If I did not violate any institutional policy, then that is a finding.

So which one is it?

As Ahmed says, "A complaint can be how you learn about institutional violence, the violence of how institutions reproduce themselves, the violence of how institutions respond to violence; yes we can be hit by it" (2021, 180).

I have become quite weary of the term "institutional courage." Those who show institutional courage to expose the wrongdoings of their institutions are portrayed as "bad actors" and as betrayers. Yet the true bad actors who cause tremendous harm remain protected. Women and BIPOC faculty and staff who refuse to protect the "secrecy" that institutions want to keep behind closed doors are also routinely charged with "unprofessionalism" and "incivility" for exhibiting institutional courage, for opening doors that MUST remain shut. Those who open the doors make the power structures anxious.

Dylan Rodriguez has written that "for most colonized peoples, 'the academy is never home'" (2012). Similarly, for all those who have stayed, left, been pushed out or fired after experiencing institutional betrayals, the academy is not a safe space. Being brave comes with a price.

As I noted earlier, this is an essay about institutional violence, institutional failures, institutional harassments, institutional betrayals—narratives of institutional disease and disorders. It is ultimately an essay about how institutions want to push those bodies out, bodies that disallow institutions to keep their secrets away from the public. And this is an essay about how institutions weaponize HR departments to use a complaint process to routinely discipline, punish, silence, and gaslight those who show institutional courage.

Works Cited

AAUP (American Association of University Professors). 2023. "Academic Freedom and Tenure: Indiana University Northwest." *Bulletin*, January 2023. https://www.aaup.org/report/academic-freedom-and-tenure-indiana-university-northwest.

Ahmed, Sara. 2021. *Complaint!* Durham, NC: Duke University Press.

Center for Institutional Courage. n.d. Accessed August 17, 2024. https://www.institutionalcourage.org/.

Cloud, Dana. 2021. "The Rhetoric of Civility as Soft Repression." In *Civility, Free Speech, and Academic Freedom in Higher Education*, edited by Reshmi Dutt-Ballerstadt and Kakali Bhattacharya, 72–88. New York: Routledge.

Conza, Sabrina. 2022. "Linfield University Finally Drops Bogus Investigation of Professor Who Still Doesn't Know the Allegations Against Her." FIRE, April 20, 2022. https://www.thefire.org/news/linfield-university-finally-drops-bogus-investigation-professor-who-still-doesnt-know.

Conza, Sabrina. 2022. "Linfield Launches Investigation of Professor's Posts Praising English Majors, Suggesting Tensions Between English and Business Departments." FIRE, March 24, 2022. https://www.thefire.org/news/linfield-launches-investigation-professors-posts-praising-english-majors-suggesting-tensions.

Flaherty, Colleen. 2022. "More Alleged Faculty Intimidation at Linfield." *Inside Higher Ed*, March 25, 2022. https://www.insidehighered.com/news/2022/03/25/professor-accuses-linfield-u-silencing-faculty-members.

Hartocollis, Anemona. "A Lawsuit Accuses Harvard of Ignoring Sexual Harassment by a Professor." *New York Times*, August 2, 2022. https://www.nytimes.com/2022/02/08/us/harvard-sexual-harassment-lawsuit.html.

Park Hong, Cathy. 2020. *Minor Feelings: An Asian American Reckoning*. New York: One World.

Rodríguez, Dylan. 2012. "Racial/Colonial Genocide and the 'Neoliberal Academy': In Excess of a Problematic." *American Quarterly* 64, no. 4 (December): 809–13. http://www.jstor.org/stable/41809528.

Spiggle, Tom. 2022. "The EEOC Sues the University of Miami for Gender-Based Pay Discrimination." *Forbes*, March 11, 2022. https://www.forbes.com/sites/tomspiggle/2022/03/11/the-eeoc-sues-the-university-of-miami-for-gender-based-pay-discrimination/?sh=648587625a8f.

Whittington, Keith E. 2019. "Academic Freedom and the Scope of Protections for Extramural Speech." *Academe* 105, no. 1 (Winter): n.p. https://www.aaup.org/article/academic-freedom-and-scope-protections-extramural-speech.

CONTRIBUTORS

Celeste Atkins is a sociologist by training, an educator by calling, and a single mother by choice. She serves as director of student engagement and recruitment in the University of Arizona (UA) Graduate College Office of Diversity and Inclusion, where she directs the IMSD program. She is also co-director/co-founder of Grad CAFE, a peer mentoring program funded by the National Science Foundation. She has been with UA in a variety of graduate student and staff positions since she began her doctoral program in 2017. Before transitioning to UA, she was full-time sociology faculty and department chair at Cochise College. Dr. Atkins has a BA in sociology from California State University, San Bernardino, and an MA in sociology from the University of Southern California, both with an emphasis on race and gender. She received her doctorate in 2021 from UA's Center for the Study of Higher Education, where her dissertation focused on the experiences of faculty from traditionally marginalized backgrounds teaching about privilege and oppression. She has over fifteen years of teaching experience at K–12 and college levels and has been honored with various awards, including the 2020–21 Dr. Maria Velez Diversity Leadership Scholarship, the 2021 Arizona Women in Higher Education Emerging Leader Award, the 2020 American Sociological Association Hans O. Mauksch Award for Distinguished Contributions to Undergraduate Sociology, and the 2019 Pacific Sociological Association Early Career Award for Innovation in Teaching Sociology. Dr. Atkins has numerous publications in the scholarship of teaching and learning, including three chapters in edited anthologies and a peer-reviewed journal article, based on her dissertation research.

Jasmine Banks has more than ten years of progressive advocacy, movement building, and organizing experience. She has spent the last five years dedicated to leading an intervention campaign, UnKoch My Campus, addressing the impact of far-right billionaires leveraging their philanthropic donations in higher education to erode democracy. During the campaign, she organized multiple campuses and coalitions, and provided movement support to hundreds of students, educators, and community activists. Jasmine has traveled to a number of higher ed institutions to speak with students and faculty about donor transparency and academic freedom. She was most recently honored to give a keynote for the Higher Education of the American Federation of Teachers. Jasmine is the founder of Generation Common Good, a movement-building organization reclaiming public education from corporations and private interests on behalf of the people and planet.

Krista L. Benson is an associate professor in the School of Interdisciplinary Studies at Grand Valley State University. Their research and teaching focuses on antiracist and decolonial feminist approaches to prison abolition and the relationship between reproductive justice and systems of care for children, including adoption, foster care, and the juvenile justice system. Their new digital humanities project explores early social media and how young people developed politics and identities related to feminism, antiracism, anticolonialism, and/or queerness.

Jessica Bishop-Royse is a health equity scholar focused on the areas of mortality, longevity, infant and maternal health, and structural racism. Her research examines the individual and contextual characteristics associated with excess risk of death and poor health for African Americans. Additionally, she has contributed to research on the education and profession of nursing. She serves as the research methodologist for the Emergency Nurses Association. Bishop-Royse joined the College of Nursing at Rush University as a statistician in February 2022 and was appointed assistant professor in April of 2022.

Samit D. Bordoloi is the equity, diversity, and inclusion manager at Sno-Isle Libraries in Washington State. Previously, he was an associate professor in the Department of Health and Community Studies at Western Washington University.

Monica J. Casper is a first-generation sociologist of gender, race, health, disability, violence, and trauma. She is the author of several books, including *The Making of the Unborn Patient: A Social Anatomy of Fetal Surgery* (Rutgers University Press, 1998), which won the C. Wright Mills Award from the Society for the Study of Social Problems, and *Babylost: Racism, Survival, and the Quiet Politics of Infant Mortality, from A to Z* (Rutgers University Press, 2022). She has published widely in the public sphere and is also a creative writer. Dr. Casper has held numerous leadership roles, including dean of the College of Arts and Letters and special assistant to the president on gender-based violence at San Diego State University. Currently serving as the dean of the College of Arts and Sciences and a professor of sociology at Seattle University, she is deeply committed to fostering inclusive and humane workplaces.

Aparajita De (she/her/hers; pronounced *Aw-paw-ra-gee-ta Day*) is an associate professor of English at the University of the District of Columbia, specializing in postcolonial literature and cultural studies. Her collection *South Asian Racialization and Belonging After 9/11: Masks of Threat* was published by Lexington Books in 2016. Her essays can also be found in *South Asian Popular Culture*, *South Asian Review*, and *Postcolonial Text*. Dr. De's most recent publication is a chapter in *Bollywood's New Woman: Liberalization, Liberation, and Contested Bodies* (Rutgers University Press, 2021). Her contribution to the *The Routledge Encyclopedia of Indian Writing in English* is targeted toward the more recent English graduate; her reviews of scholarly books are accessible in the journals *South Asian Review* and *Synoptique*.

Kathy Diehl began her professional dance career as a founding company member of the Rochester City Ballet under the artistic direction of Timothy Draper. As an award-winning choreographer and dancer, Kathy has performed with a variety of companies and presented her work nationally and internationally. She also has a professional background as a clinical social worker, and her research has primarily focused on dancer wellness, somatics, and dance pedagogy. Kathy is a Certified Movement Analyst through the Laban/Bartenieff Institute of Movement Studies, a Certified Evans Teacher through the Evans Somatic Dance Institute, a certified wellness coach, and a Registered Somatic Movement Educator through the International Somatic Movement Education and Therapy Association. She has been on faculty in both full- and part-time appointments at Idaho State University, Cleveland State University, Hobart and William Smith Colleges, Webster University, the State University of New York Brockport, Nazareth University, and University of Rochester. She began her appointment as assistant professor of dance at Colorado Mesa University in 2021.

Taylor Marie Doherty wrote her chapter while she was still a PhD student in the Department of Political Science at the University of Massachusetts Amherst (UMass Amherst) in the subfields of comparative politics and political theory. After facing continued harassment and retaliation, she left UMass Amherst and is finishing her PhD at the University of Arizona in the Department of Gender and Women's

Studies. Taylor has a graduate certificate in feminist studies from the Department of Women, Gender, Sexuality Studies at the University of Massachusetts Amherst. Her current research examines the politics of queer feminist archives across the United States and Latin America as sites of world making and protest. More broadly, her interest areas include decolonial feminisms, the nexus of Marxist, queer, and feminist theory, and the politics of desire and dissent, particularly in Latin America. She is passionate about projects of counterhistory, genealogy, critical pedagogy, community education, and university abolition. Taylor considers herself a reluctant political scientist who embraces an antidisciplinary approach.

Reshmi Dutt-Ballerstadt is the Edith Green Distinguished Professor in the Department of English at Linfield University in Oregon and also directs the Critical Ethnic Studies program. She is a teacher-scholar-activist, a public intellectual, and a cultural critic. She is the author of *The Postcolonial Citizen: The Intellectual Migrant* and is the lead editor of *Civility, Free Speech and Academic Freedom in Higher Education: Faculty on the Margins*. Her scholarship and creative writing are widely published and circulated in various literary and scholarly journals. Dutt-Ballerstadt also serves as the editor for *Inside Higher Ed*'s Conditionally Accepted, a column for marginalized faculty in higher education, and as the co-editor of *Truthout*'s Challenging the Corporate University series. She is the founder of Academic Trauma in Higher Education.

Alma Itzé Flores is an associate professor in the Undergraduate Studies in Education Department at California State University, Sacramento. Dr. Flores was born in Jalisco, Mexico, and raised in Santa Barbara, California. She is an immigrant, first-generation college student, and mother to Xoaquín and Luna. She earned her BA in sociology with a minor in education studies at the University of California,

Los Angeles (UCLA), her MA in bilingual and bicultural studies at the University of Texas at Austin, and her PhD in race and ethnic studies in education at UCLA. As a Chicana feminist teacher-scholar, her research examines the educational pathways of Chicana/o/x/Latina/o/x first-generation college students, Chicana/Latina mothers, and the development and analysis of Chicana/Latina feminist pedagogies and research methodologies.

Alanna Gillis is an assistant professor of sociology at St. Lawrence University. She researches race, class, and gender inequality in higher education and draws on her own experiences of privilege and oppression to try to make her classroom and university more equitable. She grew up in South Carolina and loves living in New England, being able to hike, cycle, and cross-country ski. She is forever indebted to the friends and mentors who saw her through the difficult time in her life she describes in this book, and she will forever admire the peer who brought the case forward to try to seek justice and faced even worse consequences than Alanna. Her chapter is in honor of all women who do not have the power to fight back, to those women who try to fight back despite the odds, and to the people who are working to dismantle these systems of oppression.

C. Goldberg (she/they/iel/ell@) is an interdisciplinary academic, versatile linguaphile, holistic wellness practitioner, and sometimes-surreptitious spoonie. An Ashkenazi settler residing in the city of Toronto/Tkaronto, C. is passionate about connecting disability advocacy with other initiatives oriented around community building and access intimacy / social justice. Keen to help foster and co-create queer- and crip-friendly spaces that are welcoming, inclusive, and fulfilling for all involved, C. has published, presented, facilitated, agitated, and ruminated on a variety of accessibility-intersecting topics, focusing especially on strategies supporting PWIVID (people with invisible and variable impairments and disabilities). C. is currently working to become a doctor of philosophy at a major Canadian institution of higher learning.

Jennifer M. Gómez is an assistant professor in the School of Social Work at Boston University (BU) and a faculty affiliate at the Center for Innovation in Social Work & Health at BU. She is a member of the Board of Directors, Scientific Committee, and Annual Conference Committee at the International Society for the Study of Trauma & Dissociation (ISSTD). In addition to being on the boards of the Center for Institutional Courage and End Rape on Campus, she is a member of the Advisory Committee of the National Academies of Sciences, Engineering, and Medicine's Action Collaborative on Preventing Sexual Harassment in Higher Education. Her research centers around cultural betrayal trauma theory, which she created as a Black feminist theoretical framework for examining the impacts of violence within the context of inequality on Black and other marginalized populations. She has published over one hundred peer-reviewed journal articles, book chapters, other scholarly writings, professional development documents, and pieces for the general public. Published by the American Psychological Association, her first book, *The Cultural Betrayal of Black Women & Girls: A Black Feminist Approach to Healing from Sexual Abuse*, won the 2024 Frank W. Putnam Outstanding Book Award from the ISSTD.

Kristina Gupta is an associate professor in the Department of Women's, Gender, and Sexuality Studies at Wake Forest University. Her research interests are in the areas of contemporary asexual identities and gender, science, and medicine. She is the author of *Medical Entanglements: Rethinking Feminist Debates about Healthcare* (Rutgers University Press, 2019), a co-editor of *Queer Feminist Science Studies: A Reader* (University of Washington Press, 2017), and the author of a number of articles published in venues such as *Signs: Journal of*

Women in Culture and Society and *Sexualities*. She is also the coordinator of Wake Forward, a group of progressive Wake Forest faculty, staff, and students. The group recently successfully campaigned to replace Wake Forest's "cultural diversity" general education requirement with a general education requirement focused on structural inequalities, including systemic racism.

Jasmine L. Harris is an associate professor and coordinator of the African American Studies program in the Department of Race, Ethnicity, Gender and Sexuality Studies at the University of Texas at San Antonio. She completed her PhD at the University of Minnesota in 2013. Her research examines Black life in predominantly white spaces, including Black students at predominantly white institutions, Black Division I football and men's basketball players at universities in the Power Five conferences, and Black sociologists producing knowledge in a white-dominated discipline. Dr. Harris has been published in major newspapers across the country, including *Newsweek*, the *Washington Post*, the *Houston Chronicle*, and the *Chicago Tribune*. In 2021, she was featured in the VICE documentary *College Sports, Inc.* Her first book, *Black Women, Ivory Tower: Revealing the Lies of White Supremacy in American Education*, was published by Broadleaf Books in 2024.

Susan Hillock (she/her) is a professor in the Department of Social Work at Trent University in Oshawa, Ontario, Canada. With over thirty years of experience, she has primarily worked with adult and children assault survivors; families coping with chronic emotional, health, and palliative care issues; people experiencing loss and grief; adolescents and families involved in the corrections system; and caregivers. Her clinical experience has included work in probation, victim/witness programs, child protection, physical/emotional rehabilitation, hospital social work, and palliative care. She has also provided professional training, supervision, and consultation for over thirty years in the fields of adult education, team assessment/building, and community mental health. At BSW and MSW levels, and in field instruction and social activism, her education and practice methods stem from feminist, critical theory, structural, queer, and anti-oppressive frameworks. Published books include *Greening Social Work Education* (University of Toronto Press, 2024); *Teaching About Sex and Sexualities in Higher Education* (University of Toronto Press, 2021); with Rick Csiernik, *Teaching Social Work: Reflections on Pedagogy & Practice* (University of Toronto Press, 2021); and, with Nick J. Mulé, *Queering Social Work Education* (University of British Columbia Press, 2016).

Doreen Hsu was at the University of California, San Diego (UCSD) for over a decade as an undergraduate psychology major and a doctoral student. She was awarded a PhD in sociology in 2024. Doreen's research and teaching focus on topics of racial and ethnic identities, sense of belonging, mental health, and access to university services among Asian American and mixed-race Asian American students. Professionally, Doreen has also served in academic program development and community leadership positions at the UCSD department-, campus-, and systemwide levels to ensure all students have equal access to success.

Jennifer Lai is an assistant professor in the Department of Sociology at the University of Vermont. She studies scientific knowledge production, and for her dissertation she investigated how knowledge about environmental risk factors is produced within the context of type 2 diabetes. Jennifer earned an undergraduate degree in engineering and then served for two years in AmeriCorps, first as an environmental engineer in Washington state and then as a classroom teaching aide in Minnesota. As a proud feminist scholar, Jennifer is particularly keen to confront scholarly practices that overtly do harm to others but is equally interested in how practices inadvertently do harm.

Amy Andrea Martinez earned her doctoral degree from the Department of Criminal Justice at John Jay College of Criminal Justice at the City University of New York. Her research interests include Mexican/Chicano gang culture, mass incarceration, third world and Indigenous qualitative research methods, U.S. (settler) colonialism, police use of lethal force, and prison/police abolition. As a first-generation, working-class, and system-impacted Xicana from Southern California, her experiences inform her commitment to decolonial research on Mexican and Chicanx families and their associations and experiences with gang and street life. Currently, she serves as a Latino Social Sciences Pipeline postdoctoral fellow at the University of California, Berkeley, within the Latinx Research Center, contributing to the advancement of Latinx scholarship in her field. Simultaneously, Dr. Martinez holds the position of assistant professor in the Justice Studies Department at San Jose State University and lecturer at the University of California, Santa Barbara.

Rebecca G. Martínez is an independent scholar, a Senior Ford Foundation Fellow, and a Fulbright Scholar. An anthropologist, her research and teaching are interdisciplinary and intersectional. Research interests include women's reproductive health / health inequities in Latin America and the United States, gender and migration studies, Latin America and gender policy, Chicanx/Latinx feminism, and critical university studies with an emphasis on diversity and higher education. Her first book, *Marked Women: The Cultural Politics of Cervical Cancer in Venezuela*, was published in 2018 and won the 2019 Eileen Basker Memorial Prize, awarded by the Society for Medical Anthropology. She has also published articles and book chapters on Chicanas' beliefs about cervical and breast cancer in Orange County, California; sexual assault on the U.S.-Mexico border; being a Latina on the tenure track; and others that reflect her varied academic interests. She also started a small business called Camino Scholars and is using her experience as a writer, researcher, and teacher to lead scholars on walking-writing workshops on the famous Camino de Santiago in Europe.

Shantel Martinez obtained her PhD in communications and media with an emphasis on Latinx communication and gender studies from the University of Illinois, Urbana-Champaign. As a practitioner-scholar, she centers storytelling and narrative practices to examine cycles of intergenerational trauma as well as survival in both familial and educational spaces. She is one of the co-editors of *Monsters and Saints: LatIndigenous Landscapes and Spectral Storytelling* and has been published in *Chicana/Latina Studies: The Journal of Mujeres Activas en Letras y Cambio Social*; *Qualitative Inquiry*; *Cultural Studies ⇔ Critical Methodologies*; *Border-Lines*; *This Bridge We Call Communication: Anzaldúan Approaches to Theory, Method, and Praxis*; *Latina/o/x Communication Studies: Theories, Methods, and Practice*; *Becoming a Diversity Leader on Campus: Navigating Identity and Situational Pressures*, and others.

Sara A. Mata is the executive director of Hispanic Serving Initiatives at Wichita State University. Dr. Mata received a bachelor's degree in sociology with an emphasis in juvenile corrections and treatment, a master's in community counseling, a master's in sociology, and a doctorate in social foundations from Oklahoma State University. Dr. Mata's personal research interests are promoting health and wellness in diverse communities, as well as advocating for institutional changes in practices impacting those dealing with a health issue. Based in cultural relevancy and engagement in the community, this work is necessary to impacting and improving care and the overall well-being of society.

Rachael McCollum is an alumna of Grand Valley State University, having studied film and video production and women, gender, and sexuality studies during her time there. Her primary research interests are in media representation of marginalized individuals and the ways that media influences and is influenced by societal power structures and structural inequity.

Wang Ping is a poet, writer, photographer, and performance and multimedia artist. Her publications have been translated into multiple languages and include poetry, short stories, novels, cultural studies, and children's stories. Her multimedia exhibitions address global themes of industrialization, the environment, interdependency, and the people. She is the recipient of numerous awards, a professor emerita of English, and the founder of the Kinship of Rivers project.

Emily Rosser (she/her) earned a PhD in gender, feminist, and women's studies from York University in Toronto, Canada. For two decades, she has worked on sexual violence and human rights in the Americas as a researcher, educator, and advocate. She has long-term interests in emotional labor, care work, and developing sustainable forms of antiracist feminist advocacy to prevent burnout and build community. Currently, Emily works in the nonprofit sector in Ottawa, Ontario, which occupies the unceded territory of the Anishinaabe Algonquin Nation. In addition, she does freelance research consulting for community organizations and is working toward the dream of writing a novel for young adults.

Angélica Ruvalcaba (she/her/ella) is an assistant professor of sociology in the Department of Social Sciences and Historical Studies at Texas Woman's University. In 2023, she graduated from Michigan State University (MSU) with a dual-major PhD in sociology and Chicano/Latino studies with a specialization in women's and gender studies. Ruvalcaba received an MA in sociology from MSU in 2020 and a BA in sociology from Texas A&M University in 2017. Her research interests include Chicana feminism, critical race theory, LatCrit, Latinx sociology, sociology of education, race/ethnicity, and immigration.

Brandy L. Simula (she/her) is a consultant, executive coach, and professional facilitator and speaker with expertise in leadership development, women's leadership, workplace well-being, and behavioral science. After academic career chapters as a faculty member and, subsequently, a faculty developer, she now develops and coaches leaders who cultivate human-centric cultures that empower people to do purpose-driven, values-aligned, highly productive work while flourishing personally and professionally. An International Coaching Federation Professional Certified Coach, Center for Credentialing and Education Board Certified Coach, and past member of the Forbes Coaches Council, her research and thought leadership have been published in *Harvard Business Review*, *Forbes*, *Newsweek*, *Inside Higher Ed*, and numerous academic journals and edited volumes. Dr. Simula was named a 2024 Emerging Culture Creator for her work in workplace well-being and mental health and a 2020–22 University System of Georgia Leadership Fellow for her contributions to leadership development.

Rashna Batliwala Singh received her BA honors degree from the University of Calcutta, her MA from Mount Holyoke College, and her PhD from the University of Massachusetts Amherst. Singh is the author of *The Imperishable Empire: A Study of British Fiction on India* (Three Continents Press, 1988) and *Goodly Is Our Heritage: Children's Literature, Empire, and the Certitude of Character* (Scarecrow Press, 2004). She has published book chapters in *Kipling and Beyond: Patriotism, Globalisation and Postcolonialism* (Palgrave Macmillan, 2010), *Chinua Achebe's Things Fall Apart 1958–2008* (Rodopi, 2011), and *The Critical Imagination in African Literature: Essays in Honor* *of Michael J. C. Echeruo* (Syracuse University Press, 2015). Singh has also contributed to *Asian American Playwrights: A Bio-Bibliographical Critical Sourcebook* (Greenwood, 2002) and the *Encyclopedia of the Jewish Diaspora: Origins, Experiences, and Culture* (Bloomsbury, 2008). In 2003, Singh received a National Endowment for the Humanities Summer Institute Grant to participate in Representations of the "Other": Jews in Medieval Christendom, a five-week institute at Oxford University. In 1998, she was one of two professors in the state awarded the Massachusetts Council for International Education Lectureship. Her last teaching assignment before retirement was at Colorado College as a visiting professor, where she taught for thirteen years in the English Department and in the Race, Ethnicity, and Migration Studies program.

Cierra Raine Sorin (she/her) completed her PhD in sociology with a doctoral emphasis in feminist studies at the University of California, Santa Barbara in 2024. She is an assistant professor in the Department of Sociology at California State University, Fresno. As a consent researcher, her work meets at the intersections of knowledge, practice, and education relating to sexuality, gender, and violence. Her various projects have focused on activist efforts within university systems to combat sexual violence and better support survivors, including her work for UC Speaks Up (a qualitative study of consent cultures, sexual violence and harassment, and institutional resources across multiple University of California campuses) and her ongoing project #metoogradschool (a multimethod study examining graduate students' experiences with sexual violence and sexual harassment while in their graduate programs). Cierra's book project is an examination of how consent operates culturally without the law as a formal mechanism of social control in BDSM communities. Using a queer feminist sociological lens, she explores how understandings of consent are constructed, shared, and enacted; the connections between consent and sexual joy; and the repercussions for consent violations in BDSM communities where legal response to harm is not desired, sought, nor expected.

Connor Spencer (she/her) is a white organizer interested in building and participating in communities and solidarities between anti-violence, anticapitalist, and justice movements across Turtle Island. Chair of Students for Consent Culture Canada (SFCC) from 2018 to 2020 and having gone through the experience that was a BA at McGill University, she is intensely interested in holding institutions accountable for the violence and power structures that they perpetuate and uphold, and in building spaces to dream and create new worlds. She currently lives, organizes, and works as a national strike and mobilization officer in the national labor movement and as an SFCC Board of Directors member on unceded Algonquin territory.

Chantelle Spicer (she/they) earned an MA in anthropology from Simon Fraser University and is co-chair of Students for Consent Culture Canada. Chantelle is dedicated to Indigenous sovereignty and futures, consent in all forms of solidarity, accountability, and care in and between our social movements. Chantelle has been involved in work with West Coast LEAF, the Downtown Eastside Women's Centre, the Nanaimo Women's Centre, and the Teaching Support Staff Union. They are also a poet, artist, and gardener. The lands Chantelle works with should be under jurisdiction of xʷməθkʷəyəm, Səl’ílwətaʔ, and Skwxwú7mesh but, due to structures of genocide that target Indigenous women and two-spirit people, are illegally claimed by Vancouver, Canada.

James M. Thomas (JT) is an associate professor of sociology at the University of Mississippi and a co-editor of the journal *Sociology of Race and Ethnicity*. He is the author or co-author of five books and over forty peer-reviewed journal articles, book chapters, and invited essays on the causes and consequences of race and racism in America and abroad. His research has been funded by the American Sociological Association, the National Science Foundation, and the Russell Sage Foundation, and has been featured in popular media outlets like the *New Yorker*, the *Washington Post*, and *Pacific Standard*. JT is deeply dedicated to public scholarship, regularly writing for mainstream outlets like the *Mississippi Free Press*, serving on the boards of nonprofit organizations, and giving public lectures on race, racism, and inequality to academic and lay audiences alike.

Mercedes Valadez is an associate professor in the Division of Criminal Justice at California State University, Sacramento. She earned a BA in criminal justice from California State University, Bakersfield; an MS in criminology and a certificate of advanced study in Homeland Security from California State University, Fresno; and a PhD in criminology and criminal justice from Arizona State University. Her research explores the intersection between the immigration system and the criminal justice system. More specifically, her work investigates disparities and discrimination in criminal justice outcomes based on race/ethnicity, nationality, and citizenship status.

Meg A. Warren is an associate professor of management at Western Washington University. She is a researcher, keynote speaker, author, and psychologist with expertise in allyship, inclusiveness, and cultural factors affecting well-being. Her award-winning research uses a positive psychology approach to study how individuals from relatively privileged groups can serve as allies to marginalized groups. Meg has published two books and over fifty journal articles and book chapters. Her research has been covered by over two hundred media outlets globally. Among other prestigious positions, she has served as the founding president of the Work and Organizations Division of the International Positive Psychology Association, co-founder of the Western Positive Psychology Association, and co-editor of the *International Journal of Wellbeing*. She serves as a faculty affiliate of the Center for Positive Organizations at the University of Michigan Stephen M. Ross School of Business and is a co-founder of its micro-community, Positive Organizational Inclusion Scholarship on Equity and Diversity.

In February 2021, **Matthew Wills** finally completed a PhD in the Department of History at the University of California, San Diego. Now he works outside of academia—a career move driven by a need to get away from a world ruled by those for whom bureaucracy, rank, and cash are king. In his years on campus, he met too many people disillusioned with what the university had become, who spent their days trying to navigate the toxic corporate strictures imposed from senior leadership, forcing aside the educational mission for which they were hired. The COVID-19 pandemic, for Matthew, revealed the total bankruptcy of current higher education leadership: its disingenuousness, its greed, its alienation from the needs of those whom it is meant to serve. He hopes for change.

INDEX